Task	Tool	Description
Encoding & Decoding Files	UUEncode, MIME	Convert binary files to ASCII and back again, so they can be sent over e-mail or Usenet.
Uncompressing Files	Archivers	Compress and uncompress files so that they can be sent over the Internet quickly.
Viewing Images and Movies	Image and Movie Viewers	Display and play images, movies, and formatted documents you find on the Internet.
Playing Sounds	Sound Players	Play sounds you find on the Internet.
Public Text Conversation	Internet Relay Chat	Talk with other people on the Internet who share your interests.
Private Text Conversation	Talk	Have a conversation with a friend online.
Voice Communication	Voice Chat	Talk to a friend or a total stranger online.
Video Communication	Internet Video	Receive and send live video images over the Internet.
Games	MUDs, Backgammon, Chess	Play games and explore new worlds with other people online.
Troubleshooting and Tuning	Diagnostic Tools	Diagnose problems and tune your Internet connection for better performance.
Write Your Own Web Page	HTML Editors	Create Web pages with a HyperText Markup Language (HTML) editing tool.

For every kind of computer user,
there is a SYBEX book.

All computer users learn in their own way. Some need straightforward and methodical explanations. Others are just too busy for this approach. But no matter what camp you fall into, SYBEX has a book that can help you get the most out of your computer and computer software while learning at your own pace.

Beginners generally want to start at the beginning. The **ABC's** series, with its step-by-step lessons in plain language, helps you build basic skills quickly. For a more personal approach, there's the **Murphy's Laws** and **Guided Tour** series. Or you might try our **Quick & Easy** series, the friendly, full-color guide, with **Quick & Easy References**, the companion pocket references to the **Quick & Easy** series. If you learn best by doing rather than reading, find out about the **Hands-On Live!** series, our new interactive multimedia training software. For hardware novices, there's the **Your First** series.

The **Mastering** and **Understanding** series will tell you everything you need to know about a subject. They're perfect for intermediate and advanced computer users, yet they don't make the mistake of leaving beginners behind. Add one of our **Instant References** and you'll have more than enough help when you have a question about your computer software. You may even want to check into our **Secrets & Solutions** series.

SYBEX even offers special titles on subjects that don't neatly fit a category—like our **Pushbutton Guides**, our books about the Internet, our books about the latest computer games, and a wide range of books for Macintosh computers and software.

SYBEX books are written by authors who are expert in their subjects. In fact, many make their living as professionals, consultants, or teachers in the field of computer software. And their manuscripts are thoroughly reviewed by our technical and editorial staff for accuracy and ease-of-use.

So when you want answers about computers or any popular software package, just help yourself to SYBEX.

For a complete catalog of our publications, please write:

SYBEX Inc.
2021 Challenger Drive
Alameda, CA 94501
Tel: (510) 523-8233/(800) 227-2346 Telex: 336311
Fax: (510) 523-2373

SYBEX

SYBEX is committed to using natural resources wisely to preserve and improve our environment. As a leader in the computer book publishing industry, we are aware that over 40% of America's solid waste is paper. This is why we have been printing the text of books like this one on recycled paper since 1982.

This year our use of recycled paper will result in the saving of more than 15,300 trees. We will lower air pollution effluents by 54,000 pounds, save 6,300,000 gallons of water, and reduce landfill by 2,700 cubic yards.

In choosing a SYBEX book you are not only making a choice for the best in skills and information, you are also choosing to enhance the quality of life for all of us.

The Internet
Tool Kit

Nancy Cedeño

SYBEX

San Francisco ■ Paris ■ Düsseldorf ■ Soest

Acquisitions Manager: Kristine Plachy

Developmental Editor: Brenda Kienan

Editor: Neil Edde

Technical Editor: Aaron Kushner

Desktop Publisher: Alissa Feinberg

Production Assistant: Renée Avalos

Indexer: Nancy Guenther

Book Designer: Lucka Zivny

Cover Designer: Ingalls + Associates

Cover Illustrator: Hank Osuna

Screen reproductions were produced with Tiffany Plus and JasCapture

Tiffany Plus is a trademark of Anderson Consulting and Software
JasCapture is a trademark of JASC Inc.

SYBEX is a registered trademark of SYBEX Inc.

Library of Congress Card Number: 95-68271

ISBN: 0-7821-1688-4

Manufactured in the United States of America

10 9 8 7 6 5 4 3 2 1

To my dad, for teaching me how to use tools, and to my mom, for not minding.

Acknowledgments

I CAN'T POSSIBLY imagine how I would have been able to survive this book without the help of my friends and associates. A special thanks to my personal sanity preservation department: Daniel Murphy, Brad Templeton, Diana Porter, and especially Craige Howlett, for keeping me sane on a daily basis.

Technical kudos to my Windows 95 and TCP/IP gurus: Robert Allen, Alex Jauch, Kent Duke, and Stew Dimon; technical editor Aaron Kushner; HTML Stud Kevin Chavaree; and my testing buddies David Goldman and Brett Arata. And a big thanks to the good folks at Sirius Connections and The Well for keeping me well-connected.

Thanks also to Neil Edde for keeping me on track, Kelli Wiseth and Steve Lipson for getting me into this in the first place, Paul Dunton and Mary Picchi for letting me finish it; Jim Howard, Paul Voisin, Annie Stephanski, Amy Hugo, Holly Jauch, Joy Giorgi, Jim Sherman, Loren MacGregor, Adele Framer, Florence Chan Leto, the alt.winsock gang (especially Ed Sinkovits and Forrest H. Stroud, for their tireless work in keeping users up-to-date on the newest and greatest Winsock applications), and all my e-mail buddies for additional moral and technical support.

And a very special thanks to my parents for unknowingly giving me the skills I needed to get to this place in my life. My mom, Marjorie, for giving me an outrageous vocabulary and a love for the English language; and my dad, Joe, for making sure that I'd never be afraid of technology.

And a round of applause for Mark P. McCahill and the University of Minnesota Gopher Software Development Team, Santanu Lahiri, Richard Kennerly, Caesar M. Samsi, Louis Aube, Peter van der Veen, Laurence G. Kahn, Peter Zander, and all the other fine developers and support folks without whom this book would not be possible.

Contents at a Glance

Table of Contents

Introduction

I'M CONSTANTLY AMAZED by the incredible variety and amount of information you can find "out there" on the Internet. Just name your subject: science, history, art, philosophy—it's all there. You can find information on everything from aardvarks to zymurgy, and most things in between. And as more and more people from all over the world are getting connected to the Internet, a thriving and incredibly exciting community of minds and ideas is evolving.

But if you venture out onto the Internet without some basic knowledge and tools, it can get pretty intimidating. I've seen more than a few people give up on the Internet before really discovering the wealth of information and communication it has to offer, simply because of a single frustrating experience. Maybe they couldn't find a file; or more likely, they found the file they needed, but couldn't read it because it wasn't downloaded correctly, or because they didn't have the right program handy to be able to process it and use it.

This book is intended to help you put together your own personalized Internet tool kit. Keep it in your pocket (well, okay, maybe it's a bit large for that) or near your computer, so if you get stuck out there on the Infobahn, you won't have to look far for the right tool for the job. There are an amazing number of Internet tools available, especially for Windows users, but if you don't know where to find them, they won't do you much good.

You may already be familiar with some of the tools I'll be discussing—FTP, Telnet, and Web browsers are all fairly common. But you may not have realized that there are many different versions of these common tools available. Still other tools are less familiar, such as file decoding and archiving tools that are fairly well-known in the Unix world, but not all that familiar to PC users. Still other tools are just now becoming popular—for example, tools that make it easy to create your own home page on the World Wide Web.

Most of the tools I'm going to talk about are written for the Microsoft Windows environment, but I'll also talk about some of the Unix tools you'll need if you get your Internet access from a system that runs the Unix operating system.

Windows on the Internet

Most Windows users probably don't realize how lucky they are when it comes to Internet tools. Developers from all over the world are writing some of the most exciting new Internet programs, specifically for Microsoft Windows users. This growing collection of tools includes Web browsers like Mosaic and Netscape, easy-to-use newsreaders like WinVN, Trumpet, and News Xpress, and FTP programs like WS-FTP that do most of the work for you.

Now you might wonder why, apparently all of a sudden, there seems to be a flood of Internet applications for Windows. It's not a coincidence. In the past couple of years, three significant events have occurred, all of which have combined to create a boon for Windows users on the Internet.

First, faster modems (14.4 kbps and higher) became available to the home PC user. Faster modems make it much easier for users to connect to Internet service providers and take advantage of the really exciting Internet applications, most of which depend on being able to transfer large graphics and sound files quickly.

Second, the media finally latched on to the "Information Superhighway" concept, which Vice President Al Gore has been advocating for years. Although the Internet today is just one part of the whole concept of a global high-speed data communications network, it is currently the electronic equivalent of the frontier. And, like the thousands of people who emigrated to California during the Gold Rush, millions are now discovering the Internet and the wealth of information it can provide.

And third, the Windows Sockets (Winsock) standard was born. This standard made it significantly easier for Microsoft Windows™ developers to write programs that allow the millions of Windows users to connect to networks that use TCP/IP (Transmission Control Protocol/Internet Protocol). And the Internet is the largest TCP/IP network the world has ever seen.

So, What Is the Internet, Anyway?

By definition, the Internet is a global network of over a thousand smaller networks that all use the Internet Protocol (IP) to communicate with each other. A *protocol* is the set of rules, or "language" that computers use to speak to one another across a network.

The word *Internet* has come to mean both the Internet of networks that "speak" IP, and the many networks that connect to it—even the ones that don't use IP, like FidoNet and BITNET.

In fact, the term *Internet* was originally coined by its developers because they needed a word to describe the network of interconnecting networks they were building.

About the Tools

There are an amazing number of Internet tools currently available for Windows users for connecting to and using the Internet. The problem with putting together a list like this is that it's always changing. For this book, I've chosen the tools and utilities that are technically superior, widely available, and popular with Windows Internet users. I've also emphasized tools that are currently in active development, since these are the ones that tend to have the best future.

With these tools especially, new versions are available almost on a monthly basis. Keep this in mind when you go to download programs. For example, if I tell you here that the current version is 1.05, and when you go to download the program, the version number is 1.08, by all means download the newest version. Most programmers include the version numbers either in the distribution filename or in the directory where the files are kept, so you can tell at a glance if the program has been updated since you last checked.

Also keep in mind that this is an awkward time to be writing a book about Windows programs, as we're in a transition period between Windows 3.1 and Windows 95. I've tested every application in this book under both Windows 3.1 and the final beta version of Windows 95. Virtually every program I tested worked just fine under both operating systems. In cases where there were problems, I mention the problem and tell you how to avoid it.

How to Use This Book

There are a number of conventions and common elements that you'll come across as you read through this book. Some of these things— notes, tips, and the dreaded warnings, for example—are there to call attention to important information; while other elements are simply there to make the instructions easier to understand.

Notes, Tips, and Warnings

The Notes, Tips, and Warnings (illustrated below) are intended to call attention to any supplementary information, helpful hints, and potential hazards that you should be aware of.

*The check mark signifies a **note**, which contains additional information you might want to know about a particular application, or just something interesting I think you might like to know.*

*The bull's-eye signifies a **tip**, which is usually a pointer to a source for more information, or a hidden feature, or just something that will make your life easier while using a particular tool.*

*The skull and cross-bones signifies a **warning**. Bad juju. Wear your Safety Belts. Avoid. Keep Away from Children. Keep Out. Do Not Try This At Home. Professional Driver on Closed Track. You get the idea.*

Type Conventions

In general, things you need to type, buttons you need to press, and dialog box fields that require user input are in **bold type**. Things that represent something you know and I don't, like *your name*, are in *italic type*. For example, I might say "type **subscribe *your name*** to get on the mailing list." That means I want you to type the word **subscribe**, and then type your name, but since I don't know what your name is, I put it in italics.

Filenames and directories are always in CAPITAL letters in DOS. Because the Unix file system is case sensitive (e.g., INDEX, Index, and index are all different filenames), and most servers on the Internet run under the Unix operating system, files and directories on servers are shown in their appropriate case. When transferring files from servers on the Internet, always keep this in mind.

Chapter Summaries

This book is organized according to tool type. I expect you'll do quite a bit of skipping around as you read through it, so here's a quick summary of the contents of each chapter:

Chapter 1: Connecting to the World Provides information about the different ways you can connect to the Internet, as well as tips for finding a good Internet service provider.

Chapter 2: Tools for Transferring Files Explains how to download files from Internet file servers using FTP, from both Unix and Windows. It includes information about the big Windows software archive sites, like CICA and SimTel, and utilities that make searching for files on these archives easier.

Chapter 3: Exploring with Telnet Covers logging into remote servers using Telnet to discover interesting databases, games, and programs.

Chapter 4: Mail, the Indispensable Tool Presents information about Unix and Windows mail programs, automated list servers, and fun things you can do with Internet mail.

Chapter 5: Reading the News Explains how to access Usenet newsgroups from Unix and Windows, and includes information about the best and newest Windows newsreaders.

Chapter 6: Burrowing with Gopher Explores how to use the Gopher information system to find information in Gopherspace on the Internet. From a Gopher client program in Unix or Windows, you can access files and information from around the globe.

Chapter 7: See the World by Web Reveals that with a good Web browser at your disposal, the world is just a mouse-click away. Web browsers come in all shapes and sizes, from simple Unix browsers to sophisticated multimedia-enabled Windows client applications.

Chapter 8: We Want Information Shows you where to start when you're having trouble finding information on the Internet. Here you'll find the tools that allow you to find things on the Internet—Web pages, Gopher menus, files, databases, and even people.

Chapter 9: Making Sense of Files Have you ever received a file via e-mail and not known what to do with it to get it to work? Well, this is the chapter for you. Here's where to go to find information about decoding (and encoding) binary files, and decompressing (and compressing) archive files.

Chapter 10: Viewers and Players Provides information on a number of different viewers and players you'll need to get multimedia-enabled on the Internet.

Chapter 11: Communicating with Netfolk Explores the world of real-time communication on the Internet. Feel like striking up a text conversation with a bunch of total strangers? Talking across the Internet with a friend using text or voice? Joining in on an Internet video-conference? Playing a game of backgammon with someone on the opposite side of the globe? Well, this is the place to find out how.

Chapter 12: Getting Deeper into Winsock Presents a more in-depth analysis of Winsock, including information on diagnostic tools, tuning your Winsock (and your communications software) for better performance, and how to save money over a SLIP or PPP connection.

Chapter 13: Staking Your Claim on the Web Explains how you too can publish material on the Internet. It's a lot easier than you might think to write your own Web page. These tools can help you to design your own presence on the World Wide Web.

Appendix A: The Unix Shell Game If you've got a Unix shell account, here's where you can find out how to get around in Unix, and how to set up your system so that you can run most of the cool Winsock applications discussed throughout this book from your plain old Unix shell account.

Appendix B: Connecting Windows to the Internet If you're new to the world of Winsock, here's where you can find out how to get connected to an Internet provider using a SLIP or PPP connection from Windows 3.1 or Windows 95.

Nuts and Bolts about the Tools

Most of the information contained in this book is about specific tools, most of them Windows applications. For each application, I'll tell you a little bit about it, why you'd want to have it, what cool or nifty things it does, and what the interface looks like. Then I'll tell you where you can get it from and what the status of the program is (shareware, freeware, fill-in-the-blankware). The location information is shown in gray shaded boxes, so you can find it quickly. And finally, I'll tell you how to install and configure each application, then give you a few quick tips for using it.

Where to Get the Tools

All of the Unix programs discussed in this book are available on most Unix systems, and are installed by your system administrator for all to use. If I mention a particular application that you don't have on your

The What's and Whys of Wares

There is an amazing variety of software out there on the Internet, just waiting for you to try. But keep in mind that while much of this software is free for you to *try*, not all of it is free to *use*.

The concept of shareware is almost as old as desktop computers themselves. Developers who didn't work for the big software development companies and didn't have access to any standard means of distributing their programs started distributing them either on diskettes at computer shows or on electronic bulletin boards (BBSs).

The concept works like this: they distribute the software for free, but request that you pay for the program if you like it and find it useful. Usually, in return for paying for and registering your copy of the software, you'll get actual diskettes, and perhaps real documentation and advance copies of new versions.

Sometimes, developers will distribute a limited version of the program for free. These versions, although often called shareware, are really more like demo versions. Usually they don't have all the features of the complete product, or they'll only function for a short time.

Other programs are freeware. Often these programs are free for individual users, but must be purchased if they are to be used for commercial purposes (i.e., you plan to make money from the product's use or distribution).

system, you'll need to talk to your administrator to find out if it can be installed.

All of the Windows programs discussed in this book are available for downloading via anonymous FTP over the Internet. If you're unfamiliar with how to use anonymous FTP, take a trip on over to Chapter 2, where I'll tell you how to do it, either from Unix, or better yet, from Windows.

How to Install the Tools

Most of the applications are distributed in compressed archive files, usually using the ZIP format. These files will always have a filename extension of .ZIP, and must be extracted using a decompression tool like

WinZip, UnZip, or PKUnZip. Other files will be self-extracting archive files. These are usually .ZIP format files that have the extraction mechanism built-in. These files have an .EXE filename extension, which means all you need to do to extract the files is run the .EXE file. When you run a self-extracting archive file, all of the files will automatically decompress into the directory where you run the .EXE file. Because of this, you don't want to run these files in a directory where you have other files, or it can be difficult to figure out which files were extracted from the archive and which were already there.

After you extract the files from the .ZIP or .EXE archive, you'll have to do one of two things, depending on the program:

- Run a SETUP.EXE or INSTALL.EXE program, which will install the program on your hard disk and create an icon for the program in Windows.

- Create a directory on your hard disk and an icon for the program in Windows manually.

Although the automatic installation programs offer the easiest means to installing programs, unfortunately very few shareware and freeware programs offer an automatic installation program. But don't fret—it's really not all that hard to install a program manually. To manually install a program in Windows 3.1 or Windows 95, you'll need to do most, if not all of the following:

- Create a directory for the program on your hard disk

- Move the archive file (.ZIP or .EXE) in to the new directory

- Extract the files

- Create an icon for the program

- Move any .DLL and .VBX files that come with the program to your WINDOWS\SYSTEM subdirectory.

If you're not that familiar with creating directories and moving files, please refer to the Windows help files and documentation to find out how. If you're unfamiliar with using archive utilities, take a side trip over to Chapter 9 for information about the various archive utilities available for DOS and Windows.

A *Few Words* about Creating Icons

Although there are several different ways to create icons in both Windows 3.1 and Windows 95, I recommend using File Manager (in Windows 3.1) or Windows Explorer (Windows 95) to do this.

In Windows 3.1, you can drag the .EXE file from File Manager over to the program group that you want the icon to appear in. When you do so, Windows automatically sets up the icon properties so that the icon will use the program's directory as the working directory, which means that Windows won't have to go searching for any support files that the program needs.

In Windows 95, you can drag the .EXE file over from Windows Explorer onto your desktop to automatically create a shortcut to the program. Shortcuts serve a similar function to program group icons in Windows 3.1, but they don't need to be in program groups—you can put them anywhere on your screen.

The time you spend putting together your own custom Internet tool kit will be well worth it in the long run. Having the right tools at your disposal will save you both time and money when you're out there cruising the Internet.

So now that we've got the formalities over with, let's get on to the fun stuff!

Connecting to
the World

IF YOU'RE LOOKING to get connected to the Internet for the first time, thinking of changing to a different kind of online service, or just wondering about the different Internet access options available, this chapter is for you. If you're savvy about the different kinds of Internet access, and you already have an account that gives you full access to the Internet, such as a SLIP or PPP account, you may want to skip this chapter and go straight to the next chapter where you can begin your quest for Internet tools.

What Do You Need to Access the Internet?

To access the Internet, you really only need four things:

- A computer, preferably one that runs Microsoft Windows
- A modem, preferably one that runs at least 14.4kbps (kilobits per second) or faster
- Connection software
- An Internet access provider

If your computer is on a LAN (local area network) that has a full connection to the Internet, you don't need a modem. All you need is your network card. If you can send e-mail to and from the Internet, you may or may not have a full (direct) connection to the Internet. Ask your system administrator to find out for sure.

The computer and modem are up to you. If you don't already have these two essential pieces of hardware, get the best you can afford, in terms of quality, reliability, speed, and performance. Remember that spending an extra few hundred dollars on a better system today may save you thousands in the long run, since a more powerful system will have a longer, more useful life.

Also, make sure you get plenty of memory (RAM) and a good size hard disk. Since both RAM and hard disks are becoming amazingly inexpensive, I recommend you get at least 16MB of RAM and a 540MB hard disk. They're like closet space—you can never have enough. Modems, too, are becoming cheaper as they're getting faster, so buy the fastest and most reliable one you can afford.

The connection software you need is completely dependent on the type of connection you have to the Internet. Some methods of access require a specific software program, while others simply require a particular type of connection software.

What's the Best Way to Connect?

There are basically three means available to the average PC user for connecting to the Internet:

- Major online services like America Online, CompuServe, Delphi, or Prodigy, all of which offer varying degrees of connectivity to the Internet among their many services.

- Corporate or educational institutions you may be affiliated with that give you an account on their network, which is connected to the Internet.

- Local and national Internet Service Providers (ISPs), who give you direct access to the Internet, usually via a Unix server, in exchange for a monthly or hourly fee.

All three options have their pros and cons. And keep in mind that the kind of Internet utilities you can, and need to use will vary depending on how you connect to the Internet.

Online Services

Nearly all of the major online services are now touting their ability to get you connected to the Internet quickly and easily, and usually offer a free trial period. But before you sign up, keep in mind that providing access to the Internet is not the primary goal of the major commercial online services, and some of them can end up costing you far more than you may realize.

Most of the big online services offer at the very least, e-mail access to the Internet, and a growing number of them are also offering access to the World Wide Web, Usenet, and FTP as well. Most of them offer their own connection software, either free or for an additional fee.

But remember that these large commercial services are primarily in the business of offering you things that you can't get from the Internet, for example, the ability to make airline reservations online.

3

Shop Around

Keep in mind that the number of options available to you are somewhat dependent on your location. If you live in a place where there's a lot of demand for Internet access, you'll tend to have more options available to you, and you'll probably pay less, because there's a lot of competition. But, if you live in a place where there is little demand, and therefore little or no competition, the number of options available will tend to diminish and your cost will probably be higher.

If there's a local computer magazine in your area, check the ads to find out more about the local providers available. Other good offline resources include user groups, and even local PC bulletin boards.

Different providers will give you different levels of support. Some provide extensive support, while others just give you basic information, and let you figure out the rest by yourself. And don't assume that the more expensive providers will give you better support. Sometimes the "little guys" will bend over backwards to help you out.

Word of mouth is generally the best recommendation for a service provider. If you have friends who are connected, find out which provider they're using and find out how well they like the service.

Another thing to look for is ease of access. Before handing over your credit card number, check out the provider's dial-in number to see how busy it gets during peak hours, such as weekday evenings.

Finally, make sure that your provider is nearby. Charges for toll calls can add up very quickly. Keep in mind that not all phone numbers in your area code may be local calls. If you're not sure, check the section at the beginning of your phone book's white pages or call your phone company to find out which exchanges within your area code are in your local (toll-free) calling area.

And I should warn you in advance that you won't be able to use most of the programs discussed in this book if you're connecting through one of the major commercial services. The interfaces that they use simply aren't compatible with the standard PC Internet access tools available.

Some of these online service providers can get expensive as well, charging you by the hour for accessing some, or all of their services. And some even charge you for the electronic mail you send and receive.

America Online   America Online (AOL) offers e-mail access to and from the Internet, access to Usenet newsgroups, a Gopher browser, and the ability to transfer files over the Internet using FTP (File Transfer Protocol). Plans for a Web browser are underway, and one may be in place by the time you read this.

The problem with AOL is that they require that you use their proprietary software to get access to the Internet, which means that you can't use most of the standard Internet tools that I'm going to talk about later in this book. In addition, they can get rather expensive. While their basic monthly charge is only $9.95 per month, it only includes 5 hours of connect time. After your 5 hours are up, you're billed $2.95 per hour for each hour you spend online. So, if you spend 20 hours online per month, expect it to cost you almost $25. For more information about America Online, call 1-800-827-6364.

CompuServe   CompuServe is one of the oldest online services, and has only just recently begun to beef up their Internet connectivity. While they've had e-mail access to the Internet for several years, they now provide access to many Usenet newsgroups, allow file transfers using FTP, and should have a Web browser in place by the time you read this.

But, like AOL, CompuServe only allows you to connect using their proprietary software, or by dialing up and interacting directly with their servers on a character-only basis, so you can't use most of the standard Internet tools here either. Compuserve is also the most expensive way to access the Internet. Although they charge just $9.95 for unlimited access to their *basic* services, these basic services *do not* include access to the Internet. For additional services such as these, you pay an additional $4.80 per hour. So, if you were to spend 20 hours online each month, it would cost you *more than $100 per month*. Compuserve recently acquired Spry, Inc., makers of the popular *Internet in a Box* package, so expect their Internet services to expand in the near future. For more information about CompuServe, call 1-800-848-8990.

Delphi Delphi has been advertising their Internet connectivity quite heavily over the past year or two. While they do offer access to Usenet news, FTP, Gopher, telnet, and the World Wide Web, your means of access is strictly character-based. And, like the other major online services, you cannot use your own Internet tools with their service.

Delphi's prices are more or less comparable with America Online's. For $23 per month, you can get access to their Internet services, and 20 hours of connect time. Each hour over that costs you $1.80. For more information about Delphi, call 1-800-695-4005.

Prodigy Prodigy was the first major online service to offer graphical access to the World Wide Web for their Windows customers. They also offer access to e-mail, Usenet newsgroups, and FTP. And, like the other services, you are only allowed to use their connection software to access these services.

Prodigy, too, is only inexpensive if you don't spend much time online. Their basic charge is $9.95 a month, for 5 hours of access time. Each hour over that costs $2.95. So, if you were to spend 20 hours online each month, it would cost you over $50. For more information about Prodigy, call 1-800-PRODIGY.

Corporate and Educational Networks

If your employer or your school is on a network that's connected to the Internet, you can probably get, at the very least, e-mail access to the Internet from any computer that's connected to that network. In some cases, your network may have a direct connection to the Internet, which allows you to run many, if not all of the Internet-based PC applications I'm going to talk about throughout the remainder of the book.

While at first this may seem like the ideal situation (because it's free), there are some drawbacks:

- If you're connecting from work, you can only access the Internet while you're at work.

What's Out There

Here are the seven most popular things to do on the Internet:

Electronic Mail lets you send and receive messages to anyone on the Internet, anywhere in the world.

Usenet Newsgroups make up an enormous, world-wide collection of online discussion groups.

FTP (File Transfer Protocol) is a way to transfer files (software, sounds, pictures, text files) to and from servers all over the world.

Telnet is a terminal emulation program that lets you log into other servers on the Internet. Many libraries have public databases available via telnet.

Gopher is a menu-driven interface to information stored and cataloged on servers that run the Gopher server software.

World Wide Web is a network of graphical, hypertext (point-and-click) documents on servers all over the world. Using a Web *browser*, or viewer such as Mosaic or Netscape, you can access Web servers, Gopher servers, and even FTP servers.

Internet Relay Chat is a network of servers that provide live chat sessions, allowing you to talk with other people all around the world.

- Many companies only provide an e-mail gateway for the majority of their employees.

- You may only get access via a Unix shell (character-based, non-graphical) account.

- Your boss may not appreciate it if you use the company's Internet connection for personal reasons.

- Your employer may have strict rules for employee conduct on the Internet.

- Many corporate networks access the Internet through a *firewall*, which limits your ability to access the Internet by restricting access into and out of your network in the interest of protecting your company's internal computing assets from outside intruders.

- If you're on a PC-based LAN (Local Area Network) that's connected to the Internet, you'll probably need additional drivers to be able to access the Internet. These drivers can often be difficult to set up properly.

But, if you can get an account for free, don't turn it down. Just keep in mind that your access may be limited. If it's not enough, you may want to look into getting your own personal account.

Because there are many different flavors of networks, I won't get into specific details about connecting to the Internet through a LAN. Talk to your network administrator to find out if your network is *directly connected* to the Internet, meaning that you can connect to Internet hosts, and run interactive Internet applications from your PC. If it is, find out if you need additional network drivers to access the Internet, and how to obtain and install them.

Keep in mind that just because you have e-mail access to the Internet doesn't mean that you have full access to the Internet. It's relatively easy for network administrators to set up an *e-mail gateway* to the Internet. An e-*mail gateway* is a single connection point to the Internet, and is only capable of transmitting e-mail. So it's relatively useless as far as running interactive applications is concerned.

If your network is behind a firewall, a few of the programs discussed in this book may not work, because they require two-way communication between your PC and the Internet. If the firewall prevents incoming queries to your workstation, you may be out of luck. A growing number of Internet applications support firewall *proxy servers*. If your firewall supports the use of proxies, you should use these applications, rather than ones that do not support proxies. Later on in the book, when I talk about specific programs, I'll point out the ones that support the use of proxy servers.

Internet Service Providers

These are the people whose sole purpose is to give you access to the Internet. But they're not all the same, and different providers offer different kinds of services.

The important things to look for in a provider are service, accessibility, and cost. Providers who run on a shoestring budget probably won't be

A Little Internet History

In July 1969, Neil Armstrong took his "one small step for man" on the Moon. Just two months later, a "giant leap for mankind" took place at UCLA, when the first computer was connected to the ARPANET. The ARPANET, named for its sponsor, the Defense Advanced Research Projects Agency (DARPA), began humbly, by connecting computers at just four sites, all of them universities: UCLA, Stanford Research Institute (SRI), UC Santa Barbara, and the University of Utah.

By 1977, there were over a hundred mainframe and minicomputers connected to ARPANET, most of them still at universities. Educational institutions loved it. It enabled researchers, professors, and students alike to share information with one another, without the need to leave their computer terminals.

Other young networks began to appear, many of them connecting to ARPANET, either directly, or through a *gateway*, which is a device that passes information between different networks.

What happened to the military, you may ask? Well, they came to the conclusion that ARPANET was getting too widespread and too uncontrollable to provide a secure means of communication. So the military split off from ARPANET in 1983, to form their own network, MILNET, which was incorporated with the Defense Data Network (DDN).

Today, there are well over 4,000,000 Internet hosts in the world. Since 1988, the Internet has grown exponentially, approximately doubling in size every year.

too concerned if you call and complain about constant busy signals. Also, if you think you'll need access from more than one location, you should probably look for a provider that offers dial up numbers in all the areas you're likely to be dialing in from.

There are basically three kinds of service you can get from Internet providers:

- Unix shell accounts
- All-in-one graphical front end accounts
- Direct connect SLIP and PPP Accounts

9

Unix Shell Accounts

Until relatively recently, the only way you could connect to the Internet was from a Unix shell account. A shell account is simply a dial-up account on a public-access server that runs the Unix operating system.

Why Unix? Most of the servers on the Internet run Unix because the "language" used on the Internet is TCP/IP (Transmission Control Protocol/Internet Protocol), which also happens to be what Unix servers use to speak to one another.

Accessing a shell account is easy. All you need is a basic terminal emulation program, like the Windows Terminal program. To the Unix server, your computer looks like a *dumb terminal*, one which is only capable of sending and receiving text characters. Consequently, all you get is a character-based interface.

Oh, and you'll need to learn a few basic Unix commands to be able to get around. A typical Unix shell interface is shown in Figure 1.1 below.

Figure 1.1:

Unix shell accounts are cheap, but how easy are they?

```
> pwd
/home/nac
> dir
dir: Command not found.
> ls -la
total 200
drwx--x--x      4 nac    cust       512 Jan 25 09:32 .
drwxr-xr-x   5128 root   wheel    87040 Jan 25 09:12 ..
drwx------      2 nac    cust       512 Jan 16 17:02 .elm
-rw-r--r--      1 nac    cust        33 Jan 14 17:14 .exit
-rw-r--r--      1 nac    cust        17 Jan  1 22:09 .forward
-rw-r--r--      1 nac    cust        64 Jan 25 09:32 .tiacf
drwx------      2 nac    cust       512 Jan  1 21:45 Mail
-rw-------      1 nac    cust      1016 Jan  1 22:35 mbox
> cd Mail
> ls -la
total 8
drwx------      2 nac   cust   512 Jan  1 21:45 .
drwx--x--x      4 nac   cust   512 Jan 25 09:32 ..
> help
help: Command not found.
>
```

On the other hand, most Unix servers have all the basic Internet tools already installed, so you really don't need much beyond your basic modem communications software.

Unix shell accounts are usually pretty inexpensive, in the neighborhood of $10 to $20 per month for unlimited access.

Emulating a SLIP Connection

While the name may not sound very exciting, *SLIP Emulation* lets you simulate a network connection over a terminal session from your PC to a Unix host computer. Okay, but what does that *really* mean? In practical terms, it means that you can run many of the graphical Internet tools described in this book, like Mosaic or Trumpet on a plain old Unix shell account. See Appendix A for information about setting up and using SLIP emulation on a Unix shell account.

Getting Graphical: NetCruiser and Pipeline

If you want a friendly, easy to use, graphical interface to the Internet, you can get an account with an Internet provider that offers an all-in-one software interface program. These programs typically give you the basic tools you'll need to get around: FTP, Telnet, e-mail, a Usenet newsreader, a Web browser, and usually a Gopher client.

Before you get too excited, keep in mind that there are some trade-offs. Although I refer to these accounts as "all-in-one" packages, that doesn't mean they give you everything you're going to need. But the latest versions of these programs do support Winsock, so if you don't like the way a particular tool works, you can use one of the tools I'll discuss later in this book in its place.

NetCruiser Netcom's NetCruiser, shown in Figure 1.2, is probably the most widely accessible and popular all-in-one graphical interface to the Internet. The NetCruiser software provides you with a Windows front end that gives you access to their NetCruiser servers.

Netcruiser has all the basic tools you'll need to access servers on the Internet: e-mail, FTP, Telnet, Gopher, WWW, and IRC client programs.

11

Figure 1.2:
Netcom's NetCruiser
makes it easy to get
around the Internet.

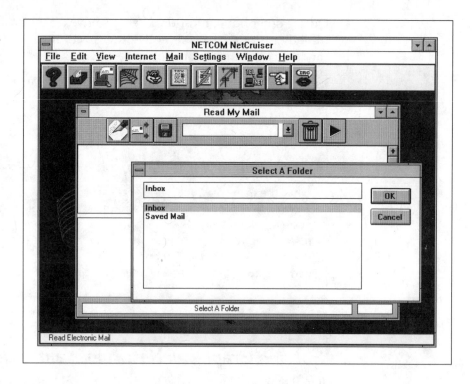

Figure 1.2:
Netcom's NetCruiser
makes it easy to get
around the Internet.

A NetCruiser account costs $19.95 per month, and includes 40 hours of
Prime Time connect time. *Prime Time* is defined as Monday through Fri-
day from 9 a.m. until midnight. If you go over the 40 hours per month,
each additional hour of Prime Time service is $2.00. For more informa-
tion, contact Netcom at 1-800-353-6600.

The Pipeline The Pipeline's *Internaut* software is similar to Netcom's
NetCruiser, and was developed for The Pipeline, an Internet provider based
in New York City, which was recently purchased by PSI, one of the largest
Internet access providers in the US. But the folks at The Pipeline also license
their software for use by other providers, such as Hooked, Inc. of San Francisco (see Figure 1.3). Typically, these providers give you a version of The
Pipeline's Internaut software specifically set up for their system.

The Pipeline's Internaut software is very easy to use, and offers all of
the basic tools you'll need to connect to a variety of services on the

Figure 1.3:

A growing number of Internet providers are offering The Pipeline's Internaut software, such as Hooked, Inc. in San Francisco.

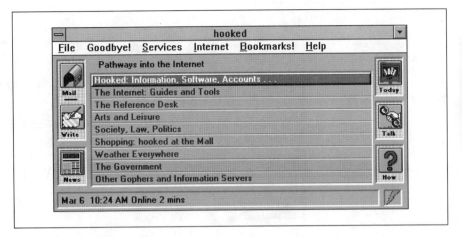

Internet, with links to all kinds of frequently wanted information and services on the Internet.

The Pipeline's Internaut software gives you access to e-mail, ftp, gopher, telnet, Usenet newsgroups, and the World Wide Web.

The amount you're charged by a service provider who licenses the Pipeline software will vary. Expect to pay between $20 and $25 per month. Both Pipeline in New York City and Hooked in San Francisco offer nationwide service via SprintNet. For more information, contact the Pipeline in New York City at (212) 267-3636 or Hooked in San Francisco at (415) 343-1233. Also, there may be a local provider in your area who licenses the Pipeline software. Check your local computer publications to find out.

Connecting with SLIP and PPP

If you want a graphical interface and the ability to run *any* Windows-based Internet program from your home PC, like the Netscape Web browser shown in Figure 1.4, you should look into getting a *SLIP* (Serial Line Interface Protocol) or *PPP* (Point-to-Point Protocol) account.

SLIP and PPP both do essentially the same thing: they simulate a network connection using a modem. In a normal network connection, you

13

Figure 1.4:
With a SLIP or PPP
connection, you can
choose from a number
of Windows Internet
tools, such as the
popular Netscape Web
browser.

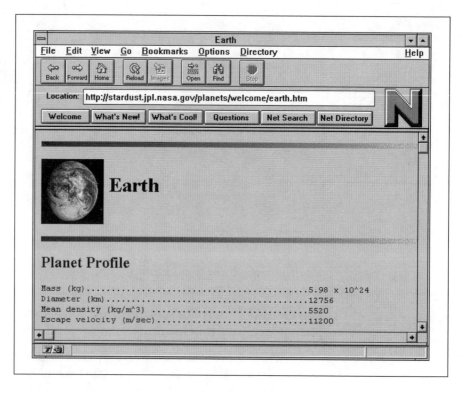

would connect your PC to the network using a Network Interface Card (NIC). The NIC plugs into your PC, and from there, connects to a cable that connects to the network.

But with SLIP and PPP, you don't need a network card. All you need to do is load the appropriate software, and your modem can take the place of a network card.

SLIP just gives you the basic connectivity, but PPP adds error checking and authentication, which makes it a more reliable protocol. Although PPP has a reputation for being more difficult to set up and configure than SLIP, there really isn't much difference between the two.

Even though PPP is more reliable, and is a defined Internet standard, SLIP tends to be more widely available, simply because it's been around longer, although support for PPP is growing.

Another option you might be given is CSLIP (Compressed SLIP), which is basically SLIP with VJ (Van Jacobson) packet header compression, which increases transfer speed.

SLIP and PPP accounts give you the most options. There are no software restrictions, which means you can select the Internet tools that you want to use. If your primary concern is cost, you can build your own Internet tool kit entirely with freeware and public domain tools. If you're more concerned with functionality, you can build yourself a "power" tool kit with a combination of freeware and shareware tools. Depending on the tools you choose, your "power" tool kit will cost anywhere from $25 to $200.

Setting up a SLIP or PPP connection takes a little more effort than the other options. But, if you can set up a modem communications program, you probably shouldn't have any trouble setting up a SLIP or PPP connection.

The cost of a SLIP or PPP connection varies widely, depending primarily on how much competition there is in your area. Expect to pay anywhere from $15 to $40 per month. Also, keep in mind that many Internet providers offer SLIP/PPP connections that include Unix shell access as well. Accounts that offer both SLIP or PPP and Unix shell access will tend to cost about $10-$15 per month more than ones which do not include shell access.

Most providers will give you connection software if you need it, usually one of the freeware packages like Chameleon Sampler. And if you're running Windows 95, you don't even need that, because Windows 95 comes with built-in SLIP and PPP connection software.

For more information about setting up a SLIP or PPP connection in either Windows 3.1 or Windows 95, see Appendix B.

Where to Next?

If you already have a SLIP or PPP connection and Winsock installed, you're ready to start putting together your Internet tool kit.

If you've got a basic Unix shell account, you might want to take a side trip over to Appendix A to find out a little more about Unix and SLIP emulation programs such as TIA (The Internet Adapter).

If you need some help installing Winsock and TCP/IP support in Windows 3.1 or Windows 95, check out Appendix B, to find out more about Chameleon Sampler, Trumpet Winsock, and Windows 95's built-in dial-up networking support.

CHAPTER

2

Tools for Transferring Files

LOOKING FOR SOME great Winsock applications to add to your personal Internet tool kit? The ultimate computer game? A recipe for salsa? Supreme Court rulings? You get them all, and much, much more, using FTP (File Transfer Protocol).

Although the name implies that it's just a *protocol* (a set of rules) for transferring files, FTP is much more than that. It's a program that lets you connect to servers around the world that run the FTP protocol, giving you access to a wide range of programs and information.

FTP is pretty straightforward. You want a file? FTP gets it for you. You can also use FTP to transfer files from your PC to a host computer, though you'll probably spend much more time downloading than uploading.

So, what kind of files can you get using FTP? Well, for one thing, you can get other tools like Web browsers, newsreaders, mail programs, and file conversion utilities. In fact, every program I'm going to talk about in this book is available via FTP.

But you can also get other kinds of information from FTP servers. For example, Microsoft Corporation, and many other software and hardware vendors, offer product information, updated drivers, and even technical support information on their FTP servers. On still other FTP servers, you can find sound files, pictures, song lyrics, legal information, recipes, and much more.

The Basics of FTP

Before getting into the Windows FTP programs, I'd like to take a little time to explain how FTP works. I'll start by discussing how to use FTP on a Unix system, since, like most Internet utilities, FTP was originally written for Unix.

If you've ever transferred files to or from another computer using a communications program on your PC, you're familiar with PC file transfer protocols, like Xmodem and Kermit, which let you download files from a host to your PC. FTP serves the same purpose, except that the FTP program does more than just transfer files. It also establishes your connection to the remote computer, logs you in, and lets you move around through directories on the remote computer.

Starting FTP

To use FTP on a Unix system, do the following:

1. When you run FTP from a Unix shell account, you'll want to start it up with the name of the FTP server you want to log into. So, if you wanted to transfer files from ftp.cica.indiana.edu, the largest archive site for Windows shareware and freeware programs, you'd type `ftp ftp.cica.indiana.edu`.

If you don't start FTP up with the name of a host, you'll get an ftp> prompt. If you want to connect to a host, you need to use the **open** command:

```
% ftp
ftp> open ftp.cica.indiana.edu
```

In either case, this will usually get you connected to the FTP server, unless the server or network is down or too busy, or if you just misspelled the server's name. When you get connected, you'll see a welcome screen and a login prompt:

```
% ftp ftp.cica.indiana.edu
Connected to winftp.cica.indiana.edu.
220-
220-     You have reached ftp.cica.indiana.edu [129.79.26.27].  All
220-     anonymous ftp transactions are logged. If you find this
220-     policy unacceptable, terminate your connection NOW.
220-
220-
220 winftp FTP server (Version wu-2.3(2) Fri Nov 18 15:25:26 EST 1994) ready.
Name (ftp.cica.indiana.edu:nac):
```

2. If you're logging in to an anonymous FTP server, enter **anonymous** at the Name: prompt.

```
Name (ftp.cica.indiana.edu:nac): anonymous
331 Guest login ok, send your complete e-mail address as password.
Password:
```

Some anonymous FTP servers will automatically append your hostname to your user ID at the password: *prompt if you just type an @ at the end of your username. You'll usually see a message to this effect when you connect to the server.*

3. Enter your e-mail address at the `password:` prompt. (You won't see your password (e-mail address) when you type it in.) Now, you're logged in to the server, and you'll probably see a second welcome screen like this one:

```
Password:
230-**    You have reached ftp.cica.indiana.edu [129.79.26.27]
230-**  C I C A - Center for Innovative Computer Applications
230-**      Indiana University in Bloomington, Indiana USA.
230-**      Sun SPARC 1  SunOS 4.1.3  28MB memory  4GB disk
230-**
230-** To request automatic help, e-mail:  ftp@cica.indiana.edu
230-**         To contact us via e-mail:  ftp-admin@cica.indiana.edu
230-**       Windows files are located in:  /pub/pc/win3
230-** Your current working directory is:  /
230-**
230-**               You are user number:  75 (of a possible 75)
230-**                   Local time is:  Wed Mar  1 22:03:42 1995 [EST]
230-
230 Guest login ok, access restrictions apply.
Remote system type is UNIX.
Using binary mode to transfer files.
ftp> █
```

4. Now you can use the old familiar `dir` command to see where you are and which directories are available:

```
ftp> dir
200 PORT command successful.
150 Opening ASCII mode data connection for /bin/ls.
total 8
dr-xr-xr-x  2 0      31           512 Feb 16  1994 bin
drwxr-xr-x  2 0       1           512 Feb 11  1994 dev
d--x--x--x  2 0       1           512 Nov 12 00:19 etc
drwxr-x--x  3 0      11          1024 Mar  1 23:00 ftpd
drwx--x--x  2 0       1           512 Feb 24 04:44 msgs
drwxr-xr-x  4 0       0           512 Feb  1 00:16 pub
drwx--x--x  3 0       1           512 Jan 31  1994 sys
drwxr-xr-x  3 0       1           512 Jan 31  1994 usr
226 Transfer complete.
ftp> █
```

 *Remember that any line that begins with **d** is a directory.*

 If the list of files is too long to display on your screen, type `ls -l |more` instead of `dir` to see the list one page at a time. Another handy trick is to use `ls -lart`, which will show all the files in order by date, with the most recent files at the bottom of the list.

20

5. Most of the time, the files that you're looking for on an anonymous FTP server are going to be in the **/pub** directory. To switch to the /pub directory, just type `cd pub`.

Beyond the /pub directory, there's no standard for directory naming. The best thing to do is look for a README *or* INDEX *file to find out what's available in the various directories. If you can't see an* INDEX *or* README *file, just type* `dir` *or* `dir |more` *to see if any of the directories listed sound like what you're looking for.*

Anonymous or Not?

There are two ways you can log in to a server using FTP: either as a regular user of that system, or as an anonymous user. If you have an account on the remote system, and you want to transfer files to or from your own home directory, just log in using your regular user ID and password. But if you don't have an account on that system and you want to get files that are kept in the server's public FTP archive, you need to log in as an anonymous user.

The anonymous FTP system has been around for a long time. It was created so that people on a system on the Internet could share files with others who didn't have accounts on there, hence the user name "anonymous." When you log in as anonymous you enter your e-mail address at the `password:` prompt so that the server's administrator can get an idea about who's using the FTP server. The anonymous FTP system relies on trust, so using your real e-mail address is your way of showing that you respect that trust.

ASCII or Binary?

When you find a file that you want, you need to set the correct *transfer mode* for the file. Most files are either *ASCII* or *binary*. There's a big difference between the two. If you try to transfer a binary file as ASCII, all you'll end up with is garbage. And if you try to transfer an ASCII file as binary, the lines won't wrap properly on your PC, because you'll lose the line breaks.

But how do you tell the difference? It's really pretty easy. Take a look at the filename extension. Here are some of the more common file types

21

you'll find around the Internet, transfer type (ASCII or binary), and how to deal with the files once you get them:

Extension:	Type:	Transfer as:	Then:
.arc	Archive	binary	Uncompress with a decompression tool like WinZip
.asc	Text	ascii	Open with Notepad or any word processor
.au	Sound	binary	Play with Wham or WPlany
.bmp	Graphic	binary	View with LView
.exe	Executable	binary	Execute
.gif	Graphic	binary	View with LView
.gz	Unix Compressed	binary	Uncompress with GNUZip of WinZip
.hqx	Apple Macintosh Encoded	ascii	Convert with UNMacIt
.jpg	Graphic	binary	View with LView
.lzh	LHarc Compressed	binary	Uncompress with LHA or Winzip
.sit	Macintosh Compressed	binary	Uncompress with UnMacIt
.tar	Unix Tape Archive	binary	Unarchive with EXTAR or WinZip
.tar.z, .taz or .tgz	Unix Tape Archive, compressed	binary	Uncompress with GNUZip, then with EXTAR or WinZip
.tif or .tiff	Graphic	binary	View with LView Pro
.txt	Text	ascii	Open with Notepad or any word processor

Extension:	Type:	Transfer as:	Then:
.uu or .uue	UUEncoded	ascii	Decode with Wincode or XFerPro
.voc	Sound	binary	Play with Wham
.wav	Sound	binary	Play with Wham or the Windows Sound Recorder
.z or .Z	Unix Compressed	binary	Uncompress with GNUZip or WinZip
.zip	Zipped Archive	binary	Uncompress with a decompression tool like WinZip or UnZip

For more information about file utilities and players, see Chapters 9 and 10.

You also might run into some of these ASCII files. All of these files can be read with the Windows Notepad or any word processor:

- INDEX
- ls-ltr
- readme
- index
- readme.txt
- .message
- 00index
- read.me
- .msg

If you want to read one of these files on screen, use `get filename |more` *to read the file on screen, one page at a time.*

Files that were created by a word processing program like Word for Windows (.doc) are usually not ASCII files, despite the fact that they contain text. Most word processors insert binary codes into the document, which won't translate properly if you transfer the file as ASCII. If you're not sure, transfer the file as binary.

A good rule of thumb for determining file type is to take a look at the extension. If it looks like an abbreviation for something, and it's not .txt or .asc, it's probably binary.

Changing the Default Transfer Mode

The default mode for the Unix version of FTP is always ASCII, so if you're transferring ASCII text files, you don't need to do anything. But if you're transferring binary files, you need to issue the **binary** or **bin** command at the ftp> prompt:

```
ftp> binary
200 Type set to I.
```

If you need to switch back to ASCII later, issue the **ascii** or **as** command:

```
ftp> ascii
200 Type set to A.
```

If you're not sure which mode you're in, use the **type** command:

```
ftp> type
Using ascii mode to transfer files.
```

Getting Files

Okay, you've found the file that you want, and set the correct transfer mode (ASCII or binary). You'll now use the get command to transfer the file. In this case, we'll download the **INDEX** file.

```
ftp> get INDEX
200 PORT command successful.
150 Opening BINARY mode data connection for INDEX (307370 bytes).
226 Transfer complete.
307370 bytes received in 22 seconds (14 Kbytes/s)
ftp>
```

Remember that most FTP servers are case sensitive, so **INDEX** is a different file than **index**.

If you're running FTP from a Unix shell account, the files you transfer using FTP will be transferred to the Unix computer you're dialed into. If you want to get these files to your PC, you'll need to execute another command to be able to transfer the files from the Unix server to your PC. Different systems use different file transfer programs. Two of the more common ones are SX *(send Xmodem) and* SZ *(send Zmodem). Check with your Unix system administrator to find out which one you should use.*

Sending Files

Although you'll probably spend most of your time downloading files rather than uploading them, there may come a time when you need to upload a file to an FTP server.

If you need to transfer a file from your system to a remote FTP server, use the **put** command. In this case, we'll upload the **Myfile.txt** file.

```
ftp> put myfile.txt
200 PORT command successful.
150 ASCII data connection for myfile.txt (199.2.134.2,1043).
226 Transfer complete.
98 bytes sent in 0.0026 seconds (36 Kbytes/s)
ftp>
```

If you're logging on as an anonymous user, you probably won't be able to transfer files to the server, unless the administrator allows anonymous users to upload files.

Logging Off

When you're done transferring files, just type **quit**:

```
ftp> quit
221 Goodbye.
```

For more information about FTP, type man ftp *at a Unix prompt to see the on-line manual. While you're running FTP, you can also type* help *at the* ftp> *prompt to see the manual, or* help command *to get a description of the particular* command.

Transferring Files
CH. 2

25

Windows FTP Programs

Windows FTP programs are great. They take a lot of the hassle out of transferring files. You can switch from ASCII mode to binary mode with a click of a mouse button, and even set the program to "redial" if the FTP server you're trying to log into is busy.

There are several Windows FTP programs available for both 16-bit Windows (3.1), and 32-bit Windows (Windows NT and Windows 95). All of the following programs use Winsock (Windows Sockets) to connect to the Internet.

FTP in Windows 95

Windows 95 comes with its own FTP application. You can find FTP in the WINDOWS directory. It works the same way as the basic Unix FTP, which I described at the beginning of this chapter.

Although it's free, I wouldn't recommend using it. It's much more difficult to use than the Windows-based FTP applications that I'll talk about next.

WS-FTP

WS-FTP, by John Junod, was one of the first FTP programs for Windows, and is the best all-around product currently available (see Figure 2.1). The program was designed to be easy to use, even for beginners; yet even experienced users will appreciate some of its more advanced features.

One of the nicest things about WS-FTP is that it allows you to save information about the FTP servers you visit most often, including the server name, anonymous login information, and directory information. It even comes pre-configured with information about 25 of the most popular anonymous FTP servers for Windows users, which saves you a lot of typing.

WS-FTP is freeware, and may be distributed freely for non-commercial use. For information on commercial use, send an e-mail message to Ipswitch at **info@ipswitch.com**.

Figure 2.1:
WS-FTP makes file
transfer over the
Internet easy.

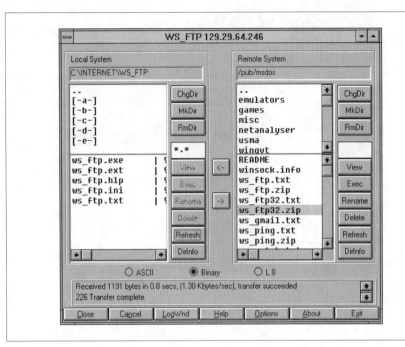

Transferring Files
CH. 2

You can get the latest version of WS-FTP via anonymous FTP from
ftp.usma.edu, in the **/pub/msdos/winsock.files/** directory. It can also be
found at **ftp.cica.indiana.edu**, in the **/pub/pc/win3/winsock/** directory.
The **ws_ftp.zip** file contains the 16-bit version for Windows 3.1, and
ws_ftp32.zip contains the 32-bit version for Windows NT and Windows 95.

*There is a Windows NT-specific version of WS-FTP, written by Larry Kahn, based
on an older version of John Junod's program. The program is essentially the same
as WS-FTP, but it will not run on Windows 3.1 or Windows 95. If you're running
Windows NT, you may want to give it a try. It's available from ftp.cica.indi-
ana.edu, in the /pub/pc/win3/winsock directory, and the filename is
wsftp32.zip.*

Installing WS-FTP

To install WS-FTP, do the following:

1. Create a **WS-FTP** directory on your hard disk.

2. Uncompress the zip file in that directory using a decompression tool such as WinZip or UnZip (see Chapter 9 for more on compression and decompression tools).

3. Create an icon for the WS_FTP.EXE file on your Windows desktop.

4. If you're running Windows 95, move the WS_FTP32.INI file to your Windows directory.

To configure WS-FTP, do the following:

1. Start up WS-FTP.

2. Click on **Cancel** to close the Session Profile Window.

3. Click on the **Options** button at the bottom of the window.

4. Click on the **Program Options** button.

5. Enter your e-mail address in the E-Mail Address field.

6. Configure other options if desired. Click on **Save**.

7. Click on **Exit** to return to the WS-FTP window.

8. To get ready to start a new FTP session, click on the **Connect** button at the bottom of the window.

If you're using WS-FTP on a network that uses a firewall server to connect to the Internet, you may need to set up WS-FTP so that it uses *PASV transfer mode*. PASV transfer mode allows the client application (in this case WS-FTP) to establish the connection to the server, which is required by most firewalls. To set this as the default, click on **Session Options**, and check the Use PASV Transfer Mode box. Click on **Save as Default** and then **Save**.

Using WS-FTP

To use WS-FTP to connect to a host, do the following:

1. If you haven't already started up WS-FTP, do so now. When you first start up WS-FTP, you'll see the Session Profile window. This window allows you to either select from a number of pre-configured FTP hosts or add a new one.

2. To connect to a host, just select the host name from the Profile Name drop-down list box, shown in Figure 2.2. If the host you want to connect to isn't listed, click on the **New** button and enter the host name.

Figure 2.2:
Just select a host from the drop-down list box in WS-FTP, and you're off!

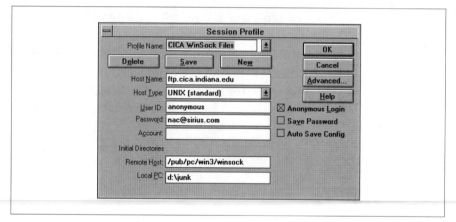

3. If it's an anonymous FTP connection, make sure the Anonymous Login box is checked. If you're connecting to your own personal account, enter your normal user ID and password in the spaces provided.

4. Click on **OK**. WS-FTP logs you in, and changes to the directory specified in the profile.

 ▶ *If you're calling a particularly busy FTP server, you can configure WS-FTP to redial by clicking on the Advanced button in the Session Profile window and entering the number of times you want WS-FTP to redial the server in the Retry box.*

Transferring Files CH. 2

If you're on a network that's behind a firewall, but supports the use of proxy servers, click on the Advanced *button on the Sessions Profile window and enter the proxy server information in the* Firewall Information *sections. When you're done, click on* OK.

Once you've connected to a host, you'll see a list of directories on the host system in the upper right hand corner of the window.

Some of the options available to you at this point include the following:

To change to a different directory, double-click on that directory in the upper right-hand section of the window.

To view a text file, such as an INDEX or README file, select the file, and click on the View button.

To transfer a file, select the file, then make sure that you have the right transfer type selected—ASCII, Binary, or L8 (VMS non-ASCII)—and double-click on the file name, or just select the file and click on the left arrow (←) button.

To transfer multiple files, select the files you want by holding down the Ctrl key while you select the files with your Left Mouse Button, then click on the left arrow button.

To exit an FTP session, click on the Close button.

WinFTP

WinFTP by Santanu Lahiri is based on an earlier version of John Junod's WS-FTP. WinFTP version 1.0, shown in Figure 2.3, is very similar to WS-FTP, and works basically the same way, with the addition of a few useful features, such as a Ping utility, which gives you the ability to send a Ping to an unresponsive FTP server. If the server doesn't answer a Ping, then it's probably not working at the moment.

As I write this, Santanu is making plans for a new and improved WinFTP version 2.0. He's planning a much snazzier interface, with performance enhancements for Windows 95. Keep an eye out for this version, which should be released sometime in the summer of 1995.

Figure 2.3:
WinFTP 1.0 is another variation on the WS_FTP theme.

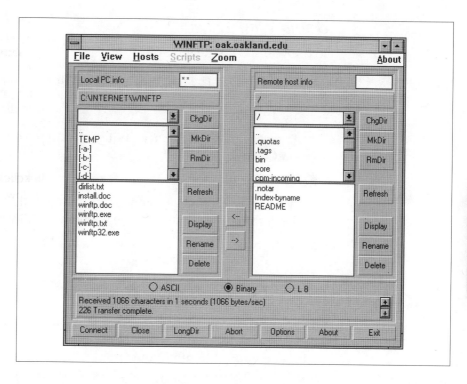

Transferring Files
CH. 2

The latest version of WinFTP can be found at **mica.chrr.ohio-state.edu** in the **/WINSOCK** directory. The **WINFTP.ZIP** file contains both the 16-bit and 32-bit versions.

WinFTP 1.0 is a public domain program, and may be freely copied and distributed. Version 2.0 will be shareware.

Installing WinFTP

To install WinFTP, do the following:

1. Create a **WINFTP** directory on your hard disk.

2. Uncompress the zip file in that directory.

3. Create an icon for the WINFTP.EXE file on your Windows desktop.

Using WinFTP

To use WinFTP, do the following:

1. Start WinFTP. The first time you run WinFTP, you'll be prompted to enter your e-mail address, as well as the default directory for file transfers.

2. Enter the name of the host that you want to connect to, then click on **Connect**.

3. Select the directory you want to go to by clicking on it.

4. To change the transfer mode, click on either the ASCII, Binary, or L8 button at the bottom of the window.

5. To transfer the file, just double click on the filename.

Anonymous FTP Archives

Okay, now that you know how to use FTP, where do you go to get files? The best place to look is at one of the big archive FTP servers. These archives contain literally thousands of shareware and freeware programs, and are usually the best place to look for just about any kind of program you'll ever need.

Here are some of the FTP archive servers I know you'll want to check out. They all carry a large number of Windows and DOS programs.

CICA Windows Archive

The Center for Innovative Computing Applications (CICA) at Indiana University is primarily a research institute focusing on developing scientific and artistic visualization and high-end computing applications. But to Windows users, the CICA Windows archive, **ftp.cica.indiana.edu**, is the single most popular anonymous FTP server on the Internet. The CICA Windows archive contains just about any shareware, freeware, or demo program for Microsoft Windows that you can imagine. The last time I looked, in early 1995, there were nearly 5,000 files in CICA's Windows archive.

The only problem with CICA is that it's *too* popular. In an average day, over 14,000 files are transferred from the server. Often, the maximum number of connections are in use (45 during the day, 75 at night). Fortunately, there are a number of anonymous FTP servers that mirror CICA's archive.

If you have problems getting into ftp.cica.indiana.edu, try one of the following servers:

- **wuarchive.wustl.edu** (MO) in the **/systems/ibmpc/win3** directory

- **archive.orst.edu** (OR) in the **/pub/mirrors/ftp.cica .indiana.edu/win3** directory

- **gatekeeper.dec.com** (CA) in the **/.f/micro/msdos/win3** directory

- **ftp.cdrom.com** (CA) in the **/pub/cica** directory

- **ftp.marcam.com** (IL) in the **/win3** directory

- **mrcnext.cso.uiuc.edu** (IL) in the **/pub/win3** directory

- **ftp.dataplex.net** (TX) in the **/.1/cica/pc/win3** directory

- **ftp.monash.edu.au** (Australia) in the **/pub/win3** directory

- **ftp.funet.fi** (Finland) in the **/pub/mirrors/ftp.cica .indiana.edu** directory

- **ftp.uni-paderborn.de** (Germany) in the **/ftp/disk2/Cica** directory

- **ftp.uni-stuttgart.de** (Germany) in the **/pub/systems/pc/ win3-cica** directory

- **ftp.iij.ad.jp** (Tokyo) in the **/pub/win3** directory

- **ftp.nectec.or.th** (Thailand) in the **/pub/mirrors/win3** directory

- **ftp.technion.ac.il** (Israel) in the **/pub/unsupported/ mswin/cica** directory

- **nic.switch.ch** (Zurich) in the **/mirror/win3** directory

- **src.doc.ic.ac.uk** (London) in the **/pub/0-Most-Packages/ windows3** directory

- **nctuccca.edu.tw** (Taiwan) in the **/PC/windows** directory
- **ftp.cyf-kr.edu.pl** (Cracow, Poland) in the **/pub/mirror/win3** directory
- **info.nic.surfnet.nl** (Netherlands) in **the /mirror-archive/ software/cica-win3** directory

Keep in mind that both the mirror sites and the directories in which they keep the mirrored files may change at any time.

Mirror Sites

Sometimes, when you try to log into an anonymous FTP server, you'll get a message like this one:

```
530-Sorry! We have reached maximum number of connections.
```

This tends to happen with very popular sites, which understandably limit the number of anonymous ftp connections they will allow at any one time. If they didn't, *their* connection to the Internet might potentially get so clogged that it would slow down to a complete halt.

If you get a message like this, there's not much you can do other than wait and try again later, or try a different site, such as a *mirror site*, if there's one available. *Mirror sites* are other FTP servers that carry relatively up-to-date copies of the files at popular anonymous FTP sites.

SimTel

The SimTel archive houses the largest collection of DOS programs on the Internet (over 10,000 files), but they offer a number of Windows programs as well, although their collection isn't as extensive as CICA's.

The SimTel server belongs to the US Army, and for security reasons is no longer accessible for direct anonymous FTP logins. However, there are a number of SimTel mirror sites. The primary mirror site is **oak.oakland.edu** at Oakland University in Rochester, Michigan.

The SimTel files are in the **/SimTel** directory, with DOS files in the **/SimTel/msdos/** subdirectory, and Windows 3.x files in the **/SimTel/win3/** subdirectory.

Secondary mirror sites of SimTel include:

- **wuarchive.wustl.edu** (MO) in the **/systems/ibmpc/msdos** directory
- **archive.orst.edu** (OR) in the **/pub/mirrors/simtel/msdos** directory
- **archie.au** (Australia) in the **/micros/pc/oak** directory
- **micros.hensa.ac.uk** (England) in the **/mirrors/simtel** directory
- **src.doc.ic.ac.uk** (England) in the **/pub/packages/simtel** directory
- **ftp.funet.fi** (Finland) in the **/pub/msdos/SimTel** directory
- **ftp.ibp.fr** (France) in the **/pub/pc/SimTel/msdos** directory
- **ftp.uni-paderborn.de** (Germany) in the **/SimTel/msdos** directory
- **ftp.cs.cuhk.hk** (Hong Kong) in the **/pub/simtel/msdos** directory
- **ftp.technion.ac.il** (Israel) in the **/pub/unsupported/dos/simtel** directory
- **ftp.cyf-kr.edu.pl** (Poland) in the **/pub/mirror/msdos** directory
- **ftp.sun.ac.za** (South Africa) in the **/pub/simtel/msdos** directory
- **ftp.sunet.se** (Sweden) in the **/pub/pc/mirror/SimTel** directory
- **ftp.switch.ch** (Switzerland) in the **/mirror/msdos** directory
- **nctuccca.edu.tw** (Taiwan) in the **/PC/simtel** directory
- **ftp.nectec.or.th** (Thailand) in the **/pub/mirrors/SimTel** directory

Keep in mind that both the mirror sites and the directories in which they keep the mirrored files may change at any time.

CICA and SimTel Archive Indexes

When you first start prowling around the popular FTP servers, it's easy to get intimidated. There are thousands of files, in many different

35

Avoiding Viruses

Sadly, viruses can happen. Although some FTP archive sites scan files before posting them for public use, you should always protect yourself from potential virus attacks by checking out files before executing them.

The best shareware virus protection is available from McAfee Associates. You can get their VirusScan program from **ftp.mcafee.com** in the **/pub/antivirus** directory. VirusScan costs $25 to register, and it's worth every penny. McAfee publishes regular updates, which include detection information on the newest viruses.

Scan your hard disk regularly, and keep suspect files in a directory by themselves until you can check them out with the most current version of VirusScan or some other virus detection utility.

directories. If you don't know exactly where to look for the file you want, you could end up searching for hours.

To make things easier for file hunters, both CICA and SimTel provide directory index files. The CICA Index file is really just a list of all the files in the CICA Windows archive. The SimTel Index files are comma-separated. Wading through these files using just a word processing program is tedious at best. Fortunately, there are utilities that will let you browse through these files easily.

The CICA Index File

CICA's Index file provides a complete listing of all the files in the **pub/pc/win3** directory and all of its subdirectories.

The CICA Index file can be found at **ftp.cica.indiana.edu** in the **/pub/pc/win3** directory. Download either the ASCII text version, **INDEX** or the compressed (binary) version, **INDEX.ZIP**, which you can uncompress using a decompression tool such as WinZip or UnZip.

The SimTel Index Files

The SimTel Archive Index is split into two files: DOS and Windows, and they're in separate directories. You can get the files in either ASCII or .IDX (comma-separated index) file formats. I recommend getting the .IDX version.

You can get the SimTel Index files from **oak.oakland.edu**. The DOS index file is in the **/SimTel/msdos/** directory, in the **SIMINDEX.ZIP** file. The Windows Index file is in the **/SimTel/win3/** directory, in the **SIMWNDEX.ZIP** file. Both files are compressed, and can be uncompressed using a decompression tool such as WinZip.

Both these .ZIP files also contain a number of other files, including copyright and other useful information files.

Anonymous FTP Archive Utilities

Index files are only as useful as the tools you have to view them with. If you're just looking at the raw text of the Index files, you won't really be able to take full advantage of their usefulness. To make your archive searches even easier, here are a couple of utilities that can help you to catalog these Index files and let you search for files offline.

SimTel Directory Viewer

The best FTP archive directory utility I've found is the SimTel Directory Viewer (SimView) by George R. Torralba (see Figure 2.4). It's a Windows utility that you can use to view any .IDX file, and even search for files offline.

Although SimView was originally designed specifically to view the SimTel Index file, you can also use it to view the CICA Index file. All you need to do is convert the CICA Index file into .IDX format. This can be done with the CNVCICA utility discussed later on in this chapter.

The SimTel Directory Viewer is freeware.

Figure 2.4:
The SimTel Directory
Viewer lets you view
and search through
FTP archive indexes
offline.

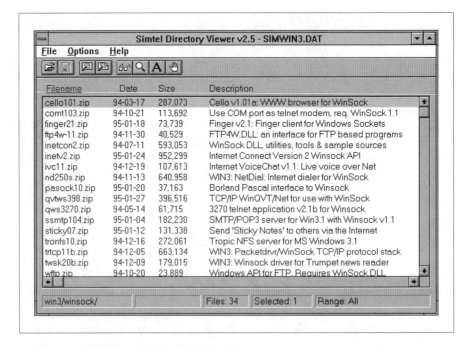

You can get it via anonymous FTP from any of the SimTel mirror sites, such as **oak.oakland.edu**, in the **/SimTel/msdos/filedoc/** directory. The current version is 2.5. Download both the **simvw25.zip** and the **simvwdll.zip** files.

Installing SimTel Directory Viewer

To install SimView, do the following:

1. Create a **SIMVW** directory on your hard disk.

2. Uncompress both the **SIMVW25.ZIP** and **SIMVWDLL.ZIP** files into this directory.

3. Move all of the .DLL files to your **WINDOWS\SYSTEM** subdirectory using the File Manager (Windows 3.1) or Windows Explorer (Windows 95). If you already have versions of these .DLL files on your system, use the newest versions.

4. Create an icon for the **SIM_VW.EXE** file on your Windows desktop.

Running The SimTel Directory Viewer

To view an Index file using SimView, do the following:

1. If you haven't already done so, download the .IDX files you want to view. (See the previous section for information about downloading these files.)

If you want to be able to view the CICA Index file, you'll need to convert it to .IDX file format first, using the CNVCICA program discussed later.

2. Put the .IDX file you want to view in the **SIMVW** directory.

3. Start up the SimTel Directory Viewer. The first time you run it, you'll get an error message stating that it's unable to find the SIM_VW.DBL file. That's okay, because SimView will create it for you. Click on **Yes** to create the file.

4. Now, select File ➤ Open or click on the File Open icon.

5. Click on the **List Files of Type** list box, and select **SimTel Data File (*.idx)**.

6. Select the .IDX file you want to view, and click on **OK**.

7. You'll then be asked if you want to convert the file. Click on **Yes**. SimView will then convert the file to .DAT format.

8. After the file is converted, SimView will open the .DAT file.

9. Double-click on any of the directories shown to see the file listings for that directory (see Figure 2.4).

10. To get back out to the directory view, just press the Esc key.

11. To find a file, select File ➤ Find or click on the magnifying glass icon. Enter your search criteria, and click on **OK**.

12. To find the next occurrence of the search text, press the F3 key.

The next time you run SimView to view this file, open the .DAT file that SimView created. Only open the file in .IDX format the first time you open the Index file.

CNVCICA

If you want to use the SimTel Directory Viewer on the CICA Index file, you need to convert the Index file from plain ASCII text format to .IDX format first. The easiest way to do this is with Peter van der Veen's CNVCICA utility, shown in Figure 2.5.

CNVCICA is public domain software.

Figure 2.5:
CNVCICA lets you convert CICA's INDEX to .IDX format so you can read it with the SimTel Directory Viewer.

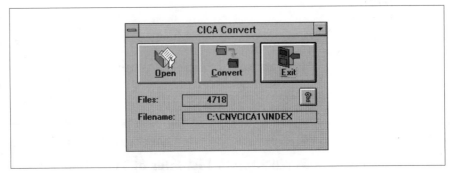

You can get CNVCICA via anonymous FTP from **ftp.cica.indiana.edu**, in the **/pub/pc/win3/ misc** directory. The current version is 1.0. Download the **cnvcica1.zip** file.

Installing CNVCICA

To install CNVCICA, do the following:

1. Copy the **CNVCICA1.ZIP** file to an empty floppy disk.

2. Uncompress the zip file on the floppy disk.

3. Run the **SETUP.EXE** file from the floppy disk to install the program on your hard disk. Accept the defaults, if possible.

Running CNVCICA

To run CNVCICA, do the following:

1. If you haven't already done so, download the CICA Index file from **ftp.cica.indiana.edu** in the **/pub/pc/win3** directory. The filename is **INDEX.ZIP**.

2. Uncompress the INDEX.ZIP file in the **CNVCICA** directory.

3. Start CNVCICA.

4. Click on the **Open** button. The Open File dialog box appears.

5. Select the INDEX file and click on **OK.**

6. Now, click on the **Convert** button. CNVCICA then converts the index file to .IDX format and renames it **CICA.IDX**. When it's done, you'll get a "converting complete" message.

7. If you want to view the file with SimView, you can then move the new CICA.IDX file to your **SIMVW** directory, and open it with SimView. (See the previous section for information about using the SimTel Directory Viewer.)

Well, now that you have the tools that will help you to put together your own Internet tool kit, it's time to get out there and start gathering!

3

Exploring
with Telnet

THESE DAYS, WHEN people talk about the Internet, they tend to focus on the really cool Internet applications—the ones that use graphics and sound for instance. By comparison, little old Telnet seems pretty dull. It's just a very basic terminal application, like the Windows Terminal.

But there are still some things out there on the Internet that you can get to by using a plain little old Telnet application. You can use Telnet to access all kinds of databases, online games, chat servers, and even electronic bulletin boards.

Also, if you have more than one account on the Internet, you can use Telnet to log into that account from another place on the Internet. For example, CompuServe is accessible via Telnet, so if I want to check my mailbox on CompuServe while I'm logged into my regular Internet account, I can telnet to **compuserve.com**, log in, and check my mail. When I log out, I'm back at my Internet account. And I don't have to hang up the phone and call CompuServe's access number to do it.

Cool Places to Telnet

Don't let the simplicity of Telnet fool you. There's a huge variety of resources available through this handy tool. Here are a few places you might want to check out.

CARL (Colorado Alliance of Research Libraries). Although CARL's main purpose is to provide an online catalog of holdings at various libraries around the US, you can also find some interesting databases here, including the *Internet Resource*, a database of information about Internet resources; and *Journal Graphics*, which offers written transcripts of many public television and radio shows. To get there, telnet to **pac.carl.org** and select **pac**.

Library of Congress. Speaking of libraries, why not check out the granddaddy of them all? The Library of Congress database is accessible via telnet. It offers a catalog of the Library's holdings, Federal legislation, copyright information, and more. To get there, telnet to **locis.loc.gov**.

HNSOURCE at the University of Kansas. A great database for history buffs, HNSOURCE offers an extensive history database, with links to other systems. To get there, telnet to **ukanaix.cc.ukans.edu** and select **history**.

Dartmouth Library Shakespeare Database. Need to look up a passage from Shakespeare? The Shakespeare database at Dartmouth Library lets you search through all of Shakespeare's plays and sonnets. To get there, telnet to **library.dartmouth.edu**. To search through Shakespeare's plays, type **select file s plays**. To search through his sonnets, type **select file s sonnets**.

First Internet Backgammon Server (FIBS). Feel like a quick game of backgammon? Then try FIBS. There are games starting all the time. The atmosphere is casual and friendly. To get there, telnet to **fraggel65.mdstud.chalmers.se**, port **4321**. Login as **guest**.

ISCA Bulletin Board. Your basic computer bulletin board, except that it's on the Internet, and it boasts over 100,000 users. If you have something to talk about, you're sure to find someone here who will listen! To get there, telnet to **bbs.isca.uiowa.edu**.

Telnet Basics

Telnet is one of the oldest applications on the Internet, with roots going back to the early 1970s. With Telnet, you can log into a remote server—either down the block or halfway around the world—and access information as if you were sitting in the same room as the computer you're accessing.

Like most everything on the Internet, Telnet originates from Unix. So I'll start out by showing you how to use Telnet on a Unix system.

Using Telnet is pretty easy. To open up a connection to a host using Telnet, just type **Telnet** and the name of the host you want to access. You should see something like this:

```
% telnet well.sf.ca.us
Trying 198.93.4.10...
Connected to well.sf.ca.us.
Escape character is '^]'.


UNIX(r) System V Release 4.0 (well)

This is the WELL

Type    newuser    to sign up.
Type    trouble    if you are having trouble logging in.
Type    guest      to learn about the WELL.

If you already have a WELL account, type your username.

login: |
```

Once you're connected, Telnet will negotiate *terminal emulation*. Terminal emulation is the method used by the remote system to display characters on your screen. If you're prompted to enter a type of terminal emulation, and you aren't sure which one to use, use VT100, as this is supported on most systems.

In most cases, the only commands you really need to know are those that are used on the remote host. Chances are that host is running Unix (see Appendix A for a sampling of useful Unix commands), although you may find other operating systems running on host servers as well, such as UMS or windows NT.

Many systems, especially databases, offer menus. If menus aren't available, see if there's a help file. Try typing **?** or **help** or just **h** to see if there's a help file.

When you're done with your Telnet session, just type **quit** or **exit**, and you'll be back at your host system.

 ▶ *Some systems use commands other than quit or exit. If quit doesn't work, try* bye *or* off.

For more information about Telnet, type man telnet *at a Unix prompt to see the online manual.*

Windows Telnet Programs

There are a surprising number of freeware and shareware Telnet programs available for Windows. Some are very basic, while others are quite sophisticated. All of these programs use Windows Sockets to connect to the Internet. In the previous chapter, you may have noticed that there were only a couple of different Winsock FTP applications to choose from. But with Telnet, you have a much wider range of choices. Many of these Telnet applications are in active development; others are useful for a specific purpose. Try out two or three of them, and see which one best fits your needs.

Some features to look for in a good Telnet program include the ability to save Telnet sessions to a file, scroll forward and backward through the text, and configure a variety of different sessions.

If you have a SLIP or PPP account that also includes access to a Unix shell, you can use one of these Windows Telnet applications to access your Unix shell when you're logged in using SLIP or PPP.

Exploring Telnet CH. 3

Telnet in Windows 95

One nice thing about Windows 95 is that it comes with its own Telnet application. You can find Telnet in your Windows directory.

It's a good basic Telnet application. Nothing fancy, but it does the job, and it's free.

COMt

COMt, by Performance Designs, takes an interesting approach to the Telnet interface. When you load COMt, it lets you use your favorite communications package as a Telnet program. So, for example, if you use Procomm for Windows, when you load COMt, you can use Procomm as your Telnet program, as shown in Figure 3.1.

If you like the features you have with your communications program, and don't want to give them up when you're running Telnet sessions over a SLIP or PPP connection, COMt is the program for you.

Figure 3.1:
COMt lets you use your favorite communications program as a telnet application.

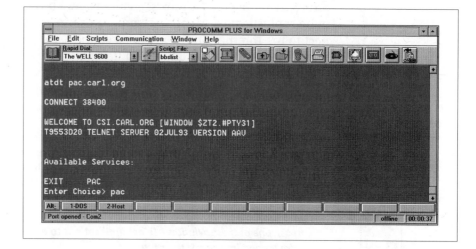

 ▶ *If you're using Windows 3.1, and you don't have a communications program, you can use the Windows Terminal program.*

COMt is shareware and costs $15.95 to register. See the **README.TXT** and **REGISTER.WRI** files that come with COMt for more information.

You can get COMt via anonymous FTP from **ftp.std.com**, in the **/customers/software/rfdmail** directory. You can also find COMt at **ftp.cica.indiana.edu**, in the **/pub/pc/win3/winsock** directory. The current version at the time of this writing is 1.05, and the filename is **comt.zip**.

Installing COMt

To install COMt, do the following:

1. Uncompress the zip file into an empty directory and run the **INSTALL.EXE** program. Accept the default settings, if possible.

2. When prompted to select a port for COMt, make sure you select an *unused* port. In fact, the documentation suggests selecting *all* unused ports, so you can open several Telnet sessions at once, each using a different COM port.

3. When the installation is complete, restart Windows.

If you select the same COM port used by your communications program, neither COMt nor your communication package will work.

Using COMt

To run COMt, do the following:

1. Start up your favorite communications program.

2. Change the COM port from the one that your modem uses to one of the unused ones you selected when installing COMt.

3. Then, all you need to do is type **ATDT** and the name of the host you want to Telnet to.

You can then use your communications program the same way you would if you were connected to a bulletin board or other host computer.

Just because your communications program supports file transfers, don't expect COMt to be able to give you this capability. Telnet is strictly a terminal emulation protocol. It does not support the ability to transfer files.

EWAN

EWAN (Emulator Without a Name), by Peter Zander, is a very easy to use Telnet program (see Figure 3.2). EWAN offers several nice features, including the ability to maximize the window to whatever size you

49

want. It also has a large scrollback buffer, which lets you easily scroll backward and forward through the text of your Telnet session. EWAN also lets you capture your entire Telnet session to a file. It offers only the basic terminal emulations—VT-100 and ANSI, but these emulations will allow you to access most host computers.

EWAN is freeware and may be distributed freely, as long as the executables are not modified. Support (via e-mail) is available to companies and large organizations for $495 per year.

Figure 3.2:
EWAN is an easy-to-use Telnet application that lets you access all kinds of interesting and fun services.

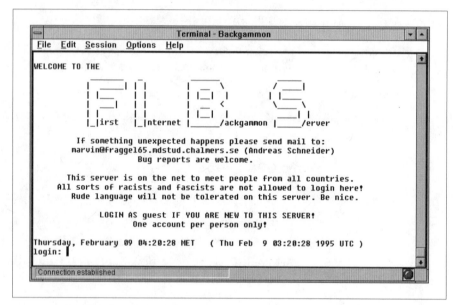

You can get EWAN via anonymous FTP from **ftp.lysator.liu.se** in the **/pub/msdos/windows** directory, or from **ftp.cica.indiana.edu**, in the **/pub/pc/win3/winsock** directory. The current version at the time of this writing is 1.052 and the filename is **ewan1052.zip**.

Installing EWAN

To install EWAN, do the following:

1. Uncompress the zip file into an empty directory.

2. Run the **INSTALL.EXE** program. Accept the default values, if possible.

Using EWAN

To use EWAN, do the following:

1. Start EWAN. When you start up EWAN for the first time, you'll see a blank list of Telnet connections.

2. To create a new connection, click on **New**. Enter the name of the Telnet host, and click on **OK**.

3. If you need to enter a special port number, you can enter it in the **Service (port)** field.

The only time you have to enter a special port number is if you're accessing something other than a standard Telnet session. If this is the case, you'll be specifically instructed to enter a port number.

4. Now just double-click on the name of the connection, and EWAN starts it up. Notice the little stoplight down in the right-hand corner of the window—when you're connected, it turns from red to green.

Telnet: The Beta Generation

Everyone seems to be writing Telnet applications these days. Here are three *beta* (pre-release) versions of Telnet applications that you can find out there on the Internet, and all they'll cost you (for now, at least) is the cost of connect time. But be warned, these programs aren't "ready for prime time" quite yet. But, who knows—maybe someday one of these Telnet apps will become a standard. Stay tuned...

The Beta Bunch

In the commercial software world, beta versions of new programs, or updates to existing programs, are usually only handed out to a small number of beta testers. There are a couple of reasons for this: for one thing, commercial software vendors don't want too many free copies of their programs floating around; but more importantly, they can't afford the negative publicity that a widely-dispersed, nasty unresolved bug could cause.

But in the shareware and freeware world, beta releases are not only acceptable—they're practically a way of life. These developers rely on input from the general public to refine and perfect their applications.

Many of the applications discussed in this book are in beta release. Because it's so easy to distribute software over the Internet, the medium tends to encourage this kind of interactive development. And user input plays an important role in the development of Internet applications. If users don't like a particular application, it won't get very far.

Some applications are called *alpha* releases. Technically, an alpha release is even further away from production than a beta release, although in most cases, they're more or less the same as betas.

And do keep in mind that because these programs aren't quite finished yet, they may be more likely to crash on you than fully completed and tested programs. This isn't to say you should avoid them—just be careful—and don't expect a lot of sympathy from the developer if the program crashes on you.

However, if you do discover a bug that hasn't been reported yet, the developer may appreciate hearing from you. Most developers include their e-mail addresses along with the documentation for their programs, so they can get your feedback.

NCSA WinTel

NCSA WinTel, from NCSA, the National Center for Supercomputing Applications at the University of Illinois, Urbana-Champaign is a very basic Telnet program (see Figure 3.3), and was originally intended to be used with their popular Mosaic Web browser (discussed in Chapter 7), but the project was apparently abandoned.

Figure 3.3:
NCSA WinTel may be a very basic Telnet program, but the things you can find with it are anything but basic.

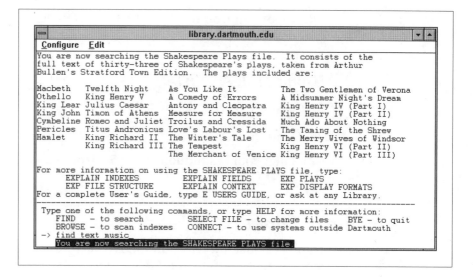

```
                          library.dartmouth.edu                     ▼ ▲
 Configure   Edit
You are now searching the Shakespeare Plays file.  It consists of the
full text of thirty-three of Shakespeare's plays, taken from Arthur
Bullen's Stratford Town Edition.   The plays included are:

Macbeth    Twelfth Night     As You Like It      The Two Gentlemen of Verona
Othello    King Henry V      A Comedy of Errors  A Midsummer Night's Dream
King Lear  Julius Caesar     Antony and Cleopatra King Henry IV (Part I)
King John  Timon of Athens   Measure for Measure King Henry IV (Part II)
Cymbeline  Romeo and Juliet  Troilus and Cressida Much Ado About Nothing
Pericles   Titus Andronicus  Love's Labour's Lost The Taming of the Shrew
Hamlet     King Richard II   The Winter's Tale   The Merry Wives of Windsor
           King Richard III  The Tempest         King Henry VI (Part II)
                             The Merchant of Venice King Henry VI (Part III)

For more information on using the SHAKESPEARE PLAYS file, type:
        EXPLAIN INDEXES         EXPLAIN FIELDS       EXP PLAYS
        EXP FILE STRUCTURE      EXPLAIN CONTEXT      EXP DISPLAY FORMATS
For a complete User's Guide, type E USERS GUIDE, or ask at any Library.
--------------------------------------------------------------------------
 Type one of the following commands, or type HELP for more information:
     FIND   - to search        SELECT FILE - to change files    BYE - to quit
     BROWSE - to scan indexes   CONNECT - to use systems outside Dartmouth
 -> find text music
  You are now searching the SHAKESPEARE PLAYS file.
```

The current version has several known bugs, some of which may prevent you from connecting to certain hosts. The only terminal emulation it supports is VT-100. But, it does work with Windows 3.1, and it's pretty small, only taking up about 40KB of hard disk space.

NCSA WinTel is freeware, and is not supported by NCSA.

You can get NCSA WinTel via anonymous FTP from **ftp.cica.indiana.edu**, in the **/pub/pc/win3/winsock** directory. The current version is beta-3, and the filename is **wintelb3.zip**.

Installing NCSA WinTel

To install NCSA WinTel, do the following:

1. Create a **WINTEL** directory on your hard disk.

2. Uncompress the zip file into that directory.

3. Next, move the **WINTEL.INI** file to your **WINDOWS** directory, and the **SCREEN.DLL** file to your **WINDOWS\SYSTEM** subdirectory.

Exploring Telnet
CH. 3

4. Create an icon for the **WINTEL.EXE** file on your Windows desktop.

Using NCSA WinTel

To use NCSA WinTel, do the following:

1. Start WinTel.

2. Enter your destination in the **Session Name** field and click on **OK**.

Trumpet Telnet

Trumpet Telnet, by Peter Tattam, is a very basic Telnet program, currently in *alpha* testing, though it's more stable than beta versions of other programs I've seen (see Figure 3.4). Like NCSA WinTel, it only offers VT-100 emulation, but it does have a couple of additional features, like the ability to open multiple Telnet connections at the same time, and the ability to change the background color.

While Trumpet Telnet is in alpha release, it will remain freeware. When it goes into production it will become shareware.

Figure 3.4:

Trumpet Telnet is a Telnet program that lets you access resources all over the globe.

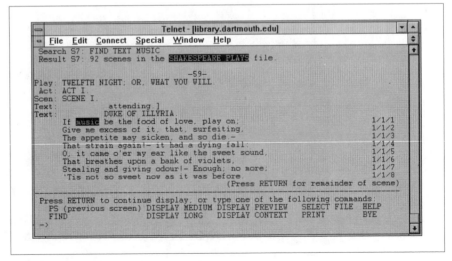

You can get Trumpet Telnet via anonymous FTP from **ftp.trumpet.com.au** in the **/ftp/pub/beta/trmptel** directory. The current version at the time of this writing is alpha-07, and the filename is **ttel0_07.zip**. Trumpet Telnet is also included in the **winapps2.zip** file in the **/ftp/pub/winsock** directory.

Installing Trumpet Telnet

To install Trumpet Telnet, do the following:

1. Create a **TRUMPTEL** directory on your hard disk.

2. Uncompress the zip file into that directory.

3. Create a TrumpTel icon for the **TRMPTEL.EXE** file on your Windows desktop.

Using Trumpet Telnet

To use Trumpet Telnet, do the following:

1. Start Trumpet Telnet.

2. Enter the host name in the **Host** field and click on **OK**.

YAWTel

YAWTel (Yet Another Winsock Telnet), by Hans van Oostrom, lives up to its name—it is indeed yet another beta-version Telnet program for Windows (see Figure 3.5). It's very basic, and is obviously still being developed, since several of the menu options don't do anything yet.

While YAWTel is in beta, and it's freeware, although it may become shareware in the future, when development is complete.

You can get YAWTel from **ftp.cica.indiana.edu**, in the **/pub/pc/win3/winsock** directory. The current version at the time of this writing is beta-02, and the filename is **yawtel02.zip**.

Figure 3.5:
YAWTel, Yet Another Windows Telnet program, is another straightforward Telnet application.

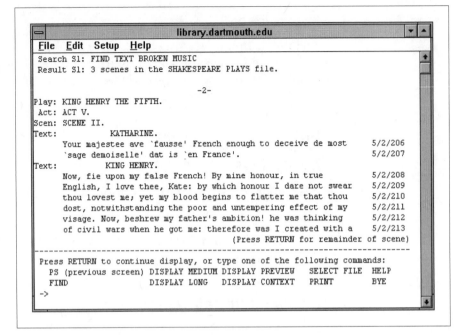

```
┌──────────────────────────────────────────────────────────────────────┐
│ ─               library.dartmouth.edu                         ▼  ▲    │
│  File   Edit   Setup   Help                                       ▲   │
│ Search S1: FIND TEXT BROKEN MUSIC                                 ▲   │
│ Result S1: 3 scenes in the SHAKESPEARE PLAYS file.                   │
│                                                                      │
│                              -2-                                     │
│ Play: KING HENRY THE FIFTH.                                          │
│  Act: ACT V.                                                         │
│ Scen: SCENE II.                                                      │
│ Text:          KATHARINE.                                            │
│      Your majestee ave `fausse' French enough to deceive de most  5/2/206│
│      `sage demoiselle' dat is `en France'.                        5/2/207│
│ Text:          KING HENRY.                                           │
│      Now, fie upon my false French! By mine honour, in true       5/2/208│
│      English, I love thee, Kate: by which honour I dare not swear  5/2/209│
│      thou lovest me; yet my blood begins to flatter me that thou  5/2/210│
│      dost, notwithstanding the poor and untempering effect of my  5/2/211│
│      visage. Now, beshrew my father's ambition! he was thinking   5/2/212│
│      of civil wars when he got me: therefore was I created with a 5/2/213│
│                                (Press RETURN for remainder of scene) │
│ ------------------------------------------------------------------- │
│ Press RETURN to continue display, or type one of the following commands:│
│   PS (previous screen) DISPLAY MEDIUM DISPLAY PREVIEW   SELECT FILE HELP│
│   FIND                 DISPLAY LONG   DISPLAY CONTEXT   PRINT       BYE │
│ ->                                                                   │
│                                                                  ▼   │
└──────────────────────────────────────────────────────────────────────┘
```

Installing YAWTel

To install YAWTel, do the following:

1. Create a **YAWTEL** directory on your hard disk.

2. Uncompress the zip file into that directory.

3. Create an icon for the **YAWTEL.EXE** file on your Windows desktop.

Using YAWTel

To use YAWTel, do the following:

1. Start YAWTel.

2. Enter the host name in the **Connect to** field and press **OK**.

Specialized Telnet Applications

These Telnet applications are not recommended for general use, but they do offer terminal emulations that you just can't find anywhere else. Most Telnet destinations on the Internet support the more common terminal emulations, like VT100 and ANSI, but occasionally, you may run into a host that requires a different emulation, like IBM 3270, or Tektronics.

CSMRLW

CSMRLW (Computer Software Manufaktur Remote Login for Windows), by Software Manufaktur GmbH of Austria, offers SCO-ANSI, IBM HFT-5151, IBM-3151, and AT386 terminal emulations. It doesn't support VT-100 emulation, which may cause problems on most systems.

I really wouldn't recommend this program unless you have a specific need for one of the emulations it supports. It doesn't offer a scrollback feature, nor does it allow you to log sessions to disk, and the documentation is pretty sparse.

You can get CSMRLW via anonymous FTP from **ftp.eunet.co.at** in the **/pub/vendor/csm** directory. The current version at the time of this writing is 3.1, the filename is **csmrlw31.exe**.

CSMRLW is a demo version of the commercial product, and will only work for 10 minutes at a time. The full version costs $99 (single user).

Installing CSMRLW

To install CSMRLW, do the following:

1. Uncompress the self-extracting executable file into an empty directory.

2. Run the **SETUP.EXE** file. Accept the default values if possible.

Using CSMRLW

To use CSMRLW, do the following:

1. Start CMSRLW.

2. Select Connect ➤ Connect to remote host. Enter the host name in the **Hostname** field and your login name in the **Loginname** field and click on **OK**.

QWS3270

For those times when you need to connect to an IBM 3270 or Tektronics 4010 terminal, you just can't beat QWS3270, by Jim Rymerson (see Figure 3.6). It's easy to use and configure, and works great as a 3270 terminal viewer for Gopher and Web browser applications (discussed in Chapters 6 and 7).

Figure 3.6:

If you ever need to connect to an IBM mainframe, QWS3270 is indispensable.

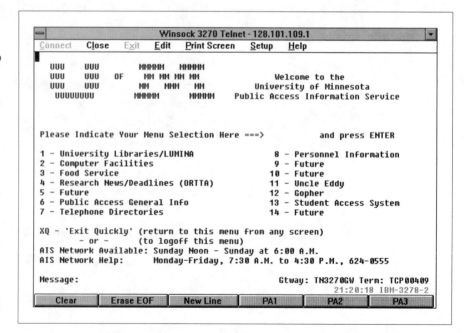

There are two versions of QWS3270. The freeware version is available via anonymous FTP from **ftp.ccs.queensu.ca**, in the **/pub/msdos/tcpip** directory. The current version at the time of this writing is 3.2e and the filename is **qws3270.zip**.

The shareware version is available via anonymous FTP from **ftp.cica.indiana-.edu**, in the **/pub/pc/win3/winsock** directory. The current version at the time of this writing is 2.0 and the filename is **qws3270.zip**.

The freeware version may be freely distributed, provided that no fee is charged. The shareware version, QWS3270X, costs $35 to register. Registration gets you priority support, upgrades, and a say in the development of future enhancements.

Installing QWS3270

To install either version of QWS3270, do the following:

1. Create a **QWS3270** directory on your hard disk.
2. Uncompress the zip file into that directory.
3. Create an icon for the **QWS3270.EXE** or **QWS3270X.EXE** file on your Windows desktop.

Using QWS3270

To use QWS3270, do the following:

1. Double-click on the QWS3270 icon.
2. Select **Connect**.
3. Enter the host name in the **Host** field and click on **OK**.

TekTel

If you have a need for Textronix T4010 terminal emulation, try TekTel. It's very basic, but it does the job.

TekTel is public domain software, and may be distributed freely.

> You can get Tektel via anonymous FTP from **ftp.cica.indiana.edu**, in the **/pub/pc/win3/winsock** directory. The current version at the time of this writing is 1b, and the filename is **tektel1b.zip**.

Installing TekTel

To install TekTel, do the following:

1. Create a **TEKTEL** directory on your hard disk.
2. Uncompress the zip file into that directory.
3. Create an icon for the **TEKTEL.EXE** file on your Windows desktop.

Using TekTel

To use TekTel, do the following:

1. Start TekTel.
2. Select Connect ➤ Open.
3. Enter the host name in the Site field and click on **OK**.

Choosing a Telnet program that you feel comfortable with is important. Even if you don't access systems via Telnet on a regular basis, you'll probably need a good Telnet program when you get your Gopher and Web browser clients going, as both of these applications can use Telnet as a "viewer" application. I'll talk about configuring viewer and helper applications in greater detail in Chapters 6 and 7.

4

Mail, the Indispensable Tool

I CAN STILL remember my first e-mail message. It was about 10 years ago, when I discovered, quite by accident, that the word processing system I used at work was actually connected to all the other word processing systems in the company by *Ethernet*. At the time, I was just starting to get into computers and had no idea what Ethernet was, but I thought it was so cool that I was able to send messages, and even documents, to my friends who were on the same network. I remember thinking how easy it was, and how incredibly cool it would be if I could send e-mail to all my friends.

Well, now I can, since most of my friends are now on the Internet. E-mail has become an important part of my life—right up there with postal mail and phone calls. I use it to communicate with friends and associates, some of them thousands of miles away. I also use it to share ideas and information with people all over the world.

And there are all kinds of things you can do with e-mail, besides sending the latest bunch of lightbulb jokes to your friends and relatives. You can get files from anonymous FTP servers, subscribe to informational and discussion mailing lists covering just about any topic you can imagine, or even send a FAX—all by just using a simple e-mail program.

How Internet Mail Works

Before getting into the specifics of different mail programs, I'd like to take a minute to talk about how mail works on the Internet.

Internet mail is transported using *SMTP* (Simple Mail Transport Protocol). Most SLIP and PPP accounts connect to a POP3 (Post Office Protocol 3) message server for incoming mail, but use SMTP to send outgoing mail.

In general, there's not much you'll need to know to connect to an SMTP or POP3 message server on a SLIP or PPP account, other than your password (usually the same one you use to log into your account).

The Trouble with Binaries

There is one peculiarity you're likely to run up against when sending mail using SMTP over the Internet—the fact that SMTP doesn't support binary files.

Binary files are comprised of 1's and 0's. If you try to open a binary file using a program that only understands ASCII characters (like the Windows Notepad), all you'll see is garbage, because the program won't understand how to display the file.

The ASCII character set, on the other hand, contains all the basic characters used in text messages: letters, numbers, punctuation, that sort of thing.

If you're not sure if a file is binary, try looking at it. Get to a DOS prompt and enter **type filename ¦ more** to take a look at the contents of the file (the ¦ more command shows you one page at a time). If you see a lot of garbage characters like those shown below, then you're probably looking at a binary file.

```
C:\WINDOWS>type redbrick.bmp |more
BMv█       υ  (           █ █                              ¢ ¢   ¢¢ ¢   ¢ ¢ ¢¢
  ¢¢¢ +++    _  _   █   _  █É██                                            █████
███         █      ████É███████           ₂██         █        ████É██████₂█
██       █₂█₂█   ██É֒█████      █₂█ Ö██₂₂Ö█   É     ₂████₂█      ██ █É₂█
   █Ü█████₂█████Ü█  █████████      █████      ███ █████████Ü██É
  ██₂█₂█████Ö ██   █      ██₂██████₂█ ÖÉ  ████Ö██₂█₂₂   █Ö█      ₂███₂Ö
█É██████É  █ █████ÖÖÖÖÖÖÖÖ       ÖÖÖÖÖÖÖ         É         Ö█████
███    █É₂É₂ ₂██  ██     ██₂█████ ₂██████████████É██₂ Ö   ████É   É₂██
  ₂██ É██ ██ ███████ É██₂█É█Ü ██₂██₂ Ü      ███₂█₂█Ü██É₂ ₂█ ██████ █
Ö██ ₂██₂█₂█   ██ ₂ █É Ö███   ███      █₂É█   █ ÉÖ██É██████₂██    ₂██₂Ö
      É█₂█████₂ ₂██ █ ₂█████████ ÖÖÖÖÖÖÖÖÖÖÖÖÖÖÖÖÖÉ
C:\WINDOWS>
```

SMTP has the same limitations as the DOS **type** command or the Windows Notepad—it simply doesn't know how to display or process binary files.

Sending Binary Files

Okay, so then how do you send binary files over the Internet? Well, some clever folks figured out how to convert binary files into ASCII characters, which can be sent via SMTP. If you want to send a binary file over the Internet, either you or your mail program must encode the file into ASCII text characters. An ASCII-encoded file looks like utter nonsense when you see it on your screen, but once a file has been encoded as ASCII, you can send it over the Internet by e-mail. When the file gets to the other end, either the mail program or the person reading the message will have to decode the file ,using the same format you used to encode it, to return it to its normal, binary condition. For more on file encoding and decoding utilities, see Chapter 9.

Mail
CH. 4

63

Unix Mail Programs

If you have a Unix shell account, there are several mail programs you can use to read your mail. The three most common are Mail, Elm, and Pine. If you have an account on a Unix system, you will have access to at least one, and probably all three of these programs.

We'll take a look at these Unix mail programs, and see how each of them processes your mail.

Mail

Mail is about as basic as you can get. To send someone mail, just type **mail username@host** at the Unix prompt. Then, you may or may not be prompted to enter a **Subject:** line. If you are, type the subject name. If you aren't, you can add one later.

Escape Commands

You can add or change the Subject: line by using an *escape command* while you're editing the mail message. An escape command is a command that you can execute from within the mail program. On most systems, escape commands must be typed at the beginning of a new line, and must begin with a tilde (~). On some systems, a different character is used, such as a colon (:). To find out which one your system uses, and to see a list of the available escape commands, type ~**?** or :**?** on a new line while you're composing a message. Some common Mail commands include:

~~	If you need to use a tilde at the beginning of a line, you need to use two, otherwise it's interpreted as a command. If your system uses a different character, such as a colon (:), the same rule applies—if you need to start a line with a that character, you need to use two (::).
~**b** *users@hosts*	Add **users@hosts** to the bcc: (*blind carbon copy*) list.
~**c** *users@hosts*	Add **users@hosts** to the cc: (*carbon copy*) list.

~d	Read in the **dead.letter** file. This file is created when your mail session is interrupted while you're composing a message, for example, if your connection to the host is terminated.
~e	Edit the message you are composing, using the default edit or program.
~f *message#*	Include a message (*message#*) from your mailbox with the message you are composing.
~m *message#*	Similar to **~f**, except that the text of the *message* is shifted to the right by one tab. This is a good option to use if you want to make it obvious that you're quoting from someone else's message.
~h	Change the header (To:, From:, Subject:, cc: list) in the message you are composing.
~r *filename*	Read a file (*filename*) into the message you are composing.
~p	Display the message you are composing on your screen.
~s*subject*	Change the Subject: line. The *subject* is the text you want to appear in the Subject: line.
~t *users@hosts*	Add *users@hosts* to the list of recipients of the message.
~v	Start up the "visual" editor—usually Vi. (For more information about Vi, type **man vi** at a Unix prompt.)
~w *filename*	Save the current message to *filename*.
~?	Print a list of available commands.
~! command	Temporarily leave the Mail program to execute a Unix *command*.
~¦ command	Pipe the current message through a *command*.

Mail
CH. 4

65

After determing what commands to implement, you can just type the text of your message. When you're done, just type a single period (**.**) on a line by itself. The message is sent immediately.

Reading Mail in Mail

To read mail using Mail, just type **mail**. You'll see a list of all of all the messages in your inbox.

```
% mail
>U   1 web-faq  Wed Feb  8 17:54  248/7721 "Your mail to web-faq@well.com"
 U   2 kgerman@marketplace.com Fri Feb 10 20:09  246/10438 "TIA News 2/10/95"
 U   3 Majordomo@and.com Thu Feb 23 13:13   40/1434 "Welcome to tankmail"
 U   4 Majordomo@and.com Thu Feb 23 13:14   39/1369 "Welcome to rbpmail"
 U   5 SFEIGIN Thu Feb 23 19:06  109/5764 "Ski Report - a fine weekend"
 U   6 Howard Davidson Fri Feb 24 16:56   96/5391 "***PARTY***"
 U   7 realbeer@and.com Wed Mar  1 07:01  186/7197 "RBPMail v1.1"
 U   8 hotwired-info@wired.com Thu Mar  2 19:34  210/8250 "HotFlash 2.08"
&
```

The ampersand (**&**) is the mail prompt. The **>** shows you which message is the current message. If you just hit the Enter key at the **&** prompt, Mail will display that message. When that message is finished displaying, you can hit Enter again to see the next message, and so on. If you want to see a different message, just type the message number and hit Enter.

There are several commands you can use at the **&** prompt. To see a list of all these commands, type **?**. The functions of these commands are shown below:

t *message#*	Display the message numbers specified (***message#***). You can specify either a single message (e.g., **t 2**) or multiple messages (e.g., **t 2-5**).
n	Display the next message
e *message#*	Edit the message(s) specified (***message#***).
f *message#*	Display the message header for the specified message(s) (***message#***).
d *message#*	Delete the specified message(s).
s *message# filename*	Append the specified message(s) to a file (***filename***).

u *message#*	Undelete the specified message(s).
r *message#*	Reply to the specified message, including all recipients of the original message.
R *message#*	Reply to the specified message, including only the original sender of the message.
pre *message#*	Mark the specified messages as new and unread.
m *users@hosts*	Compose a new message to the specified users (***users@hosts***).
q	Quit, and move all remaining messages to your mbox.
x	Quit, leaving all remaining messages in your mailbox.
h	Display message headers.
!	Temporarily leave the Mail program to execute a Unix command.
cd *directory*	Change to a different directory. If you don't specify a directory, the default is to switch to your home directory.

Your incoming mail is normally kept in a file called **inbox**. Your received mailbox file, **mbox**, is kept in your home directory. If you want to see the messages stored in your mbox file, start Mail using the **-f** switch (**mail -f**).

Other than that, reading mail from your mbox file is exactly the same as reading mail from your inbox file.

Although reading your mail with Mail can be tedious, it does have one singular advantage over the more sophisticated mail programs discussed later: It displays your messages sequentially, without any fancy formatting or pagination. This is helpful if you want to be able to capture all of your mail into a single capture file.

Just open the capture file in your communications (or Telnet) program, start up Mail and let 'em roll. You'll have to hit Enter between each message, but it's the easiest way to download mail from a Unix shell account to your PC.

For more information about Mail, type **man mail** *at a Unix prompt to see the online manual.*

When You're on Vacation

There's a nifty little Unix program that will send an automatic "I'm on vacation" message to anyone who sends mail to your account when you're away. The program is called, appropriately enough, Vacation, and is available on most Unix systems.

If you're on a Sun Unix system, you can install it by just typing **vacation** at a Unix prompt. The program will then prompt you to enter an "I'm on vacation" message, which the program stores in your home directory in a file called **.vacation.msg**. This message will be sent automatically to anyone who sends you mail while you're gone.

The program also creates a **.forward** file for you. The .forward file is normally used to automatically forward all of your mail to a different address, but Vacation uses it to process your incoming messages. When a message gets sent to your mailbox, the .forward file forwards a copy of the message to the Vacation program. Vacation then figures out who sent it, and sends that person your "I'm on vacation" message.

When you get back from vacation, all of the messages you received while you were gone will be waiting for you in your mailbox. To get rid of the Vacation message processing, just delete the .forward and vacation.msg files.

If you're on a BSD Unix system, you'll have to create the .vacation.msg and .forward files manually, and initialize Vacation by typing **vacation -i** at a Unix prompt.

For more information, type **man vacation** at a Unix prompt.

Elm

So, now that you've suffered through Mail, you're probably wondering if there's something better. There is. It's called Elm.

Elm is a much more intuitive mail program than Mail. It displays a list containing summary information about all your mail messages, and lets you use your cursor keys to move up or down through this list (see Figure 4.1). If you want to see the message under the cursor, all you have to do is hit Enter. Elm also makes it easy to create different mail folders, so you can sort your mail if you'd like.

All of the basic commands you'll need are listed at the bottom of the screen. If you need more help, just type **?**.

Elm does not support automatic encoding and decoding of binary files, unless your system administrator has installed the **Metamail** *mail handling utilities. If Metamail has not been installed, you'll have to manually encode and decode binary files using one of the utilities discussed in Chapter 9. Check with your system administrator to find out if Metamail is installed on your system.*

Figure 4.1:
Elm is an easy-to-use full-screen mail program available on most Unix systems.

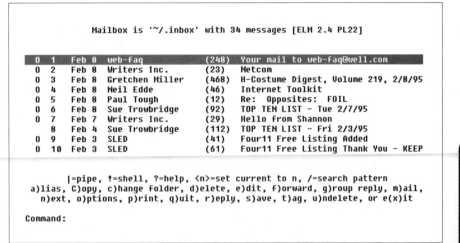

When you're done reading your messages, Elm will ask you if you want to move your read messages to your received folder. The received folder is kept in your **/Mail** subdirectory.

If you want to open your received folder later, just type **c** (change folder), and enter **=received** to open it. You need to type the equal sign to let Elm know that it's in the **/Mail** subdirectory.

*For more information about Elm, type **man elm** at a Unix prompt to see the on-line manual. You can also check out the Elm Mail FAQ (Frequently Asked Questions) list. It's available via anonymous FTP from **ftp.cs.ruu.nl**, in the **/pub/NEWS.ANSWERS/elm/** directory.*

Pine

Pine takes both the tree metaphor and the mail interface a step further (see Figure 4.2). It's very easy to use—in fact, it was designed with Unix beginners in mind. But it's also quite powerful, and is used by many a Unix guru as well. Pine offers many of the same features as Elm, plus a few additional bonuses, like automatic binary file encoding using MIME, an address book feature, and a built-in editor, Pico, which is a very easy-to-use Unix text editor.

Figure 4.2:
Pine makes sending mail in Unix easier than ever.

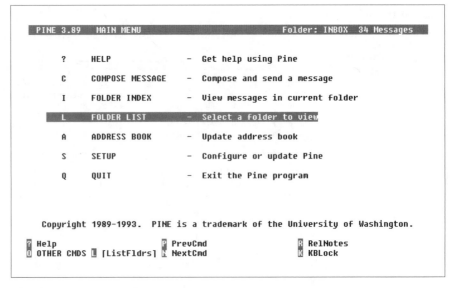

Unlike Mail and Elm, Pine does not automatically move your read messages to a different file. But if you want to move them to a different file, you can. All of the additional folders you create are kept in your **/mail** directory.

For more information about Pine, type **man pine** *at a Unix prompt to see the on-line manual.*

Editing Pine Mail Messages With Pico

When you create a mail message in Pine, the editor you'll be using is called Pico. Pico is one of the most popular, and by far the easiest text editor available on Unix systems. Other mail programs usually use more basic and difficult editors, like Ed or Edit, which only allow you to edit one line at a time.

All the commands you're likely to need are displayed at the bottom of the screen (see Figure 4.3).

Figure 4.3:

The Pico Editor is the easiest editor for non-Unix folks to learn and use. All the commands you'll need are right there on the screen.

```
┌──────────────────────────────────────────────────────────────────────┐
│  UW PICO(tm) 2.3              File: casey.txt              Modified    │
│                                                                        │
│ Casey at the Bat                                                       │
│ by Earnest Lawrence Thayer                                             │
│                                                                        │
│ It looked extremely rocky for the Mudville nine that day;              │
│ The score stood two to four, with but an inning left to play.          │
│ So when Cooney died at second, and Burrows did the same,               │
│ A pallor wreatheed the features of the patrons of the game.            │
│                                                                        │
│ A straggling few got up to go, leaving there the rest.                 │
│ With that hope which springs eternal within the human breast.          │
│ For they| thought: "if only Casey could get a whack at that,"          │
│ They'd put even money now, with Casey at the bat.                      │
│                                                                        │
│ But Flynn preceded Casey, and likewise so did Blake,                   │
│ And the former was a pudd'n, and the latter was a fake,                │
│ So on that stricken multitude a deathlike silence sat;                 │
│ For there seemed but little chance of Casey's getting to the bat.      │
│                                                                        │
│ But Flynn let drive a "single," to the wonderment of all.              │
│                                                                        │
│ ^G Get Help   ^O WriteOut   ^R Read File  ^Y Prev Pg  ^K Cut Text  ^C Cur Pos │
│ ^X Exit       ^J Justify    ^W Where is   ^U Next Pg  ^U UnCut Text ^T To Spell │
└──────────────────────────────────────────────────────────────────────┘
```

All Pico commands use the Ctrl key, which is displayed as a caret symbol (^) on the screen. If you don't see the command you want at the bottom of the screen, just press **Ctrl+G** to see the help file.

To move around in the file, you can use your cursor keys, just as you would in the MS-DOS Edit program or Windows Notepad. But you can't

71

use the PageUp and PageDown keys like you do in most DOS editors; instead, you have to use Ctrl+Y to move up and Ctrl+V to move down.

You can also use Pico outside of Pine to create and edit files. Just type **pico filename.txt**, where **filename** is the file that you want to edit.

For more information about Pico, type **man pico** *at a Unix prompt to see the online manual.*

Sending Mail Anywhere

Remember how the Internet is really comprised of many individual networks? Well, when you send mail to someone on a different network, you may need to address the message in a specific way, otherwise, they may not get the message.

For example, if you have a friend on CompuServe, and her address is 12345,6789, how would you send her mail over the Internet? If you tried sending a message to 12345,6789, it would get rejected, because Internet messages can't contain commas. So, when you send mail to CompuServe from the Internet, you need to exchange the comma for a period, and add **@compuserve.com** to the end. So, your friend's address would become 12345.6789@compuserve.com.

If you want to send mail to someone on America Online, all you need to do is add **@aol.com** to the end of that person's AOL login name.

For a complete list of Internet mail how-to's, get Scott Yanoff's Internetwork Mail Guide. It's available via anonymous ftp from **ftp.csd.uwm.edu**, in the **/pub** directory. The filename is **internetwork-mail-guide**.

Windows Mail Programs

There are currently several Winsock-compatible mail programs you can use on a SLIP/PPP or network connection that will let you connect to a POP3 or SMTP mail server. The two programs that I'll discuss are both outstanding and (surprisingly) free!

The *POP3* mail protocol is the most commonly used mail protocol for SLIP and PPP users. When you have an account that uses POP3, your mail is kept on your provider's mail server until you log in and retrieve your mail. When you retrieve your mail, using one of these mail programs, it's copied to your PC and deleted from the server.

But even though most providers use the POP3 protocol for retrieving mail, they usually use SMTP for sending mail.

If you're on a network at school or at work, don't assume that you can use one of these programs to read your mail. If your mail is stored on a different kind of server, such as a Banyan VINES, Novell, or cc:Mail server, chances are you won't be able to use these mail programs. If you're unsure, check with your system administrator.

Eudora

Eudora, originally written by Steve Dorner of the University of Illinois, is a nice little mail package (see Figure 4.4). Although it began life as a very popular freeware Macintosh mail program, it was adopted by Qualcomm, who liked the program so much, they hired Dorner and ported it over to DOS and Windows.

Figure 4.4:
Eudora is an easy to use, free mail program for Winsock.

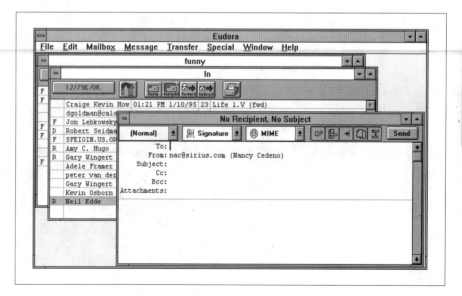

Mail
CH. 4

Because Eudora had such a wide following as a freeware product, Qualcomm decided to keep up that tradition, while at the same time developing commercial versions. You can now get both freeware and commercial versions of both the Macintosh and Windows products.

> You can get the freeware version of Eudora via anonymous FTP from **ftp.qualcomm.com**, in the **/quest/eudora/windows/1.4** directory. The current version at the time of this writing is 1.44, and the filename is **Eudor144.exe**. While you're there, you should also pick up a copy of the user manual (in Word for Windows 2.0 format), in the **/quest/eudora/windows/documentation** directory. The filename is **14Manual.exe**.

The commercial version offers more features, and real technical support, which is enticing to corporate customers. The commercial version costs $65 (single user), with substantial discounts for multiple users.

Surprisingly, the freeware version is still in active development, although Qualcomm reserves the more sophisticated features for their commercial product, like drag-and-drop attachments, extensive online help, and the ability to automatically open attachments using the appropriate application.

Installing Eudora

To install the freeware version of Eudora, do the following:

1. Create a **EUDORA** directory on your hard disk and uncompress the self-extracting executable file into that directory.

2. Make sure that you have a **set** environment variable in your **AUTOEXEC.BAT** file that sets a temporary (TMP) directory:

   ```
   SET TMP = C:\TMP
   ```

3. If you don't have a TMP directory on your hard disk, create one by typing **MD C:\TMP** at a DOS prompt.

4. Next, create an icon pointing to the WEUDORA.EXE file to your Windows desktop.

To configure Eudora, do the following:

1. Start up Eudora, and select Special ➤ Configuration.

2. Enter your e-mail address in the **POP Account** and **Return Address** fields.

3. Enter the name of your mail server in the **SMTP Server** field.

4. Enter your name in the **Real Name** field.

 If you're using TIA to access your mailbox on a Unix shell account, you'll need to find out the name of your mail server. If you're not sure what it is, ask your system administrator.

5. If you want Eudora to check your incoming mail on a regular basis, enter a number in the **Check for Mail Every __ Minutes** box. If you leave this option set at 0, Eudora will only check mail when you tell it to.

6. If you have a *Ph server* (CSO standard directory assistance) at your location, enter the name of the Ph server. Click on **OK**.

7. Finally, select Special ➤ Switches, and look over the various options, and change them to suit your preferences. I suggest changing the **Send Attachments** setting to MIME, since it is a more commonly-used encoding format than the default, BinHex, which is primarily used on Macintosh systems.

 If you are using PPP, and you aren't able to get Eudora to log into your POP3 mail server, you may need to enable Password Authentication Protocol (PAP) in your Winsock dialer. In Trumpet Winsock, the PAP option can be set under File ➤ PPP Options. Enable PAP and enter your username and password.

Using Eudora

Eudora is a very intuitive program. Your incoming mail is kept in your **In** mailbox, and your outgoing mail is kept in your **Out** mailbox. You can create additional mailboxes and folders if you'd like. Each folder can contain a number of mailboxes.

Here are some of the options available to you when using Eudora:

To check your mail manually, select File ➤ Check Mail. Eudora will log into your mail host, and ask you for your password.

If you select the Save Password option in the Switches menu (Special ➤ Switches), you'll only be prompted for your password the first time you check mail. If you're using Eudora in a non-secure location such as your workplace, you probably shouldn't set this option.

To open a message, double-click on it. If the message contains a MIME- or BinHex-encoded file, the file is automatically decoded and saved for you. Note that UUEncode and UUDecode are only supported in the commercial version.

To send a message, select Message ➤ New Message. Compose your message, and click on the Send button when you're done. Eudora keeps copies of all messages you send in your Out folder.

To attach a binary file to a message, select Message ➤ Attach Document and select the file that you want to attach.

To delete a message, select the message or messages that you want to delete, and click on the trashcan button. By default, your trashcan is only emptied when you tell Eudora to empty it by selecting Special ➤ Empty Trash. If you want, you can have Eudora empty the trash whenever you quit by selecting the Empty Trash On Quit option in the Special ➤ Switches window.

To add people to your personal address book, select Window ➤ Nicknames. Enter a "nickname" in the Nickname field, then enter the person's e-mail address in the Address(es) field, and the person's full name in the Notes field. Now, double-click on the nickname to add the person to your address book.

To send a message to someone in your address book, select Message ➤ New Message To, and select the nickname of the person you want to send the message to. From this same menu, you can forward, reply, or redirect messages to anyone in your address book.

Qualcomm has a Eudora information mailing list. To get information about product updates, just click on Help ➤ QUEST Mailing List and click on the Subscribe button to subscribe. For more information about automated mailing lists, see the end of this chapter.

FTP by Mail

For a long time, the only way I could access the Internet from work was by e-mail. If I wanted to FTP files from the Internet, I had to log into my personal Internet account from home, get the files I needed, then bring them in to work on diskettes. If only I'd known that I could FTP files using e-mail!

The following is a list of FTP-by-Mail servers. Try to choose the one that is closest to you. To get a list of commands, send a message to the server with the word **help** in the body of the message:

Server	Location
ftpmail@decwrl.dec.com	California
ftpmail@sunsite.unc.edu	North Carolina
bitftp@pucc.princeton.edu	New Jersey
ftpmail@cs.uow.edu.au	Australia
ftpmail@grasp.insa-lyon.fr	France
bitftp@vm.gmd.de	Germany
ftpmail@ftp.uni-stuttgart.de	Germany
ftpmail@ieunet.ie	Ireland
bitftp@plearn.edu.pl	Poland
ftpmail@lth.se	Sweden
ftpmail@doc.ic.ac.uk	United Kingdom

In a little while, you'll get back a message giving you instructions how to transfer files from anonymous FTP servers via mail.

Pegasus

Pegasus Mail for Windows, by David Harris, has become one of the most popular mail clients for Windows SLIP/PPP and Novell users (see Figure 4.5).

Figure 4.5:
Pegasus is a very
popular freeware mail
program for Winsock.

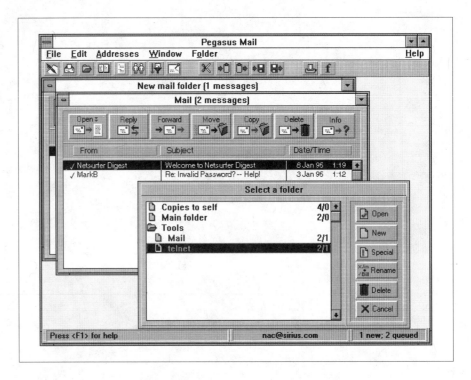

Although it's a little more difficult to install and configure than
Eudora, it is definitely worth the effort. Pegasus Mail supports UUEncode, MIME, and BinHex ASCII-encoding formats for both sending and
receiving binary messages.

> You can get Pegasus Mail via anonymous FTP from **risc.ua.edu**, in the
> **/pub/network/pegasus** directory. The current version at the time of this
> writing is 1.22, and the filename is **winpm122.zip**.

Pegasus Mail is freeware. You can order printed documentation from
the author for $125 (5 copies).

If you're on a Novell network and want to run Pegasus Mail, your mail server has to be configured to use the MHS protocol. Check with your system administrator and read the online Pegasus Mail guide, WGUIDE.EXE to find out if you can use Pegasus Mail.

Installing Pegasus Mail

To install Pegasus Mail for Windows, do the following:

1. Uncompress the zip file into an empty directory.

2. Run the **PCONFIG.EXE** file.

3. Select **Standalone Configuration** if you are connecting through a SLIP or PPP connection.

4. Follow the directions on screen. Accept the defaults, if possible.

5. Create an icon pointing to the **WINPMAIL.EXE** file on your Windows desktop.

To configure Pegasus Mail, do the following:

1. Start up Pegasus. You'll be prompted to create a mailbox. Select **Yes**.

2. When prompted, enter your user ID (without the *@hostname* part).

3. Now, select File ➤ Preferences ➤ General Settings. Enter your name in the **Personal Name** field, and your e-mail address in the **Default Reply Address** field. If desired, select additional options. When you're done, click on **OK**.

4. Now, select File ➤ Preferences ➤ Advanced Settings. Under **If WIN-SOCK.DLL is available, load it,** select **Always**. Click on **OK**.

5. Exit Pegasus Mail and start it up again.

6. Now, when you click on File, you'll see some new options. Select File ➤ Network Configuration. The TCP/IP Network Configuration dialog box appears (see Figure 4.6).

7. If you are using the POP3 mail protocol, enter the name of your mail host, your username (again without the *@hostname*), and your password in the appropriate fields.

Mail
CH. 4

Figure 4.6:
The Pegasus Mail TCP/IP
Network Configuration
dialog box.

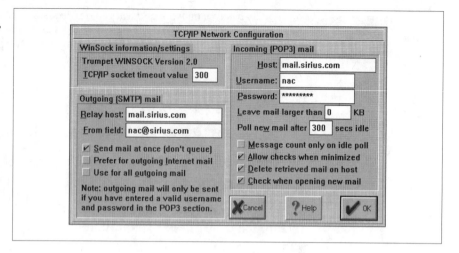

Figure 4.6:
The Pegasus Mail TCP/IP
Network Configuration
dialog box.

 ▶ If you're using TIA to access your mailbox on a Unix shell account, you'll need to find out the name of your mail server. If you're not sure what it is, ask your system administrator.

8. If you want to be able to minimize Pegasus Mail and have it check for new mail at regular intervals, enter the number of seconds you want it to wait between checks in the **Poll new mail after ___ secs idle** and check the **Allow checks when minimized** box.

9. You should also check the **Delete retrieved mail on host** option so that your mailbox on the server doesn't get too full.

10. Check the **Check when opening new mail** option if you want Pegasus Mail to check for new mail whenever you open your In box.

Using Pegasus Mail

Pegasus is similar to Eudora, in that you can have multiple mail folders, and "filing trays" which can contain a number of folders. When Pegasus checks your mail server and finds new mail, it puts the messages into the **New mail** folder. From the **New mail** folder, you can read, move, delete, copy, and reply to messages.

Here are some of the options available to you when using Pegasus Mail:

To open a message, double-click on it. If the message contains a UUEncoded, MIME-encoded, or BinHex encoded file, click on the Attachment button. You can then choose to either Save or View the attachment.

To send a message, select File ➤ New Message.

To see a list of people you've recently sent messages to, click on the **?** button. To send a message to one of these people, double-click on the name.

To attach a binary file, click on the Attach button. You can then select the file, and the encoding method for the message.

To keep copies of messages you send, check the Copy Self box in your new message. By default, Pegasus will then put a copy of the message into the Copies to Self folder. (Unlike Eudora, Pegasus doesn't keep sent messages in an "Out" folder.)

To create an address book, select Addresses ➤ Address Books and click on New. Enter a name for the address book, for example, Friends, and optionally a filename. To add users to the address book, double-click on the address book name, and click on Add. Enter the person's name, postal address and phone number (optional), and e-mail address and click on OK.

To send a message to someone in your address book, open a new message by selecting File ➤ New Message, then press F3 to open your list of address books. Double-click on the address book, then double-click on the name of the person you want to send the message to.

To delete a message, select the message and click on the Delete button.

 ▶ *There's a mailing list for Pegasus Mail users. To get on the mailing list, send a message to LISTSERV@UA1VM.UA.EDU, with the words SUBSCRIBE PMAIL firstname lastname in the body (not the subject) section. For more information about subscribing to mailing lists, see the end of this chapter.*

Mail
CH. 4

Faxing by Mail

Need to send a fax? Well, you might be able to send it from the Internet. There are currently a couple of fax services on the Internet that you can access via e-mail.

FAXiNET. This service can deliver faxes to almost any US location, and many international locations, for a fairly reasonable charge. For more information about the service and pricing, send a message to **info@awa.com**, with the word **help** in the body of the message.

TPC Experimental Fax Server. This fax service is free, but is dependent on location. As long as you want to send a fax to one of these areas, you're in luck:

Canberra, Australia (61-62)

Washington, DC (202)

Silicon Valley, California (parts of 408, 415, 510)

Riverside, California (parts of 818, 909)

University of Michigan (313)

For more information about the TPC Experimental Fax Server, including a current list of supported destinations, send a message to **tpc-faq@town .hall.org**, with the word **help** in the body of the message.

Mailing Lists

Mailing lists are a great way to get useful information, and have lively, ongoing discussions with people who share your interests.

There are mailing lists for everything from accordions (**accordion**) to Led Zeppelin (**zeppelin-l**), and more than a thousand others in between.

Most mailing list owners use an automated list server to perform the day-to-day operations of maintaining their lists. These automated servers can give you general information about the list, as well as subscribe and unsubscribe you from the list automatically. All you need to do is send the appropriate message to the list server.

There are several different list servers, but the most popular are List-serv, Listproc, and Majordomo. You can usually tell which one you're dealing with by looking at the address of the list service. If it's a List-serv, the address is usually **listserv@somewhere.com**, if it's a List-proc, it will probably be **listproc@somewhere.com**, and if it's a Majordomo, it will probably be **majordomo@somewhere.com**.

But many lists don't use this format. Some use the name **list-request @somewhere.com**. If that's the case, pay careful attention to the in-structions you're given. It could be that the owner is using something really obscure, or they just may be adding and deleting people from the list by hand.

If the list is maintained by a person, rather than by a list server, you should just send a polite note asking the list owner to add you to the list.

If you know for sure that you're dealing with an automated list server, you can use the **help** command to get more information about list server commands. Just send a message to the list server with the word **help** in the body of your message. You don't need to enter anything in the Subject: line of your message.

It's important to remember that all list servers have more than one ad-dress—don't make the mistake of sending a list server command to the list name. If you do, your "subscribe me" message will go to everyone on the list, which is quite annoying to list subscribers, and somewhat embarrassing for you.

The list server name (the one you want to send the command to) is almost always something like **listserv@somewhere.com** or **foo-request@somewhere.com**.

The name of the list itself, which is where you send messages that you want other list subscribers to receive, is usually something like **foo@somewhere.com** or **foo-l@somewhere.com**.

 ▶ *You can get a list of most mailing lists available on the Internet via anonymous ftp from **rtfm.mit.edu** in the /**pub/usenet/news.answers/mail**/ direc-tory. The file is called **mailing-lists** and is updated on a regular basis.*

Useful and Fun Mailing Lists

Here are a few mailing lists you might want to check out.

The Internet Index. Based on the *Harper's Index*, the Internet Index is a list of interesting Internet-related facts, like how many countries were accessible by electronic mail in 1994 (159) and the number of US Youth Soccer teams with Web pages (2). To subscribe to the Internet Index, send a message to **internet-index-request@OpenMarket.com**, with the words **subscribe internet-index** in the body of the message.

Netsurfer Digest. A list of interesting and fun places to visit on the World Wide Web. To subscribe to the Netsurfer Digest, send a message to **nsdigest-request@netsurf.com**. In the body of the message, put the words **subscribe nsdigest-html** for the HTML (Web-browser viewable) version, or **subscribe nsdigest-text** for the plain text version.

Winsock Users. This list provides announcements of interest to Winsock users. To subscribe to the Winsock Users list, send a message to **majordomo@mailbag.intel.com**, with the words **subscribe winsock-users** in the body of the message.

Joke of the Day. Although you won't get a joke *every* day of the year, you'll certainly get enough to give you a regular snicker fix. To subscribe to the Joke of the Day mailing list, send a message to **joke-request@tdkt.skypoint.net**, with the word **subscribe** in the body of the message.

As we've seen, mail is one of the more important and useful tools you can use on the Internet. It's a simple, yet effective way to keep in touch with friends and associates, as well as a powerful tool for information gathering.

In the next chapter, we'll take a look at Usenet newsreaders, which enable you to communicate interactively with thousands of people.

5

Reading the News

TRYING TO DESCRIBE Usenet is a difficult task. To say that it's simply a large electronic bulletin board is like saying that an ocean is simply a large lake. Anyone who's ever gone snorkeling knows that below the surface , there's a vast difference between an ocean and a lake. Similarly, when you dive below the surface of Usenet, you'll discover that it's far more complex than you may have imagined. First of all, Usenet is huge. No, beyond huge—it's enormous. There are literally tens of thousands of *newsgroups*. Each newsgroup is a discussion group, or forum covering a particular topic. Theoretically, each newsgroup covers a specific area of interest, although many of them overlap. Some newsgroups cover a very broad area of interest (*rec.food*), while others cover an exceptionally precise subject (*comp.sys.ibm.pc.hardware.chips*).

Deciphering Newsgroup Names

There are hundreds of newsgroup hierarchies, or categories. The "top level" hierarchy is the first place to look. The primary hierarchies, called the "Big Seven" are carried almost everywhere. These hierarchies are:

comp.*	Discussions relating to computers, hardware and software.
misc.*	Miscellaneous discussions and "classified ads."
news.*	News about Usenet: lists, administration, announcements.
rec.*	Recreational topics: sports, crafts, arts, food, etc.
sci.*	Scientific, medical, and physical discussions.
soc.*	Sociological and cultural discussions.
talk.*	General discussions on a variety of topics.

Beyond the top-level hierarchy, there are a number of divisions. For example, under the *comp.** level, there's *comp.databases.**, *comp.graphics.**, *comp.lang.**, *comp.os.**, and many others. And, within each of those groups, there are subgroups, such as *comp.graphics.animation*, *comp.lang.c*, and *comp.os.ms-windows.apps.utilities*.

Newsgroups that fall under one of these seven hierarchies are much more carefully controlled than other newsgroups. They must be approved by a vote of the Usenet community, which includes anyone who reads Usenet and chooses to vote.

Yet although these seven groups are traditionally called "Big," the biggest newsgroup by far—the *alt.** hierarchy—isn't one of these seven. The alt.* hierarchy isn't as strictly controlled. Technically, anyone can create an alt.* newsgroup. However, there is a certain etiquette to doing so.

If you have a burning desire to create an alt. newsgroup, read the "So You Want to Create an Alternative Newsgroup" message, posted every two weeks in the alt.answers newsgroup. This posting offers excellent advice for those wishing to create alt.* newsgroups.*

Alternative Newsgroups

Usenet legend has it that the alternative, or alt.* newsgroup hierarchy was created in 1987, after two newsgroups, rec.sex and rec.drugs were approved by vote of the Usenet community. But the administrators in charge of actually creating these newsgroups balked at creating these two groups, despite the overwhelming vote in favor of them.

So, a small group of Usenet administrators created the alt.* hierarchy, with the first two groups being alt.sex and alt.drugs. To round out the initial triumvirate, alt.rock-and-roll became the third newsgroup in the alt.* hierarchy.

Today, the number of alt.* newsgroups is in the thousands, covering a diverse range of topics. Some system administrators, however, choose not to carry alt.* newsgroups, based on the fact that a hundred or so of them contain sexually explicit subject matter.

There are also a large number of regional newsgroups. For example, groups pertaining to California are in the ca.* hierarchy, and groups for New York are in ny.*.

Important Newsgroups to Remember

There are several informational newsgroups I recommend you subscribe to, especially if you're just familiarizing yourself with Usenet:

news.announce. important	Important announcements about subjects that affect all Usenet readers.
news.announce .newusers	General information about Usenet.
alt.internet.services	Information about services and resources for Internet users.
news.answers	Hundreds of periodic informational postings from a wide range of newsgroups.
comp.os.ms-windows.*	Questions, answers, and discussion about Microsoft Windows and Windows applications.
alt.winsock	Information about Winsock applications.

A little Usenet Terminology

Here's a quick definition list for terms you'll run into when reading Usenet newsgroups:

.newsrc	A file which contains a list of all the newsgroups carried on your system, and specifying which newsgroups you're subscribed to.
followup	A posting responding to a previous posting, which will appear in the newsgroup following the original posting.
newsgroup	A discussion group for a particular topic.
NNTP	Network News Transfer Protocol. The protocol used on most Usenet news servers.
posting	A message posted to a newsgroup. Also called a message or article.

reply	A reply by mail to a person who posted a message in a newsgroup.
spam	A message that is unnecessarily posted to multiple newsgroups, when a post to one or two newsgroups would have sufficed. Spams usually come either from malicious users or amateur entrepreneurs who either don't realize or don't care how much disk space and bandwidth they're wasting on servers and networks around the world.
subscribe	Selecting a particular newsgroup so that it appears in your personal list of newsgroups.
troll	A message posted in a newsgroup specifically for the purpose of annoying and inciting the regular readers of that newsgroup.
unsubscribe	Deselecting a particular newsgroup.

Unix Newsreaders

The first newsreaders were written for Unix systems. If you're on a Unix host system, these are the newsreaders you're most likely to run across.

Read News: rn

The rn newsreader, by Larry Wall and Stan Barber, is one of the oldest newsreaders around. It's sort of like an old car. It may not be real fancy, but it gets you where you want to go (see Figure 5.1). In general, rn assumes that you want to read most of the postings in a newsgroup, while more recent newsreaders assume that you'll take a more selective approach.

The rn newsreader is available on most Unix systems.

Figure 5.1:

The rn newsreader is simple, yet effective.

```
OK (? for help): rn
Unread news in rec.food.recipes                       54 articles
Unread news in alt.internet.services                 588 articles
Unread news in rec.humor.funny                         6 articles
Unread news in alt.sports.baseball.sf-giants          56 articles
Unread news in alt.winsock                             6 articles
etc.

******  54 unread articles in rec.food.recipes -- read now? [ynq]
```

Using rn

To use rn, do the following:

1. Start rn by typing **rn** at a Unix prompt. The first time you run rn, it will display information about the program and connect you with your news server.

2. If you've never run a newsreader before, rn will create a **.newsrc** file for you. This file contains information about all of the newsgroups available at your site.

rn displays each of the newsgroups you're subscribed to in the order in which they appear in your .newsrc file. For each newsgroup, it will display header information for each message in sequential order. If you want to read the rest of the displayed message, hit the spacebar.

Here are some other commands you can use with rn:

h	Display a list of commands.
n	Go to the next unread message.
p	Go back to the previous message.
r	Reply via mail to the person who wrote the current message.
R	Same as r, except that the text of the current message is included in your reply.

f	Post a followup message to the current message.
F	Same as f, except that the text of the current message is included in your posting.
s *filename*	Save the current message to the specified ***filename***.
q	Quit, and go to the end of the message.
Q	Quit, and go to the next newsgroup. At this point, if you want to quit rn, press q.
u	Unsubscribe from this newsgroup.
$f	Post a new message to the newsgroup.

One of the biggest gripes about rn is that it shows you the messages in the order in which they were received on your local news server. Since messages are being posted from all over the world, they are received at different locations in different order. So for example, since I live in San Francisco, it's much more likely that I'll see messages posted from Oakland before I see messages posted from London.

 ▶ *For more information about rn, type* **man rn** *at a Unix prompt to see the online manual.*

Threaded Read News: trn

The trn newsreader, by Wayne Davison, is quite similar to rn. The primary difference is that trn *threads* the messages in each newsgroup. Threading means that you see them in the logical order in which they are intended to be read, with each response following the message to which it responds, as opposed to the method used by rn, which simply displays messages in the order they were received.(see Figure 5.2)

The trn newsreader is available on most Unix systems. If it isn't available on your system, and you'd like to try it, contact your system administrator to find out if it can be installed on your system.

The trn newsreader displays in "threaded" format and lets you move through messages using your cursor keys.

```
rec.arts.sf.fandom #10757 (2 + 89 more)          --(1)+-(1)
From: Loren Joseph MacGregor                        \-(1)+-(1)--(1)--(1)--(1)
+        <lmacgreg@amazing.cinenet.net>                \-(1)
[2] Re: Smileys                                  --( )+-( )--( )--[2]
Date: Thu Feb 09 00:40:46 PST 1995                  \-( )--( )+-( )--( )--[2]
Organization: David's Amazing Internet                        \-( )--[2]
+              Services - (818) 997-7500
Lines: 14
X-Newsreader: DAIS News System v0.5 (Beta)
X-Note-1: New newsreader; send complaints to postmaster@amazing.cinenet.net

--MORE--(29%)
```

Using trn

To use trn, do the following:

1. Start trn by typing **trn** at a Unix prompt. The first time you run trn, it will display information about the program and connect you with your news server.

2. If you've never run a newsreader before, trn will create a **.newsrc** file for you, containing a list of all the newsgroups available at your site.

3. When you read a newsgroup, trn starts off by showing you an overview of the threads, from which you can select the threads you want to view. To select a thread, just move your cursor to the thread you want to read, and press Enter.

In the upper right corner of the messages screen, you'll see the messages in the current thread in a tree diagram, as shown in Figure 5.2. To see the next message in the same thread, just press the right arrow key. If you want to see the next branch of the thread tree, press the down arrow key. When you get to the end of the current thread, you'll see the thread overview screen again, and you can continue with the next set of threads.

Other than that, you can use all the same commands with trn that you can use with rn.

For more information about trn, type **man trn** *at a Unix prompt to see the online manual.*

Etiquette

Some newsgroups are predominantly discussion-oriented, while others are for announcements only. Many newsgroups discourage arguments, or "flame wars," while still others actively encourage them. How can you tell the difference? Sometimes it's obvious, but other times, it's not. In general, newsgroups that have the word *announce* in their name are for announcements only, and are usually *moderated*, which means the person who administrates the group can choose which postings will appear. Newsgroups that have the word *advocacy* in them are usually meant for passionate discussions, especially the *comp.os.*.advocacy* newsgroups.

But with most newsgroups, it's hard to tell what the posting etiquette is for that group just by looking at the name. The safest thing to do is to read a particular newsgroup for a few days to get a general idea of what the discussion is like before you attempt to post to that group. You don't have to read every single message, just try to get a general feel for the atmosphere of the newsgroup before posting.

Venturing into the world of Usenet without a clear understanding of the etiquette of a particular newsgroup can get you into trouble. For more information about posting etiquette, see the *news.announce.newusers* newsgroup.

No News: nn

According to the online manual, the motto of nn is "No news is good news, but nn is better." Living up to its name, nn, by Kim F. Storm, lets you be a bit more choosy about which newsgroups and which messages within each newsgroup you want to read (see Figure 5.3).

The nn newsreader is available on most Unix systems. If it isn't available on your system, and you'd like to try it, contact your system administrator to find out if it can be installed on your system.

Figure 5.3:

The nn newsreader lets you view all the header information about messages and lets you select the messages you want to see.

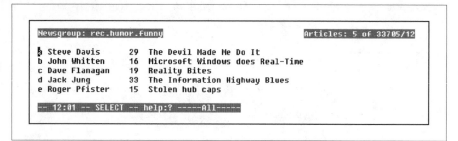

```
Newsgroup: rec.humor.funny                          Articles: 5 of 33705/12

  a Steve Davis       29   The Devil Made Me Do It
  b John Whitten      16   Microsoft Windows does Real-Time
  c Dave Flanagan     19   Reality Bites
  d Jack Jung         33   The Information Highway Blues
  e Roger Pfister     15   Stolen hub caps

-- 12:01 -- SELECT -- help:? -----All-----
```

Using nn

To use nn, do the following:

1. Start nn by typing **nn** at a Unix prompt. The first time you run nn, it will display information about the program and connect you with your news server.

2. If you've never run a newsreader before, nn will create a **.newsrc** file for you, containing a list of all the newsgroups available at your site.

3. When you first start up nn, you'll see summary information for the first 19 messages in each newsgroup, as shown in Figure 5.3. Each message will have a lowercase letter to the left of the description.

4. If you want to see that message, just type that letter and nn will mark that message to be read.

5. When you want to see the next page of headers, hit the spacebar.

6. When you get to the end of the newsgroup, hit the spacebar again, and nn will display all of the messages you marked to be read.

 *If you don't want to wait until you reach the end of the newsgroup to read the messages you've marked, press **Z**.*

Here are some other handy commands you can use with nn:

?   Display a list of all the commands available.

N   Go to the next newsgroup.

P	Go to the previous newsgroup.
F	Post a followup message to the current message.
R	Reply via mail to the person who posted the current message.
M	Mail a copy of the current article to someone.
<	Go to the previous page.
>	Go to the next page (same as spacebar).
S	Save current message to a file.
U	Unsubscribe to the current newsgroup.
Y	See a list of all the newsgroups you're subscribed to.
:post	Post a new message.
Q	Quit nn.

 ▶ *For more information about nn, type* **man nn** *at a Unix prompt, or type* **man** *if you're in nn.*

Threaded Internet Newsreader: tin

I've saved my favorite Unix newsreader for last. The tin newsreader, by Iain Lea, is just about the easiest Unix newsreader to use (see Figure 5.4).

The tin newsreader is available on most Unix systems. If it isn't available on your system, and you'd like to try it, contact your system administrator to find out if it can be installed on your system.

Using tin

To use tin, do the following:

1. Start tin by typing **tin** at a Unix prompt. The first time you run tin, it will display information about the program and connect you with your news server.

Figure 5.4:
The tin newsreader offers an intuitive way to read messages in your newsgroups.

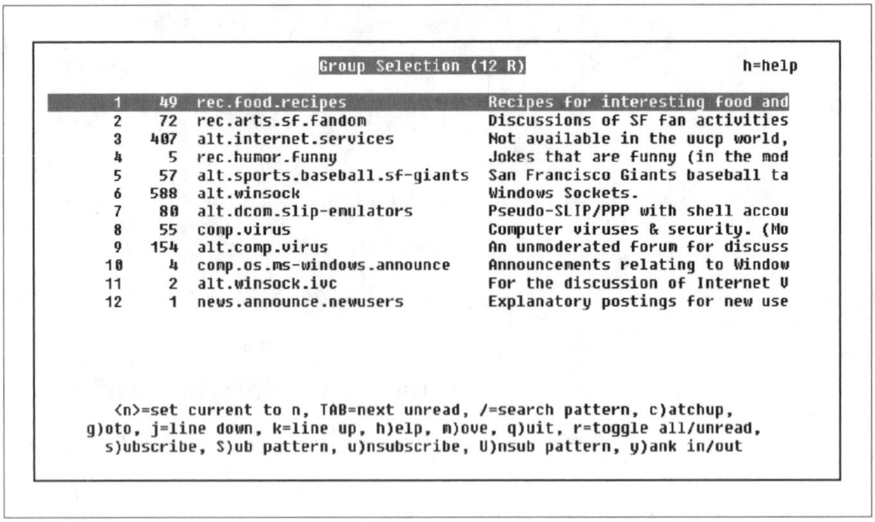

```
                    Group Selection (12 R)                      h=help
    1    49  rec.food.recipes          Recipes for interesting food and
    2    72  rec.arts.sf.fandom        Discussions of SF fan activities
    3   407  alt.internet.services     Not available in the uucp world,
    4     5  rec.humor.funny           Jokes that are funny (in the mod
    5    57  alt.sports.baseball.sf-giants  San Francisco Giants baseball ta
    6   588  alt.winsock               Windows Sockets.
    7    80  alt.dcom.slip-emulators   Pseudo-SLIP/PPP with shell accou
    8    55  comp.virus                Computer viruses & security. (Mo
    9   154  alt.comp.virus            An unmoderated forum for discuss
   10     4  comp.os.ms-windows.announce  Announcements relating to Window
   11     2  alt.winsock.ivc           For the discussion of Internet V
   12     1  news.announce.newusers    Explanatory postings for new use



       <n>=set current to n, TAB=next unread, /=search pattern, c)atchup,
       g)oto, j=line down, k=line up, h)elp, m)ove, q)uit, r=toggle all/unread,
       s)ubscribe, S)ub pattern, u)nsubscribe, U)nsub pattern, y)ank in/out
```

2. If you've never run a newsreader before, tin will create a **.newsrc** file for you, containing a list of all the newsgroups available at your site.

3. When you first start up tin, you'll see the Group Selection screen, as shown in Figure 5.4. It will display all of the newsgroups you are subscribed to. It also displays a handy list of commands at the bottom of the screen.

Here are some of the commands you can use with tin when you're at the Group Selection screen:

j or ↓	Move down a line.
k or ↑	Move up a line.
h	See a list of commands.
/	Search for text.
r	Toggle between viewing all messages, and viewing only unread messages.
y	Yank in all newsgroups—subscribed and unsubscribed.
s	Subscribe to the currently selected newsgroup.
u	Unsubscribe to the currently selected newsgroup.

To read the messages in a newsgroup, just select the newsgroup and press Enter. When you do this, you'll see the Newsgroup screen. You'll see the newsgroup name at the top of the screen.

Here are some of the other commands you can use from the Newsgroup screen:

j or ↓	Move down a line.
k or ↑	Move up a line.
h	See a list of commands.
Tab	Read the next unread article.
/	Search for text.
a	Search for an author's name.
Spacebar	Go to the next page.
t	Tag current article. Once you've tagged articles, you can perform an action on them, like save them to a file all at once.
s	Save current article (or tagged articles) to a file.
Ctrl+u	Go to the previous page.
w	Post a new article to this newsgroup.
c	Catch-up, marking all articles in the current newsgroup as read.
q	Quit, and go back to the Group Selection screen.

To read a message, just select the message and Press Enter. Now you're at the Article screen. When you're reading an article, you can do the following:

Spacebar	See the next page of the article.
t	Tag current article. Once you've tagged articles, you can perform an action on them, like save them to a file all at once.
s	Save current article (or tagged articles) to a file.
n	Read the next article.
Tab	Read the next unread article.

97

r	Reply via e-mail to the person who wrote the current message.
R	Same as r, except that the text of the current message is included in your reply.
f	Post a followup message to the current message.
F	Same as f, except that the text of the current message is included in your posting.
m	Mail a copy of the current article to someone.
w	Post a new article to this newsgroup.
q	Quit this article, and go back to the newsgroup screen.

For more information about tin, type **man tin** *at a Unix prompt to see the on-line manual.*

Posting a Test Message

If you want to post a test message, you can use one of the specific news-groups meant for this purpose. All test newsgroups are called **.test*. There's *misc.test*, *alt.test*, and regional test groups, like *ca.test*, *ba.test*, *ny.test*, and so on.

Posting a message to a test group is an easy way to test your newsreader without annoying other users with test messages.

In addition, when you post to a test newsgroup, there are servers out on the Internet that will send an automatic response back to your mailbox when they receive your posting. This is an easy way to find out how long it takes for your message to travel out to different locations.

If you don't want to receive automated response messages just put the word **ignore** in the Subject line of your test message.

Windows Newsreaders

There are a growing number of newsreaders for Windows, and all of them use Windows sockets. Newsreader choice is a matter of personal taste. I recommend trying them all out to see which one best fits your needs.

News Xpress

News Xpress, by W.L. Ken, Ng, is rapidly gaining popularity among Winsock users. For a program that is essentially still in beta testing, it's remarkably robust, and offers many attractive features, including the ability to open multiple newsgroups at the same time and automatically encode and decode binary files using UUEncode and UUDecode (see Figure 5.5).

Figure 5.5:
News Xpress is an easy-to-use and powerful newsreader for Windows.

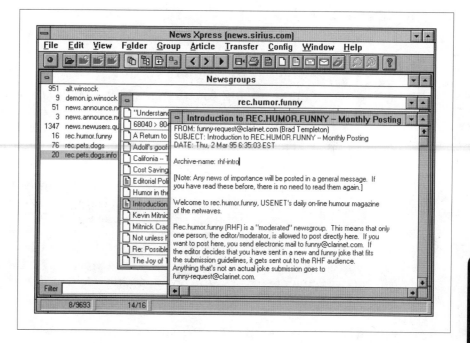

> You can get the latest version of News Xpress via anonymous FTP from **ftp.hk.super.net**, in the **/pub/windows/Winsock-Utilities** directory. The current version at the time of this writing is 1.0, beta 3, and the filename is **nx10b3.zip**.

News Xpress is public domain software and may be freely copied and distributed, provided that the program is not altered in any way.

Installing News Xpress

To install News Xpress, do the following:

1. Create an **NXPRESS** directory on your hard disk.

2. Uncompress the zip file into that directory.

3. Create an icon on your Windows desktop for the **NX.EXE** file.

Now you're ready to configure News Xpress:

1. Start up News Xpress.

2. The first time you run News Xpress, you'll be prompted to enter the name of your news (NNTP) server, SMTP (mail) server, and other important information, such as your name and e-mail address. You probably won't need to fill in your username and password in the Authentication section. When you're done, click on **OK**.

3. Select File ➤ Connect. If this is the first time you've used News Xpress, it will automatically download the names of all the newsgroups on your server. (This may take awhile.)

The next time you run News Xpress and select File ➤ Connect, you'll only see the newsgroups that you've previously subscribed to. I'll give you more information about adding additional newsgroups in the next section.

If you're using TIA to access your news server on a Unix shell account, you'll need to find out the name of your news server. If you're not sure what it is, ask your system administrator.

Using News Xpress

Here are some options available to you when running News Xpress:

To connect to your news server, select File ➤ Connect.

To subscribe to newsgroups, make sure the View ➤ All Groups option is checked, then check the boxes next to the names of newsgroups you want to subscribe to.

To unsubscribe to a newsgroup, select the newsgroup(s) you don't want to subscribe to anymore and select Group ➤ Unsubscribe.

To read messages in an newsgroup, just double-click on the newsgroup you want to read. You'll see a list of the messages in that newsgroup.

To read a message, just double-click on the listing for that message.

To search for a text string, enter the text to search for in the Filter: field at the bottom of the Newsgroups window.

To decode UUEncoded messages, select the file or files that you want to decode, then select Article ➤ Decode.

To reply to the author of a message, select or open the message, then select Article ➤ Reply.

To mail a copy of a message to someone, select or open the message, then select Article ➤ Mail/Forward.

To post a followup message to the newsgroup, select or open the message that you want to post a follow-up to, then select Article ➤ Follow-up.

To post a new message, select or open the newsgroup you want to post to, then select Article ➤ Post.

 ▶ *If you want to select multiple articles for reading, downloading, or decoding, you'll have to hold down the Ctrl key while you select them with the left mouse button.*

WinTrumpet

WinTrumpet, by Peter Tattam (of Trumpet Winsock fame), is a popular, easy-to-use newsreader for Windows (see Figure 5.6). I find it to be one

101

Figure 5.6:
It's easy to search for
and subscribe to
newsgroups using
WinTrumpet.

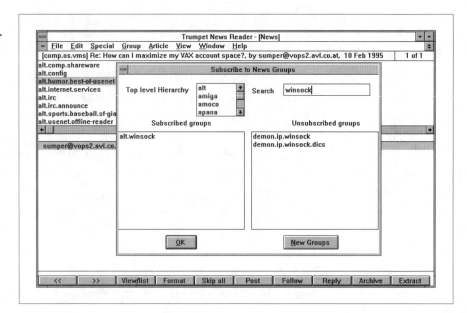

of the more intuitive newsreaders around, yet it lacks some of the sophisticated UUDecoding features available with other newsreaders.

WinTrumpet makes it easy to subscribe and unsubscribe from newsgroups, and even lets you search through your entire list of newsgroups
for all newsgroups that contain a particular text string, which can
come in real handy if you're looking for a newsgroup covering a specific topic.

You can get the latest version of WinTrumpet via anonymous FTP from
ftp.trumpet.com.au, in the **/ftp/pub/wintrump** directory. You can also
find it at **ftp.cica.indiana.edu** in the **/pub/pc/win3/winsock** directory. The
current version of the Winsock version at the time of this writing is 1.0a, and
the filename is **wtwsk10a.zip**.

If you're feeling adventurous, the current beta version is available from
ftp.trumpet.com.au in the **/ftp/pub/beta/wintrump** directory. The current beta version at the time of this writing is 1.0b Final Beta #4, and the filename is **wt_wsk.zip**. This file contains only the executable program,
WT_WSK.EXE. You must get the additional support files from the release
version.

WinTrumpet is shareware, and costs $40 to register.

Installing WinTrumpet

To install WinTrumpet, do the following:

1. Create a **WINTRUMP** directory on your hard disk.

2. Uncompress the zip file into that directory.

3. Add an icon to your Windows desktop for the **WT_WSK.EXE** program.

Now you're ready to configure WinTrumpet:

1. Start up WinTrumpet.

2. The first time you run WinTrumpet, you'll be prompted to enter setup information, including your news and mail server names, your name, and your address. If you're running WinTrumpet from a SLIP or PPP account, and you want to be able to connect to your POP3 mail server to use WinTrumpet as a mail program, be sure to enter your POP3 account name (your login name) and password.

3. When you're done, click on **OK**. WinTrumpet will then connect to your news server.

If you're using TIA to access your news server on a Unix shell account, you'll need to find out the name of your news server. If you're not sure what it is, ask your system administrator.

Using WinTrumpet

Here are some of the options available to you when using WinTrumpet:

To subscribe to newsgroups, select Group ➤ Subscribe. The first time you use WinTrumpet, it will copy a complete list of all the newsgroups on your server to your hard disk. (This may take awhile.) You can then select the newsgroups that you want to subscribe to from the list on the right side of the window.

To unsubscribe from newsgroups, select the newsgroup you don't want to subscribe to anymore and select Groups ➤ Unsubscribe.

103

To read messages in a newsgroup, just double-click on the newsgroup name. WinTrumpet will then display all the unread messages in that newsgroup. If you want to read a particular message, just double-click on that message.

To move on to the next message, click on the >> button at the bottom of the screen, or click on the View/List button to switch back to the message list view.

To reply to the author of a message, select the message, then click on the Reply button at the bottom of the screen.

To mail a copy of a message to someone, select or open the message and select Article ➤ Mail.

To post a followup message, select or open the message that you want to post a followup to, then click on the Follow button at the bottom of the screen.

To post a new message, select or open the newsgroup you want to post to, then click on the Post button at the bottom of the screen.

To save copies of messages, select the messages you want to save and click on the Archive button at the bottom of the screen.

To decode a UUEncoded message, select the message, then click on the Extract button at the bottom of the screen. WinTrumpet is unable to extract UUEncoded messages that have multiple parts.

 If you're using Trumpet Winsock and you set up your Winsock to use a Time Server, WinTrumpet will be able to show you a list of new newsgroups that have been added to your server when you select Group ➤ Subscribe.

If you aren't able to set a time server, just delete the NEWS.GRP file in your \WINTRUMP directory before you start WinTrumpet, then start it up and select Group ➤ Subscribe. Then WinTrumpet will automatically pull down a new complete list of newsgroups.

For more information about Trumpet Winsock, see Appendix B.

WinVN

WinVN, originally written by Mark Riordan, offers some very powerful features, such as the ability to open multiple newsgroups and multiple messages at the same time, in separate windows (see Figure 5.7). It also lets you automatically UUEncode and UUDecode binary files for posting, and lets you save messages to disk.

There are two versions of WinVN: 16-bit for Windows 3.1 users, and 32-bit for Windows 95 and Windows NT users.

Figure 5.7:
WinVN is a full-featured, powerful newsreader for Windows.

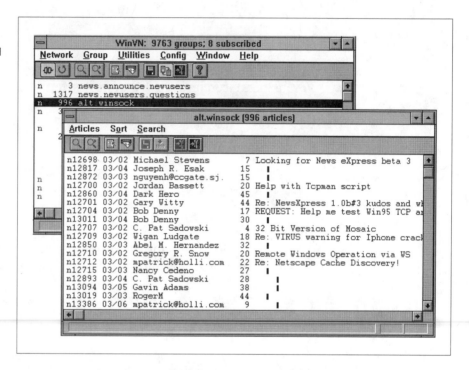

You can get WinVN via anonymous FTP from **ftp.ksc.nasa.gov** in the **/pub/winvn/win3** directory. The 32-bit version for Windows 95 and Windows NT is in the **/pub/winvn/nt** directory. This program is under very active development, with new versions appearing almost weekly. Check the dates of the files when you get to the FTP server, and download the most current version.

WinVN is public domain software and may be distributed freely.

105

The developers are uploading files with very descriptive filenames, which are longer than 8 characters. If you're using Windows 3.1, you will need to rename the file to conform to the DOS 8-character naming convention when you download it.

Installing WinVN

To install WinVN, do the following:

1. Create a **WINVN** directory on your hard disk.

2. Uncompress the zip file into that directory.

3. Create an icon on your Windows desktop for the **WINVN.EXE** file.

To configure WinVN, do the following:

1. Start up WinVN.

 If you're running Windows 95, it will prompt you to create the WINVN.INI and NEWSRC file. Click on Open then Yes to create each of these files.

2. The first time you run WinVN, it will prompt you for the name of your new server, and for your name, e-mail address and organization name. Enter this information and click on **OK**.

 Check out the README.TXT file for some additional tuning suggestions from the developers. These suggestions seem to change from version to version, so make sure you read this file when you download the newest version to get the latest helpful hints.

3. Then WinVN will start up. The first time you run WinVN, you'll be asked if you want to get the latest list of newsgroups from you server. Click on **Yes**. (Downloading this list may take awhile.)

4. You'll then be prompted to select the newsgroups that you'd like to subscribe to. Select the newsgroups by top-level hierarchy (alt., comp, rec., etc.), then select the individual newsgroups. WinVN automatically subscribes you to *news.announce.newusers* and *news.newusers.questions*.

If you're using TIA to access your news server on a Unix shell account, you'll need to find out the name of your news server. If you're not sure what it is, ask your system administrator.

Using WinVN

WinVN is very easy to use. Groups you are subscribed to are shown at the top of the list. All other groups are shown below. The number next to each group is the number of unread articles in that group.

Here are some options available to you when using WinVN:

To subscribe to newsgroups, select the newsgroups you want to subscribe to, and select Group ➤ Subscribe Selected Groups.

To unsubscribe from newsgroups, select the newsgroup(s) you don't want to subscribe to anymore and select Group ➤ Unsubscribe Selected Groups.

To read a newsgroup, double-click on the newsgroup name.

To read a message, double-click on the message header.

To reply to the author of a message by e-mail, open the message by double-clicking on it, then select Respond ➤ Compose Mail.

To mail a copy of the message to someone, open the message by double-clicking on it, then select Respond ➤ Forward Article.

To post a followup message to the newsgroup, open the message by double-clicking on it, then select Respond ➤ Followup Article.

To post a new message to the newsgroup, from the newsgroup window, select Articles ➤ New Article.

To automatically UUDecode articles, just select the articles you want to decode and click on Articles ➤ Decode Selected Articles.

 There's a mailing list for WinVN users. To get on the mailing list, send a message to **majordomo@news.ksc.nasa.gov**, *with the words* subscribe winvn *in the body of the message.*

107

Reading News Offline

An *offline* newsreader is one that lets you connect to your provider's news server, download new messages in bunches, log out, then read them while you're not online.

If you're paying by the hour for your connection, offline newsreaders can be a real money saver. Currently, there are only a couple of offline newsreaders for Windows users, but demand seems to be growing for this little niche in the newsreader market, so expect to see others. Stay tuned...

Free Agent

Free Agent, by Forte Inc., is the newest player on the newsreader block, and it's a pretty impressive player at that (see Figure 5.8). It offers internal multitasking, which allows you to perform several different tasks at once, full search capabilities, and the ability to save articles for later reading.

Free Agent allows you to read news either online or offline. When you read news online, it retrieves articles whenever you select them. When you read news offline, you can connect to get the message header lines,

Figure 5.8:
Free Agent is an impressive new online/offline newsreader.

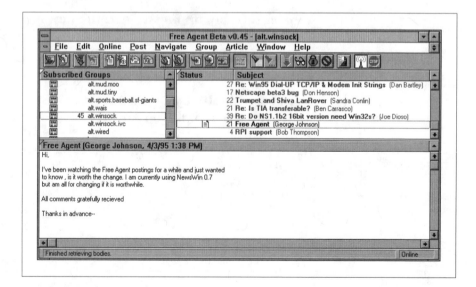

disconnect, then select the messages that you want Free Agent to retrieve for you. You can then reconnect, and download only the messages that you selected.

Free Agent allows you to mark articles you want to save, and also lets you mark certain threads to *watch*—when responses to these messages appear, Free Agent will automatically retrieve them. It also lets you mark certain threads to *ignore*—when responses to these articles appear, you won't see them.

> You can get Free Agent via anonymous FTP from **ftp.forteinc.com**, in the **/pub/agent/** directory. The current version at the time of this writing is .045 and the filename is **agent045.zip**.

Forte is releasing Free Agent as freeware for home, student, educational, and non-profit organizational use. The full product, Agent™ is available for $40, with special pricing for site licenses. The full version also includes full technical support, a mail program, a spellchecker, the ability to save messages in folders and launch other client applications like Web browsers and FTP programs.

Installing Free Agent

To install Free Agent, do the following:

1. Create an **AGENT** directory on your hard disk.

2. Uncompress the zip file into that directory.

3. Create an icon on your Windows desktop that points to the **AGENT.EXE file**. Make sure the working directory points to the AGENT directory you created.

Now you're ready to configure Free Agent:

1. Start up Free Agent by double-clicking on the Agent icon.

2. First, you'll see a copy of the license agreement. Read through it and click on **Accept**.

3. Next, you'll see the Free Agent Setup window. If you've already installed Netscape, News Xpress, Trumpet Newsreader, or Win VN, you can get configuration information from any of these programs by clicking on the **Use Information From Another Program** button. Otherwise, enter the name of your news server and mail server, your e-mail address and full name in the spaces provided. Select your time zone from the list box. Click on **OK**.

4. You'll then be asked if you want to connect to your news server now and download a list of newsgroups. Click on **Yes**. (This may take awhile.)

5. Now, select File ➤ Preferences. Look through the available option tabs and select your preferred options.

6. If you'd like to set up Free Agent for offline news reading, click on the **Online Operation** tab and click on **Configure for Offline Operation**.

Using Free Agent

Here are some of the options available to you when using Free Agent:

To see what each of the buttons does, move the mouse cursor over the button. A little description box will appear for each button.

To find newsgroups, click on the Find button.

To subscribe to newsgroups, double-click on the group you want to subscribe to. You'll be prompted to either view articles or subscribe to the group. Select Subscribe to Group.

To unsubscribe from newsgroups, select the newsgroup you don't want to subscribe to anymore and click on the depressed Subscribe to Group button.

To retrieve message headers for a group, double click on the group. You'll be prompted to view articles or subscribe to the group. Select either Sample 50 Article Headers or Get All Article Headers.

To read an unread message (shown in red) , double-click on the article header.

To decode an encoded message or messages, select the messages and click on Launch Binary Attachments.

To reply to the author of a message, double-click on the message you want to respond to, and click on the Post Reply via Email button.

To mail a copy of the message to someone, double-click on the message you want to forward, and select Post ➤ Forward via E-mail.

To post a followup message to the newsgroup, double-click on the message you want to follow up, and click on the Post Follow Up Article button.

To post a new message, click on the Post New Article button.

To mark a message for retrieval, click on the Mark for Retrieval button.

To retrieve marked messages, click on Get Marked Article Bodies.

WinQVT

WinQVT, by QPC Software, includes a newsreader, mail program, Telnet, and FTP, all wrapped up into one package, which is nice if you like all-in-one solutions (see Figure 5.9). The only problem with all-in-one

Figure 5.9:
The WinQVT/Net
newsreader.

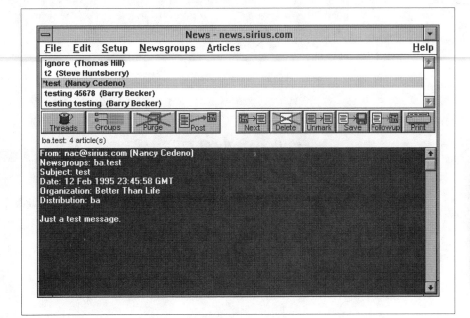

solutions is that they don't necessarily do all things well. WinQVT is no exception to this rule. This newsreader is good, but it's not great.

In the version I tried, the newsreader was quite slow, especially compared with the other available programs, and it doesn't support the ability to reply to or forward messages via e-mail, despite the fact that WinQVT comes with a mail program.

Of the other applications, the Telnet program is quite good, comparable to standalone Telnet programs such as EWAN or Trumpet Telnet, and it's the only Winsock Telnet program I've found that supports rlogin, which is similar to Telnet, but offers better security. The FTP program is just a Windows version of the basic Unix FTP program, which requires you to use text commands to transfer files. The mail application is quite functional, but doesn't have the features of programs like Eudora and Pegasus.

There are versions for both Windows 3.1 running Winsock as well as a version for Windows NT and Windows 95.

> You can get WinQVT via anonymous FTP from **biocserver.bioc.cwru.edu**, in the **/pub/windows/qvtnet** directory. You can also get it from **ftp.cica.indiana.edu** in the **/pub/pc/win3/winsock** directory. The current version of the Winsock-compatible 16-bit program at the time of this writing is 3.98, and the filename is **qvtws398.zip**. The filename for the 32-bit version for Windows NT or Windows 95 is **qvtnt398.zip**.

WinQVT is shareware, and costs $40 to register ($20 for students).

Installing WinQVT

To install WinQVT, do the following:

1. Create a **WINQVT** directory on your hard disk.

2. Uncompress the zip file into that directory.

3. Then, move the **VT220.FON** file to your WINDOWS\SYSTEM directory.

4. Create an icon for the **QVTNET16.EXE** file on your Windows desktop.

To configure WinQVT, do the following:

1. Start up WinQVT. You'll see a configuration screen.

2. Enter the \WINQVT directory in the **Hosts File Directory** field and click on **OK**.

3. You'll then be asked if you want to set up a default printer. Do so if you have one connected. It will use your default printer unless you tell it otherwise.

4. Now, click on Setup ➤ News. Enter your news hostname in the **Host** field. Also enter your e-mail address and name in the **Post From** field, and an organization name in the **Organization** field, if you'd like. Click on **OK**.

5. Then, click on Setup ➤ Mail. Enter your mailbox account name in the **Default Mailbox** field, your e-mail address in the **Return Address** field, and your mail server name in the **SMTP Host** field. Click on **OK**.

6. To start WinQVT's newsreader, click on Services ➤ News. You'll be asked if you want to read articles from disk or from the server. If this is the first time you're using WinQVT, select **Read articles from Server**.

7. To subscribe to newsgroups, select Newsgroups ➤ Subscribe. You'll be asked if you want to download a list of newsgroups. Select **Yes**. (Downloading this list may take awhile.)

If you're using TIA to access your news server on a Unix shell account, you'll need to find out the name of your news server. If you're not sure what it is, ask your system administrator.

Using WinQVT

Here are some options available to you when using WinQVT's newsreader:

To subscribe to additional newsgroups, select Newsgroups ➤ Subscribe. You'll be asked if you want to download a list of newsgroups.

113

In the version I tested, 3.98, you can only subscribe to new newsgroups when you are in Groups view. If you're reading articles in a newsgroup and you want to add additional newsgroups, you need to switch to Groups view by clicking on the Groups button first. Then you can select Newsgroups ➤ Subscribe to subscribe to additional newsgroups.

To unsubscribe from newsgroups, select the newsgroups that you don't want to subscribe to anymore and select Newsgroups ➤ Unsubscribe.

To read the messages in a newsgroup, double-click on the newsgroup you want to read. WinQVT will only show you the first five messages. To see more, click on the Articles button.

To save a message, double-click on the message you want to save, and click on the Save button.

To post a followup message, select the message that you want to post a followup message to, then click on the FollowUp button.

To post a new message, select the newsgroup that you want to post a message to, then click on the Post button.

The newsreader market seems to be booming right now, almost as much as the Web browser market (see Chapter 7). Of course, for users like us, this is great, because we benefit from a greater selection of applications.

And Usenet itself is booming. New newsgroups are getting added every day. While some are just pointless pranks perpetrated by bored college students, others are really quite useful and necessary.

CHAPTER

6

Burrowing
with Gopher

gopher n. 1. Any of various short tailed, burrowing mammals of the family Geomyidae, of North America. 2. (Amer. colloq.) Native or inhabitant of Minnesota: the Gopher State. 3. (Amer. colloq.) One who runs errands, does odd-jobs, fetches or delivers documents for office staff. 4. (computer tech.) Software following a simple protocol for tunneling through a TCP/IP internet.

—Gopher Software Development Team at the University of Minnesota

GOPHER WAS QUITE a revolutionary development on the Internet when it first appeared in 1991. It was the first widely-available, easy-to-use client application for finding information on Internet servers. With Gopher, you could search for information from all over the Internet with just a few keystrokes. Originally designed for use by University of Minnesota students, Gopher provides a simple, menu-driven interface to servers around the world that run the Gopher server software. Many sites, primarily at Universities, have adopted the Gopher server software, and have used it to create links to their anonymous FTP servers, as well as to text-based information, images, sounds, and even movies.

Since that time, the World Wide Web has become vastly more popular, due primarily to its appealing graphical interface. Yet the simple Gopher is still a major force on the Internet.

The immediate appeal of Gopher is that it's easy to use, even for novices. If you can use a menu system, you can use Gopher. Gopher offers much more than just an easy-to-use interface, however. It's also fast. In fact, you can often transfer a file faster using Gopher than with either FTP or a Web browser client application.

And using a Gopher client is a good way to explore the Internet. There's a lot of information out there on Gopher servers, and once you start to explore, you'll probably soon discover something you didn't realize was available on the Internet.

Places to Go Gophering

Take some time to explore with Gopher to get an idea of the kinds of things you can find. If you find one you like, make sure to create a bookmark for it, using your Gopher client program, so that you'll be able to find it again. Here are just a few of the thousands of places you can get to using Gopher. Often, one Gopher menu will lead you to several others located throughout the world.

University of Minnesota Gopher Home. Don't know where to start? Then try the mother of all Gophers, the U of M's Gopher Home. From here, you can find links to every Gopher server on the planet. To get there, point your Gopher client to:

> **gopher.micro.umn.edu, Port 70.**

CMU's English Server . From Carnegie-Mellon University's English Department, this Gopher server offers links to all kinds of interesting topics. You can find anything from the complete text of Charlotte Bronte's *Jane Eyre* to dissertations subjects from Medieval carpentry to *Beverly Hills 90210*, with lots of other stuff in between. To get there, point your Gopher client to:

> **english-server.hss.cmu.edu, Port 70.**

C-SPAN Gopher . The Cable-Satellite Public Affairs Network, or C-SPAN as it's more commonly known as, offers schedule information for their television programming as well as general information about US politics. To get there, point your Gopher client to:

> **c-span.org, Port 70.**

Digital Picture Archive . From the Delft University of Technology in the Netherlands, this is an absolutely enormous archive of images. Here you can find everything from a digital Mona Lisa to images of Jupiter. To get there, point your Gopher client to:

> **olt.et.tudelft.nl, Port 1251.**

The University of Iowa Weather Machine . Everything you'll ever need to know about the weather in your area or just about anywhere else on the planet, including satellite photos (in the Images directory). To get there, point your Gopher client to:

wx.atmos.uiuc.edu, Port 70.

The Yucks Digest Archives . Archives of Internet guru Gene Spafford's *Yucks Digest*, a semi-regular Internet publication of jokes, amusements, and just all-around funny stuff. To get there, point your Gopher client to:

gopher.cs.purdue.edu, Port 70, Path (Selector) 1Purdue_cs/Users/spaf/yucks/gopher.

Unix Gopher

The original Unix gopher is very easy to use. Just type **gopher** at a Unix prompt to start it up. You'll see the Gopher *Home* server menu first. The Home server is the starting point for your Gopher searches. Chances are, you'll either see a Gopher Home menu designed specifically for your system or you'll see the original Gopher Home server at the University of Minnesota, gopher.micro.umn.edu (see Figure 6.1).

To go to a specific Gopher server, just start up Gopher with the name of that server. For example, to go directly to the original University of Minnesota Gopher Home, just type:

```
% gopher gopher.micro.umn.edu
```

To move through the menus, just use your ↓ and ↑ keys to move to the line you want. Or, you can just type the number of the line. To see what lies behind the currently selected menu item, just press Enter.

Each item can lead to a number of different places, either on your current server, or halfway across the planet. If you've never burrowed through the Internet with Gopher before, I recommend taking some

Figure 6.1:
Gopher Home, at
the University of
Minnesota.

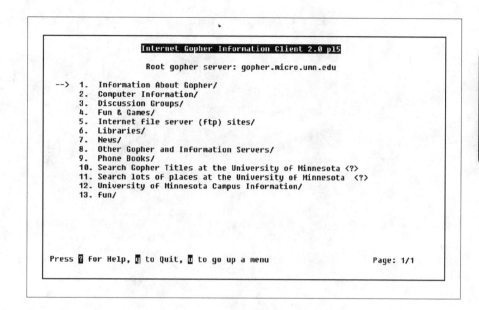

```
            Internet Gopher Information Client 2.0 p15

              Root gopher server: gopher.micro.umn.edu

  -->   1.  Information About Gopher/
        2.  Computer Information/
        3.  Discussion Groups/
        4.  Fun & Games/
        5.  Internet file server (ftp) sites/
        6.  Libraries/
        7.  News/
        8.  Other Gopher and Information Servers/
        9.  Phone Books/
       10.  Search Gopher Titles at the University of Minnesota <?>
       11.  Search lots of places at the University of Minnesota  <?>
       12.  University of Minnesota Campus Information/
       13.  Fun/




  Press ? for Help, q to Quit, u to go up a menu          Page: 1/1
```

time to poke around and see what's out there. You'd be amazed at all the different places Gopher can take you. And, you can add *bookmarks* to Gopher pages, making it easy to go back to places you want to visit again.

Here are some handy Unix Gopher commands to remember:

↓	Down a line.
↑	Up a line.
Enter	View item.
u	Up to the previous menu.
PageDown	Down a page.
PageUp	Up a page.
/	Search for an item in the menu.
m	Go back to the Main Menu.
a	Add a bookmark for the current page.
v	View your bookmark list.
q	Quit Gopher.

119

Publicly Accessible Gophers

If your local system doesn't have its own gopher, you can use telnet to get to one of the following public Gopher servers. Try to find one that's nearby—you'll get much better response time than you will from one that's far away.

Location	Telnet to	Log in as
California	infoslug.ucsc.edu	infoslug
Illinois	ux1.cso.uiuc.edu	gopher
Michigan	gopher.msu.edu	gopher
Minnesota	consultant.micro.umn.edu	gopher
Australia	info.anu.edu.au	info
Chile (in Spanish)	tolten.puc.cl	gopher
Equador (in Spanish)	ecnet.ec	gopher
Japan	gan.ncc.go.jp	gopher
Sweden	gopher.sunet.se	gopher

If you get a password: prompt, just press Enter.

For more information and announcements about Gopher, check out the **comp.infosystems.gopher** newsgroup on Usenet.

Windows Gophers

There are several Gopher client programs for Windows. They all offer an easy point-and-click interface, and they are all Winsock (Windows sockets) applications.

Burrow with Gopher CH. 6

Setting Up Viewers

You'll need to configure *viewers* for all of the Windows Gopher clients described in this chapter, and for all of the Web Browsers described in the next chapter.

Viewers are helper applications, such as picture viewers, sound players, and telnet programs. The viewers that are included with Windows, such as the Media Player or the Sound Recorder, are usually already defined for you. But if you want to change to a different viewer, or add viewers that aren't already configured, you'll need to configure them yourself, since you're the only one who knows where they're located on your hard disk.

Configuring viewers isn't all that difficult. It's really just a matter of deciding which viewers you want to use with different file types, and then configuring your Gopher or Web client application so that it will be able to find them.

There are several different image, video, and sound viewers described in Chapter 10 that you'll want to check out. Telnet applications are also useful viewer applications for Gopher and Web browser clients. For more information about telnet applications, see Chapter 3. You can configure some file decoding and uncompression tools as viewers as well (see Chapter 9 for more information).

Each application offers a different method for configuring viewer applications. I've included instructions for configuring viewers for each Gopher and Web client application discussed in these two chapters.

BCGopher

BCGopher, by Edmond C. Greene of Boston College, offers a nice, straightforward, graphical interface to Gopher servers around the world (see Figure 6.2). It offers the ability to select Gopher menu items by a simple double-click of the mouse, and automatically starts up viewer applications when needed. For example, if you double-click on a text item, BCGopher automatically opens the file using the Windows Notepad.

Figure 6.2:
When You Start Up
BCGopher, Your First
Stop Will Be Boston
College's InfoEagle
Gopher Server.

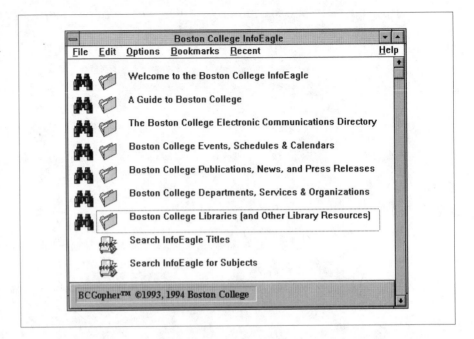

BCGopher is available via anonymous FTP from **bcinfo.bc.edu**, in the **/PUB/BCGOPHER** directory. When you log into the ftp server, use **anonymous** as the login name and **guest** as the password (*do not* use your e-mail address, as you would with other anonymous FTP servers). The current version at the time of this writing is 0.ß, and the filename is **BCG08BA3.EXE**, which is a self-extracting archive file..

Technically speaking, BCGopher is still in beta testing, although I ran it for some time without experiencing any problems.

Installing BCGopher

To install BCGopher, do the following:

1. Create a **BCGOPHER** directory on your hard disk.

2. Run the self-extracting archive file in that directory to uncompress the files.

3. Create a BCGopher icon on your Windows desktop for the **BCGOPHER.EXE** file.

To configure BCGopher, do the following:

1. Start BCGopher.

2. Select Options ➤ Configuration. If you'd like to use the Boston College Gopher as your Home menu, leave the Default Server field as is. If you'd like to use a different Gopher server as your home gopher, you can do that as well. Enter the Gopher name, Gopher address (i.e., gopher.micro.umn.edu), and Port number (usually 70). You should also check the **Connect on Startup** box, and change the **Default Download Directory** to \BCGOPHER.

3. Then, select File ➤ New Gopher and click on Connect. You should then connect to the Gopher you specified in the Configuration window.

To configure a new viewer application, do the following:

1. If you're not already in the Configuration window, select Options ➤ Configuration. Click on the application type that you want to configure at the bottom of the Configuration window, and click on **Edit**.

2. Click on **Browse** to find viewers on your hard disk. You can then select the appropriate viewer for each filetype. (For information on viewers, see *Setting Up Viewers* earlier in this chapter.

3. When you're done configuring viewers, click on **Close Configuration**.

Using BCGopher

Take a look at the BCGopher main window shown in Figure 6.2. Any menu option marked with the binoculars icon is on the current server, and any option that has a file folder icon is a menu. The sheet of paper icon identifies a text file. (For more information about the icons used in BCGopher, press F1 to see the help file.)

123

Here are a few options available to you when using BCGopher:

To see to a Gopher menu item, just double-click on it.

To go back to the previous menu item, click on the large arrow button at the bottom of the screen.

To see information on the current menu item, select Options ➤ Descriptor Box.

To change to a different Gopher server, select File ➤ New Gopher and enter the Gopher you want to jump to.

To add a Bookmark for the current menu page, select Bookmarks ➤ Add. Then, the next time you select Bookmarks, you'll see the Bookmark you added at the bottom of the list.

To edit your Bookmark list, select Bookmarks ➤ List.

HGopher

HGopher, by Martyn Hampson, was one of the first Winsock Gopher clients, and offers many nice features, such as the ability to switch between the current Gopher menu and your list of bookmarks with a single click of your mouse button. HGopher also supports a wide range of application types and viewer applications (see Figure 6.3).

Figure 6.3:
HGopher was one of the first Gopher clients for Windows.

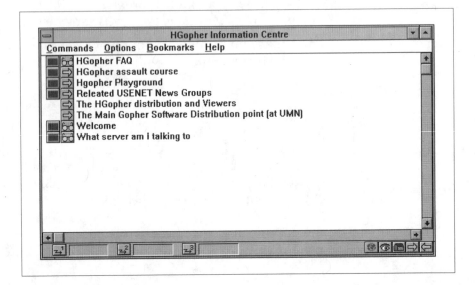

> You can get HGopher via anonymous FTP from **ftp.cica.indiana.edu**, in the **/pub/pc/win3/winsock** directory. The last freeware version is 2.3 and the filename is **hgoph23.zip**.

The rights to HGopher were purchased by FTP Software, Inc. in 1994, and HGopher is now a commercial product. The older version of HGopher, available from ftp.cica.indiana.edu, is freeware and can be freely distributed.

Installing HGopher

To install HGopher, do the following:

1. Create an **HGOPHER** directory on your hard disk.

2. Uncompress the zip file into that directory.

3. Create an HGopher icon on your Windows desktop for the **HGOPHER.EXE** file.

To configure HGopher, do the following:

1. Start up HGopher. You'll see a menu of options. This is your default bookmark file DEFAULT.GBM.

2. Select Options ➤ Gopher Setup. If you'd like to enter a home Gopher to start out with, enter its name in the **Gopher Server** field. If you'd like to use the Imperial University Computing Centre Gopher as your Home menu, click on **Factory**. Click on **OK**.

To configure a new viewer application, do the following:

1. Select Options ➤ Viewer Set up. Select the file type on the left side of the screen and enter viewer information on the right side. Make sure that you enter the full path for each viewer.

2. To automatically load the selected file in the viewer, type **%f** after the viewer executable name in the **Viewer** field. Make sure that the **Disabled** box is unchecked once you've entered viewer information for a particular file type.

3. When you're done configuring each viewer, click on the **Accept** button at the bottom of the screen.

For more information about HGopher, check out the bookmark for the HGopher Information Centre. This Gopher is located at the Imperial College Centre for Computing Services (gopher.ic.ac.uk), the home of HGopher.

Using HGopher

Here are some useful options available to you when using HGopher:

To go to a new Gopher menu item, just double-click on the Gopher menu item that you want to go to.

To switch between Gopher view and Bookmark view, click on the first icon at the bottom right corner of the window. If you see a globe, you're in Gopher view. If you see a set of books, you're in Bookmark view.

To go back to the previous menu, click on the left arrow at the bottom right corner of the window.

To go forward to a link you've just visited, click on the right arrow.

To go back to your home Gopher, click on the house icon.

To download linked files rather than view them, click on the eye. It changes to a folder. Now whenever you click on a linked file, you will be prompted to save the file on your hard disk.

To see where you've been, click on Commands ➤ History. HGopher will then display a menu showing you all of the menus you have visited since starting up HGopher.

To create a bookmark for the current menu, select Bookmarks ➤ Mark Menu.

To jump to a new server, load your bookmarks menu by selecting Bookmarks ➤ Show Bookmarks. Then, select Bookmarks ➤ Create Bookmark. Enter the Gopher server name in the **Description** field, the address (i.e., gopher.micro.umn.edu) in the **Host** field, and the Port (usually 70) in the Port field.

PNLInfo Browser

The PNLInfo Browser, from the Information Systems and Services department at Pacific Northwest Laboratory, is a simple, friendly, yet powerful Gopher client for Windows (see Figure 6.4). It's easier to set up than many of the Gopher clients I've tried, and it's quite configurable, allowing you to change fonts and viewers easily.

Figure 6.4:
The PNLInfo Browser is a simple, friendly Gopher client for Windows.

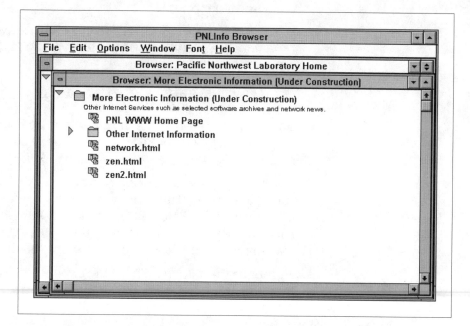

You can get PNLInfo Browser via anonymous FTP from **ftp.pnl.gov**, in the **/pub/pnlinfo/win** directory. The current version at the time of this writing is 1.05 and the filename is **ib105.exe** which is a self-extracting archive file.

PNLInfo Browser is freeware, and may be freely distributed, provided that the documentation is included and it is not sold for profit.

127

Installing PNLInfo Browser

To install PNLInfo Browser, do the following:

1. Create a **PNLIB** directory on your hard disk.

2. Run the self-extracting archive file in this directory to uncompress the files.

3. Create an InfoBrowse icon for the **INFOBRWS.EXE** file on your Windows desktop.

4. Move the **INFOBRWS.INI** file to your WINDOWS directory. Then, move the **XWI320.DLL** and **XWI320TE.DLL** files to your WINDOWS\SYSTEM directory.

To configure PNLInfo Browser, do the following:

1. Start InfoBrowser. The first time you start up PNLInfo Browser, you'll be connected to the Pacific Northwest Laboratory Home menu.

2. If you'd like to use the Pacific Northwest Laboratory Gopher as your Home menu, leave the Home Browser section as is. To change the default Home Gopher, select Options ➤ General Setup. Enter the Gopher name, Gopher address (i.e., gopher.micro.umn.edu), and Port number (usually 70). Click on **OK**.

3. To change the default font, select Font and choose a new font from the list of options.

To configure a new viewer application, do the following:

1. Select Options ➤ Viewer Setup.

2. To add a viewer, select the file type from the left side of the window, and click on **Select Viewer**.

3. You'll then be able to search for the appropriate viewer on your hard disk, when you find it, select it.

4. By default, you'll only see an abbreviated list of viewers. If you want to see the entire list, click on the **More Choices** button.

5. When you're done, click on **OK**.

Using PNLInfo Browser

Have a look around the PNLInfo Browser window shown in Figure 6.4. Notice the icons to the left of each menu item. A folder icon means that the item leads to another menu. A sheet of paper icon means that the item is a text file, and a graphic icon means that the item is a picture. For more information about these icons, or about anything else in Info Browser, press the F1 key at any time.

Here are some options available to you with PNLInfo Browser:

To jump to a Gopher menu item, just double-click on it. PNLInfo Browser will then open a new window displaying the item. To go back, just close the current window.

To see an expanded view of a Gopher menu item, click on the right-pointing triangle. Info Browser will then display the contents of that menu in outline format, within the context of the original Gopher menu.

To jump to a different Gopher server, select Options ➤ General Setup and enter the Gopher server name in the Name field, the address (i.e., gopher.micro.umn.edu) in the Server field, and the port (usually 70) in the Port field.

To add a bookmark for the currently selected menu, select File ➤ New Bookmark. To see your list of bookmarks, select File ➤ Show Bookmarks.

To print the current menu, select File ➤ Print List. If you're viewing a document, just select File ➤ Print.

PNLInfo Browser offers an online tutorial. Just click on File ➤ Show Tutorial to connect to the PNLInfo Tutorial menu.

WGopher

WGopher, created by the Computer Services Centre of the Chinese University of Hong Kong, is a very basic Gopher client for Windows. It isn't really fancy (see Figure 6.5), but it does have all of the basic features, and it is currently in active development.

Figure 6.5:

WGopher is a Gopher
client currently under
development from the
Chinese University of
Hong Kong.

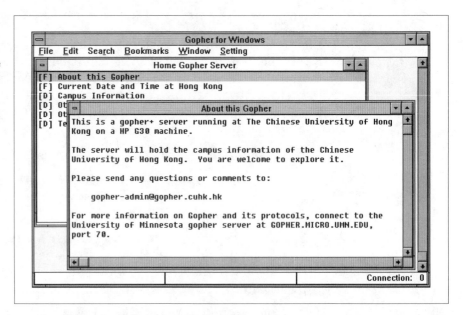

Figure 6.5:

WGopher is a Gopher client currently under development from the Chinese University of Hong Kong.

You can get WGopher via anonymous FTP from **ftp.cuhk.hk**, in the **/pub /gopher/PC** directory. The current version at the time of this writing is 2.32, and the filename is **wgoph232.exe**, which is a self-extracting archive file.

WGopher is freeware, and may be freely distributed, provided that that no fee is charged for the program and all documentation, copyright and permissions information is included with the program.

Installing WGopher

To install WGopher, do the following:

1. Create a **WGOPHER** directory on your hard disk.

2. Run the self-extracting archive file in this directory to uncompress the files.

3. Create a WGopher icon for the **WGOPHER.EXE** file on your Windows desktop.

To configure WGopher, do the following:

1. Start WGopher.

2. Select Setting ➤ Configuration. If you'd like to use the Chinese University of Hong Kong's Gopher as your Home menu, leave the Host Name as is. To change the default Home Gopher, enter the Gopher address (i.e., gopher.micro.umn.edu), and Port number (usually 70). Click on **OK**.

3. To change the default font, select Setting ➤ Fonts. The standard Windows font dialog box appears. Select the font you want to use and click on **OK**.

To configure telnet and image viewer applications for WGopher, do the following:

1. Select Setting ➤ Configuration.

2. Enter a standard telnet application in the Telnet Application field, a 3270 telnet application in the TN3270 Application field, and an image viewer in the Image Viewer field. Click on **OK**.

Using WGopher

WGopher is a very basic Gopher client application, but it does support all of the common Gopher functions. Notice that each menu item has a letter alongside it. An [F] means that the item is a file, and a [D] means that the item is a directory.

Here are a few options available to you when you use WGopher:

To go to your Home Gopher, select File ➤ Home Gopher. Unless you changed the Home Gopher, this option will take you to the Home menu at the Chinese University of Hong Kong.

To switch to a new Gopher server, select File ➤ New Gopher. Enter the Gopher name in the **Window Title** field, the address (i.e., gopher.micro.umn.edu) in the **Host Name** field, and the port number (usually 70) in the **Port Number** field.

To print a menu or document, select File ➤ Print. Unfortunately, in the version I tried, 2.3.2, the result was not very readable. Hopefully, they'll fix this in future versions.

To create a bookmark for the current menu item, select Bookmarks ➤ Open Bookmarks. The Bookmarks window appears. Now switch back to the Gopher window, and select Bookmarks ➤ Set Bookmark.

To jump to a bookmark, select Bookmarks ➤ Open Bookmarks, then double-click on the bookmark item you'd like to jump to.

WSGopher

I'd been seeing rave reviews for WSGopher, by Dave Brooks, in the alt.winsock newsgroup for months, but I didn't get around to installing it until recently. Now I understand why folks have been raving about it. WSGopher, shown in Figure 6.6, is an excellent Gopher client for Windows, and is clearly head and shoulders above the rest.

Figure 6.6:
WSGopher is clearly the leader of the Windows Gopher pack.

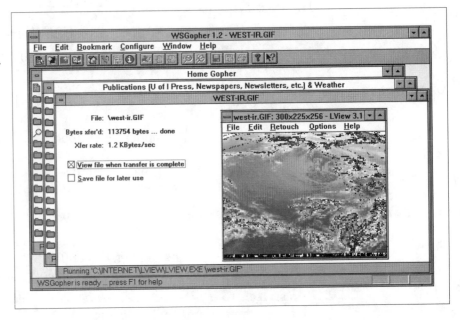

WSGopher offers all the best features of the other Gopher clients, plus many others. You can open multiple menu windows at the same time, and switch between them with a click of your mouse button. It allows you to not only print menus and documents, but preview the page layout before printing. It comes pre-configured with hundreds of book-mark references, and makes it easy for you to add your own book-marks as well.

> You can get WSGopher via anonymous FTP from **dewey.tis.inel.gov** in the **/pub/wsgopher** directory. The current version at the time of this writing is 1.2 and the filename is **wsg-12.exe**, which is a self-extracting archive file.

WSGopher is freeware, and may be freely distributed provided that no fee is charged for its distribution. The author maintains copyright to the program and its source code.

Installing WSGopher

To install WSGopher, do the following:

1. Create a **WSGOPHER** directory on your hard disk.

2. Run the self-extracting archive file in this directory to uncompress the files.

3. Create a WSGopher icon on your Windows desktop for the WSGOPHER.EXE file.

To configure WSGopher, do the following:

1. Start WSGopher. The first time you start WSGopher, it connects you to the Gopher server at the University of Illinois, Urbana-Champaign.

2. If you'd like to keep the University of Illinois Urbana-Champaign Gopher as your Home menu, you don't need to do anything. If you'd like to change your Gopher Home to a different server, se-lect Configure ➤ Home Gopher Server. Enter the Gopher address (i.e., gopher.micro.umn.edu), and Port number (usually 70) in the **Server #1** and **Port** fields. Click on **OK**.

To configure viewer applications for WSGopher, do the following:

1. Select Configure ➤ Viewers. Enter a file extension, such as .JPG or .WAV, and click on the (...) button to search for and select the appropriate viewer on your hard disk.

2. After you have selected a viewer, click on the Add button to add it to the list of viewers. When you're done, click on **OK**.

Using WSGopher

Take a look around WSGopher. To the left of each menu item, you'll see an icon identifying the item. A file folder icon means that the item points to another Gopher menu. A sheet of paper means that the item is a text file. And a spyglass means that the item is a search field. For more information about icons and options, press the F1 key at any time.

Here are some of the options available when using WSGopher:

To get more information about anything in the WSGopher window, click on the cursor help button. Your mouse cursor turns into a Question mark cursor. Now, any time you click on something, help information about that item will appear.

To jump to a new Gopher server, select File ➤ New Gopher Item. Enter the name of the Gopher server in the Title field, the address (i.e., gopher.micro.umn.edu) in the Server Name field, and the port (usually 70) in the Port field.

To view the bookmark list, select Bookmark ➤ Fetch, then just click on the bookmark you want to jump to and click on OK.

To add a new bookmark, select Bookmark ➤ Add Bookmark. You'll see a list of categories to add your new bookmark to. If you need to enter a new bookmark category, enter the new category name in the Name field and click on the Create button. Otherwise, just select a category and click on OK.

To print the current menu list, select File ➤ Print.

To see what the printout will look like, select File ➤ Print Preview.

To change the page setup before you print, select File ➤ Page Setup.

The real value of Gopher is the information you can find when using it. The number of Gopher servers on the Internet is still growing at a rate of around 100 per month. With thousands of Gopher servers on the Internet already, it should be obvious that Gopher is one Internet resource that will be around for a while.

7

See the World
by Web

THE POPULARITY OF the World Wide Web has been increasing at an astounding rate. No other Internet-based network has had the kind of immediate impact and appeal as the Web.

What makes the Web different than other Internet-based networks is that it's very approachable, even for someone who would otherwise be afraid of computers. At the same time, it is a powerful research and educational tool for the most seasoned computer veteran. To navigate through the Web, you just click on a highlighted word or phrase, and you are transported to another place. For example, if I'm reading about the works of Lewis Carroll, and I click on the words _Alice's Adventures in Wonderland_, I might see this:

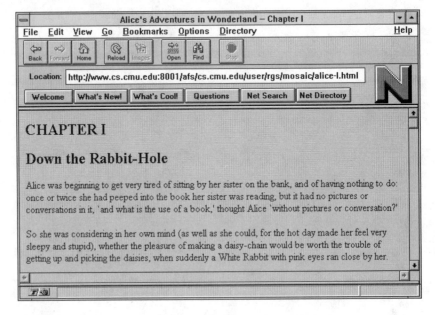

Because it uses _hypertext links_ to allow you to move from one information page to another, it's easy to navigate through the Web—you almost never have to take your hand off the mouse—and it allows you to view not only text, but also pictures, sounds, and movies.

"Surfing" the Web has become just about the most popular thing to do on the Internet. With each click of the mouse, you can access a new link to another page of information, one that may be on the same server, or halfway around the world. Click on another spot, and you'll be able to download a picture. Click on still another, and you can send an e-mail message to someone.

Another reason for the Web's enormous popularity is that it's relatively easy for anyone to create their own *page* of information on the Web. I'll talk more about tools for creating Web pages in Chapter 13.

With your Web browser, you can also access anonymous FTP sites, Gopher servers, and even read Usenet newsgroups. But this isn't to say that Web browsers make other Internet tools obsolete. For example, if I plan on doing some heavy-duty Gophering, I use a Gopher client, because it's easier and quicker. After all, Gopher clients are designed for viewing text only, so they don't have all the extra overhead required to display graphics, as the Web browsers do. Just remember, while you can use a crescent wrench to drive in a nail, a hammer will do the job faster.

How the Web Happened

The World Wide Web project was begun by Tim Berners-Lee at CERN (the European Laboratory for Particle Physics) in Geneva, Switzerland in 1989, with the first Web server coming online in November 1990.

Now, you might wonder why an organization dedicated to research in particle physics would begin a project to build a network of hypertext information servers all over the world. But, it does make sense—after all, CERN is primarily a research organization, and as such, they're very interested in collecting and distributing information. The World Wide Web was designed specifically to make this task as easy as possible, especially for researchers who may not be all that familiar with computers.

To ensure that the WWW project would be a success, the team knew that the system would have to be both easy to use and easy to implement. Well, they succeeded. There are now tens of thousands of Web servers all over the world, and many different *browsers*, which are the client programs you use to connect to Web servers. And putting together a Web page is very easy. For more information about putting together Web pages see Chapter 13.

Browsers That Do Unix

If you're on a Unix shell account, you have a couple of different options for getting to the Web. The first, Lynx, is simply a character-only Unix Web browser, while the second, SlipKnot, gives you a Windows front-end for Lynx, and doesn't require Winsock.

Lynx

Lynx was one of the first Web browsers, and is still the only one you can run in a character-only environment. It was originally developed by Lou Montulli, Michael Grobe, and Charles Rezac of the Distributed Computing Support group in the Academic Computing Services department at The University of Kansas.

Although Lynx is about as basic as you can get in a Web browser, it does do the job, and it's actually much faster than most graphical Windows Web browsers, simply because it doesn't have to display the pictures. But don't despair. Lynx does give you the option of saving embedded files—pictures, sounds, and movies—in your home directory on your Unix server, so you can download them to your PC and look at them later, if you'd like.

Using Lynx

To start up Lynx, just type **lynx** at a Unix prompt, followed by the address of the web server you'd like to visit. For example, to get to the home of the Web at CERN in Switzerland, you'd type **lynx http://www.w3.org**. You'll then be taken to the WWW Home page, as shown in Figure 7.1.

If you don't have any specific destination in mind, you can just type **lynx**, and you'll start out at the Lynx home page at the University of Kansas, **http://www.cc.ukans.edu.**

You'll find that there's a handy list of commands at the bottom of the screen. If you need more help, just type **h** or **?** to see the online help file.

Here's a few options available to you when using Lynx:

To move to the next highlighted link, use the down cursor key (↓). To move back up, use the up cursor key (↑).

Figure 7.1:

With Lynx, you can cruise the Web from a Unix shell account.

```
                                           World-Wide Web Home (p1 of 3)

                      [IMAGE] WORLD-WIDE WEB HOME

Announcement: 4th WWW conference [IMAGE]
Clarification on security protocols [IMAGE]

Welcome to the web about the web, with everything you ever needed to
know or pointers to it. This server is supported by the WWW team at
CERN, the originators of WWW, with the help of collaborators
worldwide.

About The Web Project

Everything you need to know about the W3 is on the web. A few selected
jumping off points:
   * The definitive WWW project page
   * A list of client software, and documentation
   * A list of server software, and documentation
-- press space for next page --
  Arrow keys: Up and Down to move. Right to follow a link; Left to go back.
  H)elp O)ptions P)rint G)o M)ain screen Q)uit /=search [delete]=history list
```

To go on to the next page, press the spacebar.

To follow the current link to the linked Web page, use the right cursor key ($\rightarrow$).

To go back to the previous link, use the left cursor key ($\leftarrow$).

To search for a text link on the current page, enter /. You'll then be prompted to enter the text to search for. Hit Enter, and if the text you entered appears in a link, Lynx will take you to it.

To download an image, select the image link and type **d**.

SlipKnot

SlipKnot, by Peter Brooks, offers an interesting way to get around the strictly character-based interface of the Unix shell when using the World Wide Web. SlipKnot runs on your PC under Windows, but it communicates with Lynx running on your Unix host, allowing you to navigate the Web with a Windows front-end (see Figure 7.2).

If you have a Unix shell account, but don't have TIA (discussed in Appendix A) for running Windows applications, SlipKnot is a nice alternative.

I should also mention that SlipKnot is not a Winsock application, and doesn't require any additional software. In fact, SlipKnot even includes

141

its own terminal communications program, which you can use in place of your normal communications program when you access your Unix host for text-only communications.

> You can get SlipKnot via anonymous FTP from the SimTel Windows archive at **oak.oakland.edu**, in the **/SimTel/win3/internet** directory. The current version at the time of this writing is 1.0, and the filename is **slnot100.zip**, although by the time you read this, version 1.1 should have been released.

SlipKnot is shareware, and registration costs $29.95, with 10% of your registration fees donated to refugee relief.

Figure 7.2:
SlipKnot allows Unix shell account users to access the Web with a Windows front end, without the need for SLIP or any additional software, such as Winsock.

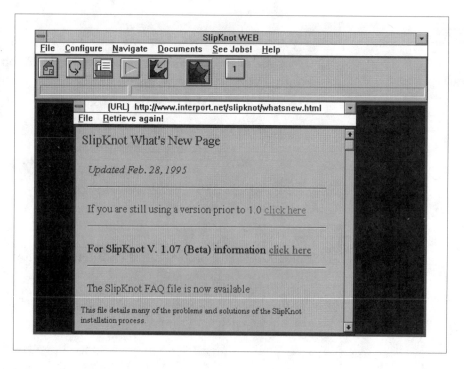

URLs and How to Use Them

The URL, or *Uniform Resource Locator*, is Web-ese for address. Anything you want to get to on the Web has a URL.

You've probably noticed that all the Web page references you see begin with **http://**. What does it mean? Well, HTTP stands for *HyperText Transfer Protocol*, which is the protocol used to transfer Web pages over the network. When you start out the name of a link with **http://**, it simply tells your browser that you want to go to a Web page that uses HTTP.

Similarly, if you were going to a Gopher server, the URL for the link would begin with **gopher://**, and if you were going to an FTP site, it would begin with **ftp://**.

Installing SlipKnot

The installation procedure for SlipKnot is a bit complicated, but that's because you need to test a couple of things before you can use it. Follow these directions carefully. The default configuration will work on most Unix hosts, but if you run into trouble, the Help file included with SlipKnot should be able to guide you through any problems you might encounter.

Before installing SlipKnot, disconnect from your Unix host, because you'll be using SlipKnot to dial up your host after you install the program.

To install SlipKnot, do the following:

1. Uncompress the zip file into an empty directory.

2. Run the **SETUP.EXE** program.

To configure SlipKnot, do the following:

1. Start up SlipKnot. You'll see a reminder about how to register the program, and a message about the Help documentation. Click on **OK** to close both these messages. Then you'll see the SlipKnot Terminal screen.

143

2. Select Setup ➤ Communications to configure your modem. Select the COM port used by your modem, and click on **OK**. Unless you are a modem expert, leave the other modem settings alone, as they will work with most modems.

3. Select Setup ➤ Host to configure your connection to your Unix host. A message will appear asking you to make a copy of the SAMPLE host file. Click on **OK** to close the message. The Host Settings window then appears:

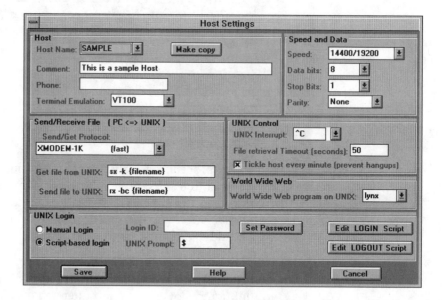

4. Click on **Make a copy**, and enter a name for your host. Enter a description of the host in the **Comment** field, if you'd like.

5. Enter your username in the **Login ID** field. Then click on **Set Password** to enter your password. You'll have to enter your password twice to ensure you entered it correctly.

6. Leave the other settings alone for now. These settings should work on most Unix hosts. If they do not work on your host system, check the Help file by selecting Help ➤ Contents from the SlipKnot menu bar for troubleshooting information.

7. Click on **Save** to save your configuration settings. You're returned to the SlipKnot Terminal screen.

Now you're ready to test SlipKnot.

1. Click on the **Connect** button at the bottom of the SlipKnot terminal screen. SlipKnot will start your modem, dial your Unix host computer, and log you in. When it's done, you'll see your regular Unix prompt.

2. Test SlipKnot's ability to transfer files from your host by first creating a small file to transfer. To do this, type **date >sliptest.tmp** at the Unix prompt. This will create a small file containing today's date. Make sure it's there by typing **cat sliptest.tmp**. If you see the contents of the file, which should be the current date, then the file was created properly.

3. Select Communications ➤ Get File From Host, and enter **sliptest.tmp** in the **Get UNIX file** field. Click on **PC: Save As** to save the file as **SLIPTEST.TMP**, and click on **OK**. Then, click on **Go** to start the file transfer. If the file is transferred properly, you'll see a message to this effect; If it isn't, you'll see an error message. At that point, check the SlipKnot Help file by selecting Help ➤ Contents for information about troubleshooting file transfer problems.

Using SlipKnot

If you aren't already connected, click on the **Connect** button at the bottom of the SlipKnot terminal screen . Once you're connected, you can click on the **World Wide Web** button.

SlipKnot will display the SlipKnot information page stored in your SLIP-KNOT directory. From there, you can go to the SlipKnot What's New page by clicking on the **Get "What's New"** hypertext link.

Here's a few useful options for SlipKnot:

To display your local SlipKnot home page, click on the house icon.

To see all the links you've visited recently, click on the looping arrow icon.

To see your bookmarks, click on the folder icon.

To move forward or backward within your open pages, just click on the page you want to go to.

To retrieve a page from the Internet, click on the green web icon.

Touring the Web in Windows

Take your pick. There are currently eight different Web browsers for Microsoft Windows, and they all use Windows Sockets (Winsock). Some are freeware, others are shareware, and still others are demo versions of commercial products. Some have more bells and whistles than a cheap carnival ride, while others are as plain as an Amish horsecart.

This is another one of those areas where personal preference plays more of a role than anything else. Try a couple of them out, or all of them if you feel up to it. Kick the tires, even slam the doors a few times. I'm sure you'll find one that suits your particular taste.

Cello

Cello, by Thomas R. Bruce of the Legal Information Institute at Cornell Law School, is a very basic, simple Web browser for Windows. Although I'm sure many people will find Cello far too plain (see Figure 7.3), it's the simplicity of the program that accounts for its greatest feature: speed.

Another big advantage of Cello is that it goes real easy on your computer's system resources, consuming less than 1MB of disk space.

You can get Cello via anonymous FTP from **ftp.law.cornell.edu**, in the **/pub/LII/Cello** directory. The current version at the time of this writing is 1.0, and the filename is **cello.zip**.

Cello is freeware, and may be freely distributed for non-commercial use.

Figure 7.3:

Cello may be plain and
simple, but it lets you
navigate the Web with
ease, visiting places
like this Ansel Adams
exhibit at U.C. Irvine.

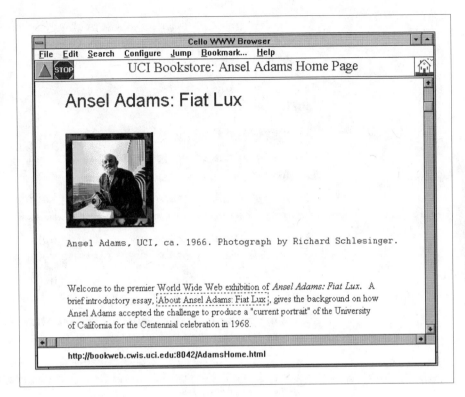

Installing Cello

To install Cello, do the following:

1. Create a **CELLO** directory on your hard disk.

2. Uncompress the zip file into this directory.

3. Create an icon for the **CELLO.EXE** file on your Windows desktop.

To configure Cello, do the following:

1. Start up Cello. You'll see the Cello banner. Click anywhere on it to close it. The Welcome page will the appear.

2. To configure Cello to be able to send mail, select Configure ➤ Your E-mail Address and enter your address in the space provided. Then select Configure ➤ Mail Relay and enter your mail server in the space provided.

3. To configure Cello so that it will fetch newsgroups from your local news server, select Configure ➤ News Server and enter your news server in the space provided.

Using Cello

Here are some of the options available with Cello:

To go to a linked page or image, click on the text surrounded by dashed lines.

To jump to a new page, select Jump ➤ Launch via URL, and enter the URL you want to jump to, then click OK.

To see where a link leads to, click the right mouse button over the link. A message box appears showing you the URL for the link.

To jump back to the previous page, click on the upward pointing triangle icon in the upper left corner of the screen.

To search the current page for a text string, select Search ➤ Current File, then enter the search string and click on OK.

To add a bookmark for the current page, select Bookmark... to see the Cello: Bookmarks dialog box. Then click on the Mark Current Document button.

To jump to a bookmark you've already added, select Bookmark... and click on the Jump button.

You can see a complete list of the Frequently Asked Questions (FAQ) about Cello by jumping to URL **http://www.law.cornell.edu/cello/cellofaq.html**.

InternetWorks

InternetWorks, originally written by Booklink, Inc., is an impressive, full-featured Web browser, which also comes with a built-in mail program and newsreader (see Figure 7.4). In December 1994, America Online bought out Booklink, and incorporated them into their NaviSoft subsidiary.

Figure 7.4:
InternetWorks is the upstart kid on the Web block.

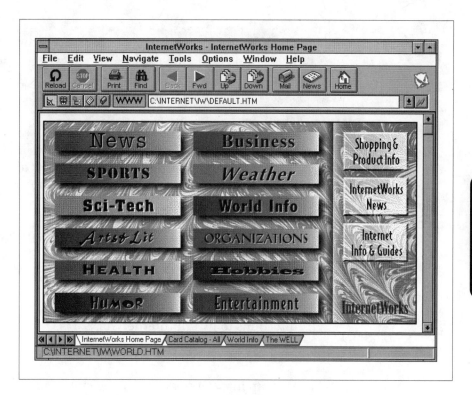

InternetWorks received *Byte Magazine's* "Rookie of the Year" award at the Fall 1994 Comdex trade show. And deservedly so. It's an impressive, if rather disk-heavy product, consuming over 2MB of disk space.

InternetWorks was also one of the first Web browsers to support Microsoft's OLE (Object Linking and Embedding) version 2.0, which allows you to create active, interactive links between different kinds of files. In fact, Microsoft adopted Internet Works' OLE technology for its Word Internet Assistant HTML editor, discussed in Chapter 13.

The mail program is comparable to mail programs like Eudora and Pegasus, and includes support for binary file transfers using UUEncode and MIME.

The newsreader doesn't have the extensive features offered by stand-alone products like WinVN and News Xpress, but it's perfectly adequate for just browsing the news.

149

The beta version of InternetWorks is available via anonymous FTP from **ftp.booklink.com** in the **/lite** directory. The current version at the time of this writing is Beta 7, and the filename is **beta7.exe**, which is a self-extracting archive file.

Although InternetWorks is a commercial product, and currently retails for $99, the beta version will remain available as a free demo.

Installing InternetWorks

To install the demo version of InternetWorks, do the following:

1. Put the self-extracting archive file into an empty directory, and run it to expand the setup files.

2. Run the **SETUP.EXE** program. Follow the Setup program's directions to install InternetWorks.

To configure InternetWorks, do the following:

1. Start up InternetWorks. You'll see the default home page, which is loaded from your hard disk.

2. Select Options ➤ User and enter your user information and the locations of your news and mail servers.

3. To configure viewers, select Options ➤ Viewers. Select the application type, then select the **Use External Viewer** option button and click on **Browse** to search for the appropriate viewer application on your hard disk. (For more information about configuring Viewers, see *Configuring Viewers* at the end of this section.)

4. If you're on a network that supports proxies, which allow you to connect to the Internet despite being behind a firewall, you can set up InternetWorks to use proxies by starting up InternetWorks and selecting Options ➤ Proxy Servers. Enter the proxy server information and click on **OK**.

Using the InternetWorks Web Browser

From the InternetWorks main screen, click on one of the colorful hypertext "buttons" shown on the InternetWorks Home Page to see the next link. InternetWorks stores many pages of information on your hard disk. Both the main home page and these other pages contain links to other pages on your hard disk and on the Web itself.

Notice that when you jump to a page on the Web that has embedded graphics, the images load in waves, gradually becoming clearer and more focused as they load. Some Web browsers force you to wait until all the graphics have been loaded into memory before they display the page. With gradual image loading, you don't have to wait.

Here are a few options available with InternetWorks:

To see where a link leads, just wave the mouse pointer over it and the link location will display at the bottom of the window.

To jump to a new page, enter the address you want to jump to in the field at the top of the window, just below the button bar.

To create a new card catalog (similar to the bookmark feature in other browsers), select Tools ➤ Create Card Catalog ➤ HTML. Then select File ➤ Save As to save your catalog. The default filename extension is .HTX.

To open a previously saved Card Catalog, use the File ➤ Open Local File to open it.

To download a page if it isn't loaded correctly, click on the Reload button.

To search for a text string on the current page, click on the Find button and enter the text string.

Using the InternetWorks Messaging System

The InternetWorks Messaging System includes a mail program and a newsreader. You can start it up from within InternetWorks itself by clicking on either the Mail or News button. The InternetWorks Messaging System window will appear, as shown in Figure 7.5.

151

Figure 7.5:
InternetWorks also includes a combination mail and newsreader program.

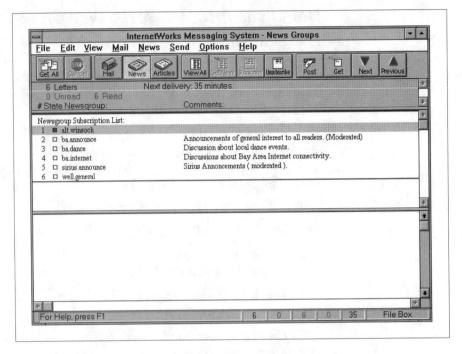

If you want to use the mail and newsreader program, you'll need to configure it first. To configure the mail and newsreader program, do the following:

1. From the InternetWorks Messaging System window, select Options ➤ User. Enter information about your mail and news server, including your mail server password if needed.

2. Then select Options ➤ General. Select your preferred default options.

3. To get a master list of all newsgroups, select View ➤ All Newsgroups. Then select News ➤ Get List of All Newsgroups.

In the version I tried, Beta 7, InternetWorks was unable to pull down an entire list of the newsgroups on my news server. It seems to be limited to around 3,000 newsgroups.

Here are a few things you can do when using the Messaging Center:

To check your news server for mail, click on the Check button.

To send a new message, click on the Send button and enter your new message. If you want to attach a binary file to the message, click on the File button at the bottom of the screen.

To read newsgroups, click on the News button.

To add a new newsgroup, select News ➤ Add Newsgroup. Once you've added a newsgroup, double-click on its name to see the articles in the newsgroup.

To print an article, select the article and click on Print.

To send a reply via e-mail to the currently selected message, click on the Reply button and enter your message.

To post a followup message to the newsgroup for the currently selected message, click on Followup and enter your new message.

To post a new message to the currently selected newsgroup, click on Post and enter your new message.

You can see a complete list of the Frequently Asked Questions (FAQ) about InternetWorks at **http://www.booklink.com/faq.htm**.

Configuring Viewers

Just like with Gopher client programs, you need to configure external viewers for use with Web browsers. I've included information about installing viewers with the installation instructions for each browser that supports external viewers.

For more information about viewer programs suitable for use with different sound, image, and movie files, see Chapters 9 and 10. For information about Telnet viewer applications, see Chapter 3.

NCSA Mosaic

NCSA Mosaic for Windows, by the National Center for Supercomputing Applications at the University of Illinois, Urbana-Champaign, was the first widely used Web browser for Windows. Despite being eclipsed in popularity by newer Web browsers, NCSA Mosaic is still worth checking out. And it's still under active development, with new features being added every month or so. The current version at the time of this writing is 2.0, Beta 3, and is quite impressive, offering features such as a built-in newsreader and the ability to send e-mail directly from Mosaic.

NCSA Mosaic, shown in Figure 7.6, offers an easy to use interface that includes the ability to quickly save the current page to disk, and view or copy information about a link by just clicking the right mouse button.

The Windows version of NCSA Mosaic is but one of several flavors currently available. There are also versions for Macintosh computers and Unix workstations that use the X Window System (a popular graphical user interface for high-end Unix workstations).

Figure 7.6:
NCSA Mosaic was one of the first Web browsers for Windows, and is still one of the most popular.

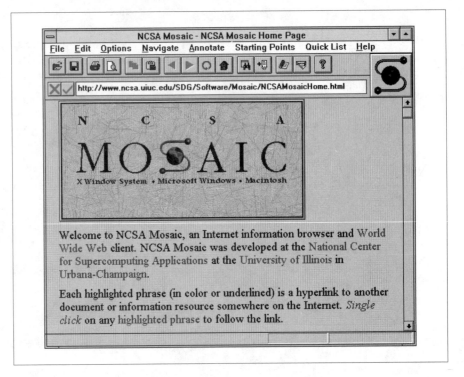

154

The one problem with NCSA Mosaic is that the most current version for Windows relies on the Windows Win32s API (Application Programming Interface). Win32s is the API which allows 16-bit Windows 3.1 users to run certain 32-bit Windows applications.

The reason it's a problem is because it's an additional installation hassle. Some users may experience problems running Win32s. Also, it uses up an additional 2MB of hard disk space. Since Mosaic itself consumes nearly 2MB of disk space, the total package comes to over 4MB. If you're timid about installing big drivers, you may want to pass on this browser.

On the other hand, if you're running Windows 95 or Windows NT, you'll love NCSA Mosaic, because it takes full advantage of these 32-bit operating systems, and runs much faster than its 16-bit cousins.

> You can get NCSA Mosaic via anonymous FTP from **ftp.ncsa.uiuc.edu**, in the **/Web/Mosaic/Windows** directory. The current version at the time of this writing is Version 2, Beta04, and the filename is **mos20b3.EXE**, which is a self-extracting archive file.
>
> If you're running Windows 3.1, you'll also need to pick up the most current copy of Win32s, which is also available in the **/Web/Mosaic/Windows** directory. The current version at the time of this writing is Version 1.25, and the filename is **w32sole.EXE**, which is also a self-extracting archive file.
>
> Also keep in mind that if you're using Windows 3.1, when you upgrade to a newer version of NCSA Mosaic, you'll probably need to install a newer version of Win32s as well, since the two go hand-in-hand.

NCSA Mosaic is freeware, and there is no charge for non-commercial use.

Installing NCSA Mosaic

If you're using Windows 3.1, you first need to install Win32s. If you're running Windows 95 or Windows NT, you can skip to the next set of steps.

To install Win32s, do the following:

1. Before you start, disconnect from the Internet and close all open applications.

2. Put the self-extracting archive file containing the Win32s setup files (**W32SOLE.EXE**) into an empty directory, and run it to expand the setup files.

3. Run the **INSTALL.BAT** file. This will expand all of the Win32s install files into their appropriate subdirectories.

4. Change to the **DISK1** subdirectory and run the **SETUP.EXE** file. Accept the defaults if possible. When it's done installing, the Setup program will automatically reboot Windows.

5. Delete all of the setup files that were created when you ran the INSTALL.BAT file in Step 3.

Now that you Windows 3.1 users have Win32s in place, you can get down to the business of putting NCSA Mosaic onto your computer. To install Mosaic, do the following:

1. Put the self-extracting archive file containing the NCSA Mosaic setup files (**MOS20B1.EXE**) into an empty directory, and run it to expand the setup files.

2. Run the **SETUP.EXE** file to install NCSA Mosaic. Accept the defaults, if possible.

3. Restart your Winsock and TCP/IP network software, and reconnect to your Internet provider.

4. Start NCSA Mosaic. Mosaic will automatically connect you to the NCSA Mosaic home page at the University of Illinois, Urbana-Champaign.

5. To configure viewers, select Options ➤ Preferences, and click on the **Viewers** tab. Select the application type from the drop down list box, and click on **Browse** to search your hard disk for the appropriate viewer application. When you're done, click on **OK**. (For more information about configuring Viewers, see *Configuring Viewers* earlier in this chapter.)

6. If you're behind a firewall that supports proxy servers, you can configure proxies by selecting Options ➤ Preferences, and clicking on the **Proxy** tab. When you're done, click on **OK**.

7. If you want to be able to read Usenet newsgroups or send e-mail from Mosaic, for example, to send someone an interesting page or URL, you need to configure your user information. Select Options ➤ Preferences, and click on the **Services** tab. Enter your e-mail address and the names of your mail and news servers in the appropriate fields. To subscribe to newsgroups, click on **Subscriptions**, then **Update** to pull down a complete list of newsgroups from your server, then select the ones you want to subscribe to. When you're done, click on **OK**.

The single most common problem experienced by first-time NCSA Mosaic users is the GROWSTUB error. This is caused by a bug in the original release of the POINTER.DLL file that comes with the Microsoft Mouse driver version 9.01. To get the corrected version of the POINTER.DLL file, use anonymous FTP to **ftp.microsoft.com***. The correct version is in the* **/Softlib/MSLFILES** *directory, and the filename is* **HD1061.EXE***, which is a self-extracting archive file. The file contains the POINTER.DLL file and a README.TXT file which contains instructions for updating the driver.*

Using NCSA Mosaic

The first thing you should do with NCSA Mosaic is explore, using the pre-configured links that are included with the application. To access these links, select **Starting Points** from the menu bar. From there, you can go to all of NCSA's important home pages, the central WWW project pages at CERN, or any number of interesting Web pages, Gopher servers, and even Archie servers, which let you search for files on anonymous FTP servers all over the Internet. (For more information about Archie, see Chapter 8.)

Here are a few handy options you'll want to be familiar with when running NCSA Mosaic:

To see what each of the buttons in the button bar does, hold the mouse pointer over each button for a few seconds. A little pop-up box appears, describing each button.

To see where a link leads, just wave the mouse pointer over it and the link location will display at the bottom of the window.

To enter a new link, just highlight the current URL in the field at the top of the window, delete it, type in the new URL, and press Enter.

To add the current page to your *Hotlist* of bookmarks, select Navigate ➤ Add Current to Hotlist.

To see a complete list of saved links, select Navigate ➤ Hotlist Manager. The Mosaic Hotlist Manager window appears. From there, you can select any of the pre-configured links, as well as ones you've added to your Hotlist.

To read Usenet newsgroups, select File ➤ Newsgroups.

You can see a complete list of the Frequently Asked Questions (FAQ) about NCSA Mosaic at **http://www.ncsa.uiuc.edu/SDG/Software/WinMosaic /FAQ.html**.

Netscape

Netscape, by Netscape Communications Corporation, is currently the hottest Web browser around. The development team for Netscape included several of the same programmers who originally designed NCSA Mosaic and Lynx.

Netscape Communications very wisely hired these sharp young developers away from the academic arena and let them go wild. In many respects, we can see where they learned from their mistakes—Netscape, shown in Figure 7.7, is quite a robust program, and offers some very desirable features, including the ability to send URLs and the text of Web pages via e-mail. And in more recent releases, it's become incredibly fast—easily as fast as the less graphical Web browsers like Cello.

Netscape's features include the ability to load graphics files in waves, which makes pages load faster, and page caching, which increases speed. Netscape also changes the color of links that you've visited recently from their original blue to pink, so you know that you've been there before. You can also read Usenet newsgroups directly from Netscape.

Figure 7.7:
Netscape is currently
the front runner in the
Web race.

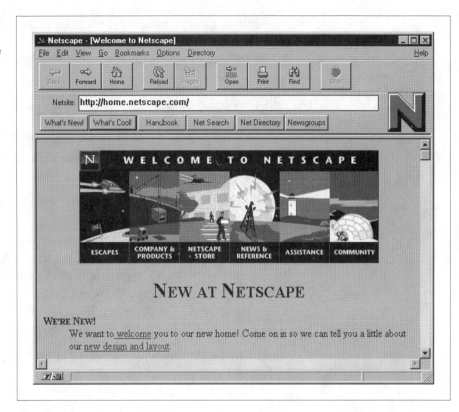

In addition, considering how powerful Netscape is, it's rather surprising that it only takes up just a little over 1MB of disk space.

Like NCSA Mosaic, Netscape comes in two additional flavors: one for the X Window System for Unix and one for the Macintosh.

Netscape is available via anonymous FTP from **ftp.netscape.com** in the **/pub /netscape/windows** directory. The current version at the time of this writing is 1.1, and the filename is **n16e11.EXE**, which is a self-extracting archive file.

159

Netscape for Windows is shareware, and costs $39 to register, although it is free for use by students and employees of non-profit companies. Registration gets you printed manuals and real technical support.

Installing Netscape

To install Netscape, do the following:

1. Put the self-extracting archive file into an empty directory, and run it to expand the setup files.

2. Run the **SETUP.EXE** file. Accept the defaults, if possible.

To configure Netscape, do the following:

1. Start Netscape. You'll see the Netscape Licensing Agreement. Read through the terms of the agreement, and, if you agree with them, click on **Accept**. Then, Netscape will start, and connect up with the Netscape Welcome page.

2. Select Options ➤ Preferences. The Preferences window is displayed.

3. Under **Mail and News**, enter your mail server name, full name, and e-mail address in the spaces provided. If you want to be able to use Netscape to read newsgroups from your news server, enter your news server name in the space provided.

4. If you're behind an Internet firewall that supports proxies, select **Proxies** from the list box and enter your proxy server information as well.

5. To configure viewers for use with Netscape, select **Helper Applications** from the list box in the Preferences window.

6. To configure a Telnet viewer application, select **Applications and Directories**, and enter your preferred Telnet application in the space provided. (For more information about viewer configuration, see *Configuring Viewers* earlier in this chapter.)

Using Netscape

When you first start Netscape, it will connect up with the Welcome to Netscape page. From there, you can get more information about

Netscape, including press releases and pointers to documentation pages and a wide range of Internet information resources.

You'll probably notice that when you start up Netscape that a second Netscape icon will appear minimized on your desktop. This is the Netscape cache. You can't maximize this icon, but it will disappear when you close Netscape. The caching helps to speed up the reloading of pages. When you go back to the previous page, Netscape can read it from the cache, rather than from the Internet, which is much faster.

Also notice the six buttons just above the document viewing page: **Welcome**, **What's New**, **What's Cool**, **Questions**, **Net Search**, and **Net Directory**. These buttons will all automatically take you to different pages on Netscape Communications' server. Check 'em out—you'll find all kinds of interesting and useful information and links behind those buttons.

Here are some other useful commands you'll need when using Netscape:

To see where a link leads, wave the mouse pointer over it and the link location will display at the bottom of the window.

To jump to a new page, enter the URL for the page in the field at the top of the window.

To go back to the previous page, click on the Back button.

To go forward to the next page, click on the Forward button.

To reload the current page, click on the Reload button.

To search for a text string on the current page, click on the Find button and enter the text string in the Find What: field, then click on the Find Next button.

To mail the current page to someone, select File ➤ Mail Document.

To read Usenet newsgroups, select Directory ➤ Go to Newsgroups.

The World by Web CH. 7

161

If Netscape starts seeming a little slow after a while, you may need to empty the disk cache. Select Options ➤ Preferences, and select Cache and Network. *Click on the* Clear Disk Cache Now *button. A confirmation box will appear. Click on* Continue *to empty the cache. They aren't really doing you any good, they take up a lot of space on your hard disk, and they can slow down Netscape considerably. If you find that this becomes a perpetual problem, you can lower the size of the disk cache from the default of 5MB down to something more reasonable, like 2MB (2000 kilobytes) from the* Cache and Network *option.*

You can see a complete list of the Frequently Asked Questions (FAQ) about Netscape at **http://home.netscape.com/home/faq_docs/faq_client.html**.

Spry's AIR Mosaic Express

This is a demo version of Spry's popular AIR Mosaic program, which is just one product in their suite of Internet applications. The demo is fully functional, except that you're limited to making only six jumps outside of Spry's Web server.

AIR Mosaic Express, shown in Figure 7.8, was originally based on source code from the 16-bit version of NCSA's Mosaic, and it does bear a striking resemblance to earlier versions of NCSA's browser.

AIR Mosaic also doesn't take up a lot of disk space—only about 1.3MB.

> You can get the AIR Mosaic demo via anonymous FTP from **ftp.spry.com** in the **/vendor/spry/demo/AirMosaicDemo** directory. The current version at the time of this writing is 03.09.05.08, and the filename is **AMOSDEMO. EXE**, which is a self-extracting archive file.

The demo version of AIR Mosaic is free, but limited to six external links per session. The full version costs $29.95, and can be ordered from Spry online at **http://www.spry.com/order-info.html**.

Figure 7.8:

Spry's AIR Mosaic
Express is a demo
version of their popular
Web browser.

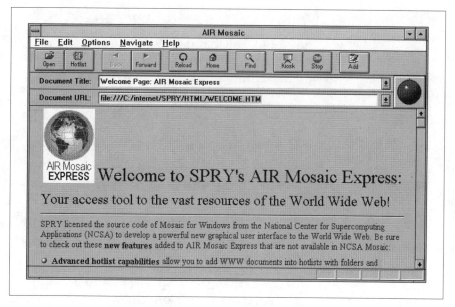

Installing AIR Mosaic Express

To install the AIR Mosaic demo, do the following:

1. Put the self-extracting archive file into an empty directory, and run it to expand the setup files.

2. Run the **SETUP.EXE** file. Accept the defaults, if possible.

To configure AIR Mosaic Express, do the following:

1. Start AIR Mosaic Express, you'll see a window warning you about the limitations of the demo version. Click on **OK** to close the window.

2. To configure viewers, select Options ➤ Configuration, and click on the **Viewers** button. Select the application type from the list box, and click on **Browse** to search your hard disk for the appropriate viewer application. (For more information about viewers, see *Configuring Viewers* earlier in this chapter.)

3. If you're on a network that's behind an Internet firewall that supports proxies, you can configure proxy servers by selecting Options ➤ Configuration, and clicking on the **Proxy Servers** button.

163

Using AIR Mosaic Express

The AIR Mosaic Express Welcome page describes the features of AIR Mosaic, and offers links to Spry's Web pages. Here are a few useful options available when using AIR Mosaic:

To see where a link leads, just wave the mouse pointer over it and the link location will display at the bottom of the window.

To jump to a new URL, select File ➤ Open URL and enter the URL for the page.

To view your hotlist of saved links, click on the Hotlist button. AIR Mosaic comes with a number of pre-configured links worth checking out.

To add the current URL to your hotlist, select Navigate ➤ Add Document to Hotlist.

To maximize the display area to encompass your entire screen, click on the Kiosk button. Press Esc to return to the normal view.

To find a text string on the current page, click on Find, and enter the text string in the Find What field, then click on Find Next.

When you've reached your maximum of six external links, a dialog box will appear giving you two options: order the full package, or exit the browser.

For more information about Spry's AIR products, check out **http://www .spry.com**.

WinWeb

One of the newest entries in the Web browser race, WinWeb by EINet, is a very basic Web browser that lacks some of the more sophisticated features of the other browsers available. However, it is free, so who's complaining?

Because WinWeb, shown in Figure 7.9, isn't as feature-rich as some of the other browsers, it goes real easy on the system resources. If you've only got 4MB of RAM installed, this is the browser for you, as it only takes up about 1MB of hard disk space.

Figure 7.9:
WinWeb is a simple Web browser, ideal for less powerful PCs.

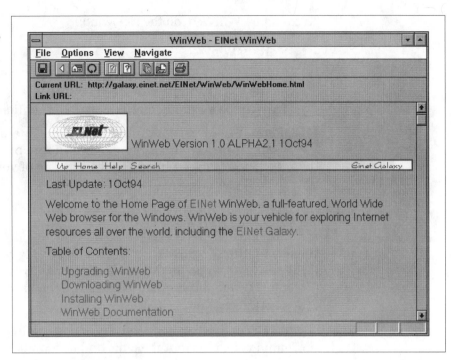

You can get WinWeb via anonymous FTP from **ftp.einet.net**, in the **/einet/pc** directory. The current version at the time of this writing is 1.0, alpha 2.2, and the filename is **winweb.zip**.

WinWeb is freeware, and there is no charge for non-commercial use.

Installing WinWeb

To install WinWeb, do the following:

1. Create a **WINWEB** directory on your hard disk.

2. Uncompress the zip file in this directory.

3. Create an icon for the **WINWEB.EXE** file.

To configure WinWeb, do the following:

1. Start up WinWeb.

2. To configure viewers, you need to edit the **WINWEB.INI** file in your WINDOWS directory. See the WINWEB.WRI (Windows Write format) file for more information about configuring viewers.

3. If you're on a network that's behind an Internet firewall that supports proxy servers, you can configure proxies by selecting Options ➤ Proxy Server. Enter the name of your proxy server in the appropriate field, and click on **OK**.

Using WinWeb

When you first run WinWeb, it will automatically connect you with EINet Galaxy Web page. This page offers links to many interesting places, and even allows you to search through its database for links that may interest you.

You'll notice that when you load a new page, a little window will pop up, letting you know that the page and its graphics are loading. This is nice, because if a page is just loading slowly, you won't think that it (or Windows) has just stopped working.

Here are some handy commands you can use in WinWeb:

To see the URL for the current page, select View ➤ URL Display.

To jump to a new page, select Navigate ➤ Load URL. Enter the new URL in the field provided and click on OK.

To see a list of all the pages you've visited during your session, select Navigate ➤ History List.

To add the URL for the current page to your hotlist, select Navigate ➤ Hotlist, then click on Add Current Page.

To see your hotlist, select Navigate ➤ Hotlist. Select the entry you'd like to jump to, and click on Goto. To see the URL for the entry, click on Edit.

To search for a text string on the current page, click on the ? button. Enter the text string you want to search for and click on OK.

▶

For more information about WinWeb, check out the WinWeb home page at **http://galaxy.einet.net/EINet/WinWeb/WinWebHome.html**.

Starting Points

When I first got on the Web, I soon discovered that the best way to keep up with it's many changes and permutations was to frequent the various *What's New* lists.

These are some of my favorite lists of new and interesting things. You should check them out on a regular basis.

NCSA's *What's New List*. The oldest what's new list on the Internet, NCSA's list is a websurfer's dream. Updated three times a week, and pulling in approximately 300 new listings per week, this one is definitely worth checking out. To get there, pint your Web browser to:

http://www.ncsa.uiuc.edu:80 /SDG/Software/Mosaic/Docs /whats-new.html.

Netscape Communications *What's Cool List* . Although Netscape's list isn't as complete as NCSA's, it does offer some of the coolest spots on the Web. To get there, pint your Web browser to:

http://home.mcom.com /home/whats-cool.html.

Yanoff's *Internet Services List*. Scott Yanoff's *Special Internet Connections* list has become legend on the Internet. The list includes not only Web pages, but Gopher sites, databases, games, and resources for almost anything you can think of. His list is also posted twice a month to several newsgroups, including *alt.internet.services* and *news.answers*, but if you're looking for something in particular, you should use the Web version. To get there, pint your Web browser to:

http://www.uwm.edu/Mirror/inet.services.html.

What's New at Yahoo. Updated daily with approximately 100 new links per day, the Yahoo what's new list at Stanford University offers a wealth of new and interesting links. To get there, pint your Web browser to:

http://akebono.stanford .edu/yahoo/new.html.

Stroud's Consummate Winsock Apps List. To see what's new with Winsock applications, check out Forrest Stroud's Consummate Winsock Application List. To get there, pint your Web browser to:

http://bongo.cc.utexas .edu/~neuroses/cwsapps.html.

Best of the Web . These awards are presented every year at the W3 Conference, and honor what the judges feel are the best sites on the Web. Their goal is to promote the use of the Web by showing some of its highlights and help information providers by demonstrating what can be accomplished using this medium. To get there, pint your Web browser to:

http://wings.buffalo.edu /contest/.

Mirsky's Worst of the Web. Had enough of the best? Try the worst! Amusingly bad links, updated daily, and with commentary from Mirsky himself. To get there, pint your Web browser to:

http://turnpike.net/metro /mirsky/Worst.html.

Useless WWW Pages. Paul Phillips has put together an amazing list of totally useless Web pages. Some of them are hopelessly out of date ("Submission Deadline November 12, 1993!"), while still others are just plain useless to begin with. To get there, pint your Web browser to:

http://www.primus.com/staff/paulp/useless.html.

Exploring the Web can become quite addictive. There are millions of places to visit, and the Web itself changes shape almost on a daily basis, as pages are added, deleted, and moved. Don't be too dismayed if your favorite site disappears one day. Chances are, it's just been moved, or is taking a temporary vacation.

Keeping up with the changing Web can be challenging, but fortunately there are lots of tools you can use to search the Web for new and changed destinations. I'll talk about these in the next chapter.

And, if you're thinking of doing your own Web page, check out Chapter 13, where I'll discuss some of the more popular tools for creating your own Web pages.

The World by Web CH. 7

8

We Want Information

TRYING TO FIND information on the Internet can sometimes feel like looking for the proverbial needle in the haystack. There's just so much stuff out there, it's often hard to know where to look first.

Fortunately, there are folks out there who are working hard to make finding things on the Internet easier. This chapter discusses the tools that have come out of these efforts.

If you've ever done research in a library, you probably know that different libraries will have a different set of books on any given subject. And even within the same library, there are different methods of finding information on a particular subject. You may have to look in a couple of different card catalogs, or search an online database, before you find all the information you need.

Finding information on the Internet is no different. Some of the search tools are very specific. Archie, for instance, is designed specifically to find files on anonymous FTP servers; others, like the Lycos and World Wide Web Worm *search engines*, will find Web, Gopher, FTP, and telnet links.

So how do you figure out which one to use? Well, you should probably try two or three methods to find the information you need. *World Wide Web search engines* are huge databases of links available from the Web. These links include Web pages, Gopher menus, and FTP sites. Different search engines use different methods of collecting and cataloging links, so they'll all find a different set of links for the same search criteria.

Once you've done a few different searches, you'll learn which ones are best at finding a particular kind of information. When I go searching for information, I usually start my searches with a Web search tool, like Lycos, or I go hunting through the Yahoo directory at Stanford or CERN's directory in Switzerland.

If it starts looking like some of the information I need is on Gopher servers, I switch over to my Gopher client and search using Veronica or Jughead. And, if I need to search for a particular file, and I can't find it on one of the big archive sites, like CICA or the SimTel mirrors discussed in Chapter 2, I go hunting with Archie.

In each of the following sections, I'll cover a different set of information tools. For each set of tools, I'll describe what kinds of information they can help you find, and how to access them.

Searching on the Web

There are a number of search engines on the World Wide Web, and I highly recommend that you start any search for information or files with one or more of them. Why? Because Web search engines will find more than just references to Web pages—they'll also find FTP and Gopher links as well.

But don't just rely on one search engine for all your searches. All the search engines use pre-compiled databases of URLs, and each one uses a slightly different methodology for collecting links for its database. Also, the searches themselves are slightly different. Some search engines have a standard way of searching for information, while others let you take a little more control of the search criteria.

Lycos

The Lycos™ search engine at Carnegie Mellon University is one of the best around. The name Lycos comes from the Latin name for the Wolf Spider, *Lycosidae*. The Wolf Spider catches its prey not by using a web, but by pursuit. Similarly, Lycos lets you actively pursue information on the Web rather than wander around, waiting to happen upon a choice morsel.

As of March 1995, the Lycos database contained well over 2 million unique URLs. These URLs are added by the people who run Web servers. You can search the Lycos database using either a standard interface, or a forms-based interface, shown in Figure 8.1.

When you search using the forms-based interface, you can set additional search options, such as the maximum number of hits (results) and the minimum number of search words that must be found.

Using Lycos

To perform a search using Lycos, do the following:

1. Set your Web browser to URL **http://lycos.cs.cmu.edu**.

2. Select the Lycos catalog. You can choose from either the small catalog, or the large catalog. You can also select whether to do a plain search, which only allows you to enter search words, or the

search form, which allows you to specify additional options. I recommend using the search form, because it gives you greater control over how the search is performed.

3. Enter your search keyword(s) in the **Query:** field. If you want Lycos to find an exact match for your keyword, put a period at the end of it. For example, if you wanted to find all pages that referenced the word *cat*, you'd enter **cat.** (note the period); but if you wanted it to also find *cats, catalogs,* etc., you'd just enter **cat**, without the period.

4. There are some additional options available, if you'd like.

- If you want to see more (or less) than 10 results, change the number in the **Max-hits** field.

- If you've entered multiple search keywords, and you want Lycos to find only those entries that include more than just one of your keywords, enter the minimum number of keywords in the **Min-terms** field.

- If you want to change the minimum score for entries from the default of 0.2 (out of 1.0), change the entry in the **Min-score** field. (The score is based on how many of your search words are found, how many times they occur, and how close to the top of the document they appear.)

- If you want to only see a brief description of each hit, check the **Terse output** box.

5. Now, just click on the **Start Search** button.

Most searches take only a minute or two. The amount of time it takes depends both on the complexity of your search and on the server load at the time you submit your search.

When your search is complete, you'll see listings for each result, beginning with the highest scoring entry, and going on from there. Each entry includes an active link to the resulting page, so all you need to do to get to it is click on the link.

> *For more information about Lycos, check out the Frequently Asked Questions list at* **http://lycos.cs.cmu.edu/lycos-faq.html**.

WWWW: The World Wide Web Worm

The World Wide Web Worm, by Oliver McBryan of the University of Colorado at Boulder, is another excellent Web search engine (see Figure 8.2). The Worm works a little differently than Lycos. It actively goes out and searches for links, but it only finds those that are linked to something that it already knows about. It allows you to search for keywords in titles of Web pages, in the embedded links in pages, or in the full text of the page itself.

Using WWWW

To start the Worm on its quest, do the following:

1. Set your Web browser to URL **http://www.cs.colorado.edu /home/mcbryan/WWWW.html**.

175

THE INTERNET TOOL KIT

Figure 8.2:
The World Wide Web Worm, or W4, is a search tool you can use to burrow through the Web.

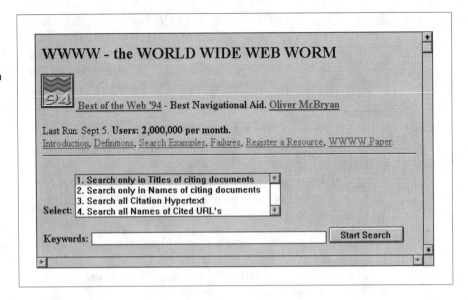

2. Select the type of search you want to perform from the options below:

   - **Search only Titles of citing documents** searches for keywords in the titles of documents in the database

   - **Search only in Names of citing documents** searches for keywords in the URL names of documents in the database

   - **Search all Citation Hypertext** Ssearches for keywords in all text included in documents in the database

   - **Search all Names of Cited URL's** searches for keywords in all URLs referenced within each document in the database

3. Enter the search keyword(s) in the **Keyword** field.

4. Click on the **Start Search** button.

Most searches will take only a few seconds, but the amount of time it takes depends on the complexity of your search and the load on the server at the time you submit your search.

The results you get will just be hypertext links to the pages referenced in the results.

 ▶ *For some additional information about formulating keyword queries, check out the Search Examples at* **http://www.cs.colorado.edu/home/mcbryan /WWWWintro.html**.

Gopher Search Tools

These search tools allow you to perform searches in *Gopherspace*, which is the collective name for the world-wide network of Gopher servers. With Gopher search tools, you can find either Gopher menus, or items in those menus, which may include text documents, graphics, or other kinds of files.

Veronica

Veronica, which stands for *Very Easy Rodent-Oriented Net-wide Index to Computerized Archives*, is a Gopher-based search engine. Veronica, shown in Figure 8.3, makes it easy to find information on Gopher servers all over the world.

As of January 1995, the Veronica database contained links to over 5000 Gopher servers, with over 15 million items.

Using Veronica

To search through Gopherspace with Veronica, do the following:

1. Point your Gopher client to any Veronica server. If you don't have one handy, you can use the mother of all Veronica servers at **veronica.scs.unr.edu**.

2. Many Gopher servers give you a couple of different Veronica query options. Select one of the following:

   - **Search Gopherspace using Veronica** searches all listings in all Gopher menus in the Veronica database. Select this option for most queries.

177

Figure 8.3:
Veronica can help you find the information you want in Gopherspace. If you're searching for a broad subject, confine your search to Gopher menus only; otherwise, you could end up with thousands of hits.

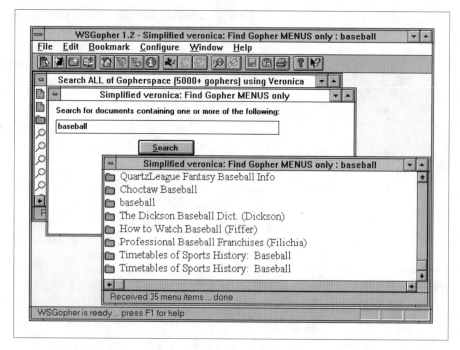

- **Search High Level Menus (or Search Gopher Directories) in Gopherspace using Veronica** searches the high-level Gopher menus in the Veronica database. Select this option if your query is for something that would otherwise turn up too many results, for example, if you were searching for *Internet* or *Gopher*.

3. You'll be prompted to enter keyword(s). Enter your keyword(s). Veronica only finds Gopher items that have your keyword(s) in the *title*. Fortunately, you can use **and** and **or** to be more specific in your search. So, for example, if you were looking for Gopher items on colleges and universities, you'd probably want to use the keywords **college or university**, so that you'd get all items that had *either* of these words in the title.

4. Press **Enter** to start your search.

Veronica processes your request, usually in less than a minute, and presents you with a customized menu of all the Gopher items that matched your search criteria.

178

For more information about Veronica, see the Veronica FAQ, which is available from **gopher.veronica.unr.edu.** *Select* **Search ALL of Gopherspace (5000+ gophers) using Veronica,** *then* **Frequently Asked Questions (FAQ) about veronica** *to see the latest copy of the FAQ.*

Jughead

Jughead, which stands for *Jonzy's Universal Gopher Hierarchy Excavation And Display,* was written by Rhett "Jonzy" Jones of the University of Utah Computer Center. Jughead, shown in Figure 8.4, is similar to Veronica, except that it only searches specific areas in Gopherspace, while Veronica searches all of Gopherspace.

Using Jughead

To perform a search using Jughead, do the following:

1. Point your Gopher client to any Jughead server. If you don't have one handy, you can use **gopher.utah.edu**, and select **Search menu titles using jughead**, then **Search other institutions using jughead**.

2. Select the Gopher server that you want to search using Jughead. You'll be prompted to enter the keyword(s).

3. Enter the keyword(s) that you want to search for and press Enter.

If your keyword matches an item on that Gopher server's menu, you'll see the menu item listed. You can then just use that link to go to the item.

For more information about Jughead, see About Jughead *at* **gopher.utah.edu,** *under* Search menu titles using jughead.

WAIS

WAIS™, Wide Area Information Server, was originally developed in a partnership between Thinking Machines Inc., Apple Computer, Dow Jones, and KPMG Peat Marwick in 1991. Currently, there are two versions

179

Figure 8.4:
Jughead lets you search through individual Gopher servers.

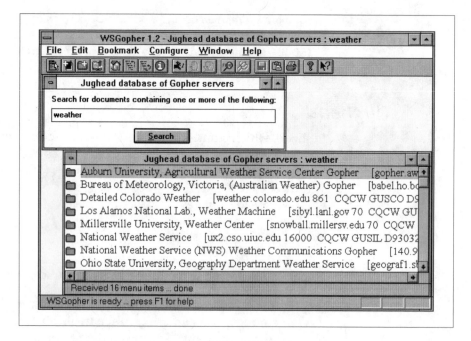

of the WAIS server software, a commercial version—WAISserver™—available from WAIS, Inc., and freeware version—freeWAIS—by the Clearinghouse for Networked Information Discovery and Retrieval (CNIDR). There are currently about 300 servers running a version of the WAIS software. WAIS is different from Veronica and Jughead, in that it searches the entire text of documents. And, it can run on WWW servers, using the WAISGate server software.

The only problem with WAIS is that it only finds information on servers that are running WAIS, which is great if you need to find something that's on a WAIS server. But if the information you're looking for isn't on a WAIS server, it won't do you much good. Fortunately, there are databases of WAIS databases, so you can find out quickly if the kind of information you're looking for is available via WAIS.

You can access WAIS databases using several different front end programs. The easiest ways are by using the WAISGate Web gateway or by getting either a shareware or freeware WAIS front end application.

WAISGate

WAISGate is a service provided by WAIS, Inc., and provides an easy to use front-end for WAIS (see Figure 8.5). It's ostensibly an example of how the WAIS server and Web gateway software work, but it's also a handy reference tool for the online researcher.

Figure 8.5:
WAISGate lets you conduct full text searches of WAIS database information from the Web.

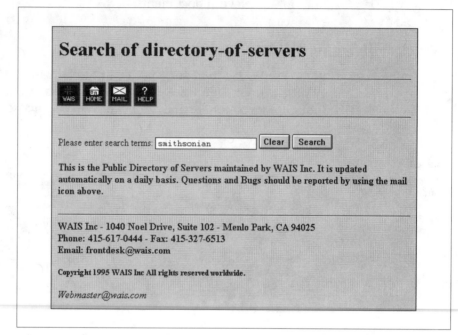

Search of directory-of-servers

Please enter search terms: smithsonian   Clear   Search

This is the Public Directory of Servers maintained by WAIS Inc. It is updated automatically on a daily basis. Questions and Bugs should be reported by using the mail icon above.

WAIS Inc - 1040 Noel Drive, Suite 102 - Menlo Park, CA 94025
Phone: 415-617-0444 - Fax: 415-327-6513
Email: frontdesk@wais.com

Copyright 1995 WAIS Inc All rights reserved worldwide.

Webmaster@wais.com

Using WAISGate

To perform a search using WAISGate, do the following:

1. Set your Web browser for URL **http://server.wais.com/ newhomepages/waisgate.html**.

2. To find out if a subject you're interested in is indexed by WAIS and available by WAISGate, select the **directory of servers** option.

3. Enter your search keyword(s) in the field provided.

Information CH. 8

4. Click on the **Search** button. If there's a match, you'll get three re-sponses—a note about the database you just searched, the WAIS database .SRC filename, and a query report for your search.

5. Click on the link to the database. You'll see another search field. Enter your search keywords for the database in this field.

If the information you're searching for is in the database, you'll see links to the relevant documents.

EINet winWAIS

If you use WAIS often, you might want to look into using EINet win-WAIS, shown in Figure 8.6. winWAIS is a Windows front end for WAIS, that allows you to search a variety of WAIS databases.

Figure 8.6:
EINet winWAIS lets you search through WAIS databases direct from your PC.

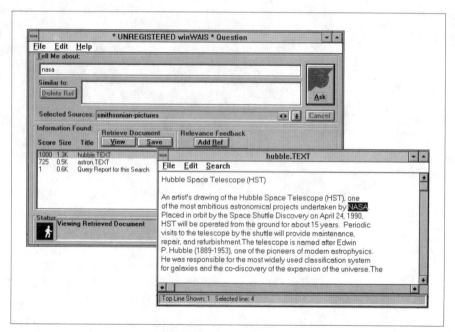

EINet winWAIS is available from **ftp.einet.net**, in the **/einet/pc** directory. The current version at the time of this writing is 2.04, and the filename is **EWAIS204.EXE**, which is a self-extracting archive file.

EINet winWAIS is shareware, and costs $35 to register, although you are allowed to evaluate it for 30 days before registering.

Installing EINet winWAIS

To install EINet winWAIS, do the following:

1. Uncompress the self-extracting archive file into an empty directory.

2. Run the **SETUP.EXE** file. The Setup program will prompt you to install the EINet winWAIS executable files in your Windows directory. However, in the interest of keeping your Windows directory from getting too cluttered, I recommend having Setup create a new directory for these files, such as **EINWWAIS**. Other than that, accept the defaults, if possible. If the Setup program discovers that you have a more recent version of any of its support files, it will alert you of this fact, and allow you to use the newer version that you already have installed, which is recommended.

Using EINet winWAIS

To use EINet winWAIS, do the following:

1. Start up EINet winWAIS. You'll see a registration reminder message. Click on **OK** to close this message window, or **Register** to register the program. The winWAIS main screen is displayed.

2. To select a new WAIS database , choose Edit ➤ Select Sources. Select the **Directory of Servers at Thinking Machines Inc.** to search for a particular WAIS database.

3. Enter your search keyword(s) in the **Tell Me about:** field and click on **Ask**.

Information
CH. 8

183

4. If your search is successful, you'll get at least three responses—a note about the database you just searched, one or more WAIS database .SRC files, and a query report for your search.

5. Double-click on the .SRC filename. A WAIS Source Description window will appear displaying information about the database. It asks you if you want to add this database to your list of sources.

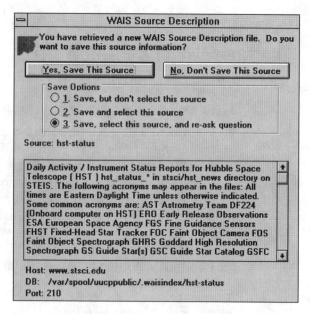

6. Click on **Yes, Save This Source** to save the source in your list of sources.

7. Now, repeat steps 3 and 4 to query your selected database.

8. When you find a listing for a document or another WAIS database .SRC file that you want to view, just double-click on the listing to display the document.

USGS WinWAIS

USGS WinWAIS is quite similar to EINet winWAIS. The interface is quite similar, and it works in basically the same way (see Figure 8.7).

USGS WinWAIS is freeware, and may be freely distributed.

Figure 8.7:
USGS WinWAIS is a freeware WAIS database search tool for Windows.

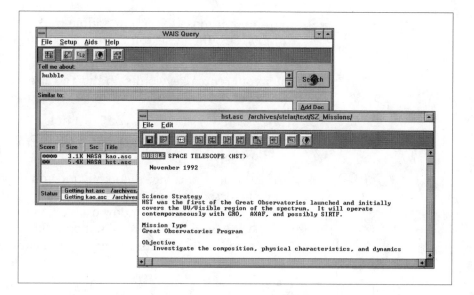

You can get USGS WinWAIS via anonymous FTP from **ridgisd.er.usgs.gov**, in the **/software/wais** directory. The current version at the time of this writing is 2.4, and the filename is **wwais24.exe**, which is a self-extracting archive file.

Installing USGS WinWAIS

To install USGS WinWAIS, do the following:

1. Uncompress the self-extracting archive file into an empty directory.

2. Run the **SETUP.EXE** program. Accept the defaults, if possible.

Using USGS WinWAIS

To use USGS WinWAIS, do the following:

1. Start up WinWAIS. The WinWAIS main screen is displayed.

2. Select File ➤ Select Sources to pick a source database.

3. To find a database to search, double-click on **D of S Directory of Services**, then click on **Done**. This brings you back to the WinWAIS main screen.

4. Enter your search keyword(s) in the **Tell me about** field and click on **Search**.

5. If your search is successful, you'll get at least three responses—a note about the database you just searched, one or more WAIS database .SRC files, and a query report for your search.

6. Double-click on the .SRC filename, and you'll see a window showing you a description of the WAIS database. At the bottom of the screen, you'll also see a window asking you if you want to add this .SRC file as a new source database. Click on the **Add This Source** button to add this database, then close the window.

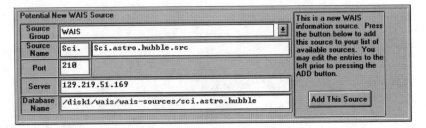

7. Repeat steps 2 through 5 to select and search the new database.

8. When you find a listing for a document or another WAIS database .SRC file that you want to view, just double-click on the listing to display the document.

Hytelnet

Hytelnet is a hypertext front end for telnet-based information. It lets you search through a database of telnet-based information sources, such as library and other databases.

The easiest way to access Hytelnet is via a Web browser interface. The best one I have found is the one at EINet, shown in Figure 8.8.

Real News on the Internet

If you're looking for real news on the Internet, such as Associated Press and Reuters news articles, stock reports, computer industry news, and even daily comics and features, the only source is ClariNet. ClariNet offers newsfeeds via Usenet news to Internet providers, corporations, non-profit organizations, and schools for a small monthly fee.

Find out if your Internet provider carries the ClariNet newsgroups (clari.*). If not, ask them why. For more information, check out their Web page at **http://www/clari.net**.

Figure 8.8:
The ElNet Hytelnet Gateway makes it easy to find telnet-based resources on the Internet.

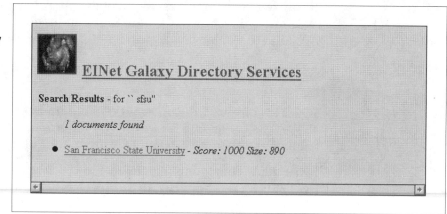

ElNet Hytelnet Gateway

To use the ElNet Hytelnet Gateway, do the following:

1. Set your Web browser to URL **http://galaxy.einet.net/ hytelnet/HYTELNET.html**.

2. Enter your search keyword(s) in the space provided.

3. If your search is successful, you'll be presented with a list of search results.

187

4. Click on the result you want to see, and you'll see a description of the Telnet link, along with information about what login name and password to use.

5. Click on the Telnet link, and, if you have configured a telnet program to use with your Web browser, your Telnet application will start up, and you can log in to the server.

Information Directories

Well, there will probably come a time when you won't be able to find what you're looking for using the search tools I talked about so far.

When that happens, your best bet is to go prowling through one of the extensive information directories on the Internet. My two favorites are the original directory at CERN in Switzerland, home of the World Wide Web, and the Yahoo directory at Stanford University.

CERN

The CERN directory, a.k.a. The WWW Virtual Library, is the mother of all Web directories (see Figure 8.9). It's organized by subject, with subject indices either residing at CERN, or at some other institution.

To get there, point your Web browser to URL **http://www.w3.org/ hypertext/DataSources/bySubject/Overview.html**.

From there, all you need to do is click on the general subject of your choice.

Yahoo

The Yahoo directory at Stanford University is another excellent subject-based directory (see Figure 8.10). Yahoo is great if you're looking for information on a particular subject, but it's also a lot of fun to just wander around in. And if you're looking for adventure, it even offers a random Web link. Click on the button, and you could end up anywhere.

To get to Yahoo, point your Web browser to URL **http://akebono .stanford.edu/yahoo/** or **http://www.com**.

Figure 8.9:
Stuck? Check out The
WWW Virtual Library at
CERN.

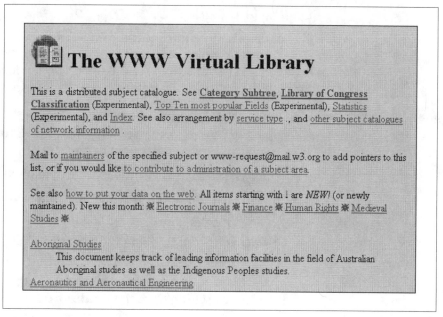

Figure 8.10:
The Yahoo Directory at
Stanford University is
an excellent resource
for finding information
on the Internet.

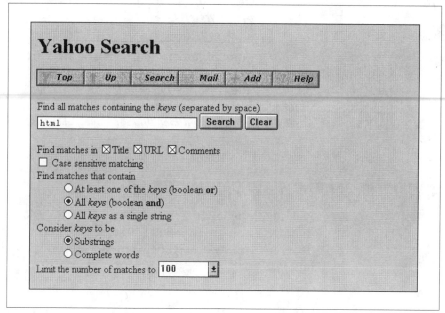

Using the Yahoo Search Tool

One of the nicest features of the Yahoo directory is its search tool. If you're not sure which directory listing to look under, your best bet is to do a quick keyword search for the subject you're looking for. To search through the entire Yahoo database, do the following:

1. Either click on the **Search** button from any page in the Yahoo directory, or set your Web browser to URL **http://akebono .stanford .edu/yahoo/search.html**.

2. Enter your search keyword(s) in the field provided.

3. If you'd like, you can also fine tune your search criteria using these options:

   - If you want to do a case sensitive search, check the **Case sensitive searching** box.

   - If you want to change the and/or settings, select your preferred setting from the **Find matches that contain** section.

   - If you want to search for exact words rather than substrings, change the setting under **Consider keys to be** to **Complete words**.

   - If you want to see fewer (or more) responses, change the number under the **Limit the number of matches** setting.

Tired of the same old links? Click on the A Random Link *button at the top of each Yahoo directory page. You could be transported to Rome, Paris, or Kalamazoo. Who knows, you might even find something of special interest to you.*

Finding Files with Archie

As I mentioned earlier in the chapter, Archie is a service that helps you to find files on anonymous FTP servers from all over the Internet. It was begun by faculty and students at McGill University in Montreal, Canada in 1991.

Dictionaries

Need to look up a word? Look no further than your computer's Internet connection. There are several dictionaries on the Internet. Here are just a few:

The Free Online Dictionary of Computing. This has become one of my personal favorite Web reference spots. It's a communal computing dictionary. If you find it useful, and you have a definition for one of the as-yet undefined words, send it on to the editor, Denis Howe. To get there, point your Web browser to:

http://wombat.doc.ic.ac.uk/.

The Jargon File. Sometimes referred to as the "Hacker's Dictionary," the Jargon File is a must-visit reference spot for anyone interested in computing folklore. In its pages, you'll find definitions for such things as the *Obfuscated C Contest* and *bit rot*. Like the *Webster's Dictionary*, there are several different versions out there. This one is my favorite, since it allows you to both search and roam with ease. To get there, point your Web browser to:

http://www.phil.uni-sb.de/fun /jargon/index.html.

The Devil's Dictionary. Ambrose Bierce's classic work of etymology, in glorious HTML. If you've never read the Devil's Dictionary, here's a sample:

AGE, n. That period of life in which we compound for the vices that we still cherish by reviling those that we have no longer the enterprise to commit.

To get there, point your Web browser to:

http://www.vestnett.no /cgi-bin/devil).

For more pointers to dictionaries, and other works of reference, check out the Yahoo directory of Reference works at **http://akebono.stanford.edu/ yahoo/Reference/.**

Archie depends on anonymous FTP system administrators who register their sites with Archie servers all over the world. The service is strictly voluntary, but a significant number of sites do register with Archie, which updates its database every month.

191

There are three basic ways to get to Archie: by Telnet, by the World Wide Web, and by using the Winsock Archie client WS-Archie. I'll describe each of these methods in the following sections.

Using Archie by Telnet

Searching an Archie database by Telnet isn't the most efficient way to get the job done, but Archie is universally accessible via Telnet (see Figure 8.11).

Figure 8.11:

You can use Archie to help you find files on FTP servers all over the world.

```
unl-archie> set search sub
unl-archie> find unzip
# Search type: sub.
# Your queue position: 95
# Estimated time for completion: 33:08
working... \

Host ftp.germany.eu.net    (192.76.144.75)
Last updated 03:31  9 Sep 1994

    Location: /pub/comp/msdos/mirror.rus/emtex/disk1
        FILE    -rw-r--r--    22022 bytes  00:00  4 Oct 1990  pkunzip.exe


    Location: /pub/infosystems/www/einet/pc/winweb
        FILE    -rw-r--r--    22022 bytes  12:39 27 Jul 1994  pkunzip.exe


    Location: /pub/mail/pine/PC-PINE
        FILE    -rw-r--r--    22022 bytes  18:06 13 Aug 1994  pkunzip.exe
```

To perform an Archie search via Telnet, do the following:

1. Type **telnet** at the Unix prompt, followed by the address of an Archie server near you (see list of Archie servers at the end of this section), like this,

   % `telnet archie.sura.net`

2. At the login prompt, type **archie**. If you get a password prompt, just press Enter. If the server isn't too busy, you'll be connected, and you'll see an **archie>** prompt. If the server is too busy, you'll either have to try again later, or try a different Archie server.

3. Now, you should set Archie for the type of search you want to do. The type of search depends on whether you know the exact name of the file you're looking for, or if you only know part of the name. If you know the exact name, type **set search exact**. If you only know part of the name, type **set search sub**.

4. Then, just type **find *filename***, where ***filename*** is the name (or part of the name) of the file you're looking for.

The amount of time required to complete your search will depend on the complexity of your search, the number of results you get, and how busy the Archie server is when you submit your request. It's not uncommon for Archie searches to take 30 minutes or more, especially when the server is busy.

If your search is successful, you'll see a list of Anonymous FTP sites that have the file you're looking for. Write down the FTP site name and the directory where the file is located, and then you can start up FTP and download the file.

Archie Servers

At the time of this writing, the available Archie servers are:

archie.sura.net	Maryland
archie.unl.edu	Nebraska
archie.ans.net	New York
archie.rutgers.edu	New Jersey
archie.internic.net	New Jersey
archie.au	Australia
archie.edvz.uni-linz.ac.at	Austria
archie.univie.ac.at	Austria
archie.uqam.ca	Canada (in French)
archie.cs.mcgill.ca	Canada
archie.funet.fi	Finland

Information   CH. 8

193

archie.univ-rennes1.fr	France
archie.th-darmstadt.de	Germany
archie.ac.il	Israel
archie.unipi.it	Italy
archie.wide.ad.jp	Japan
archie.kr	Korea
archie.sogang.ac.kr	Korea
archie.uninett.no	Norway
archie.rediris.es	Spain
archie.luth.se	Sweden
archie.switch.ch	Switzerland
archie.twnic.net	Taiwan
archie.ncu.edu.tw	Taiwan
archie.doc.ic.ac.uk	United Kingdom
archie.hensa.ac.uk	United Kingdom

Try using the one that's closest to you; however, if it's too busy, there are plenty of others to choose from.

Archie by Web

An easier way to do Archie searches is to use the ArchiePlex gateway to Archie servers from the World Wide Web. To get to ArchiePlex, point your Web browser to **http://web.nexor.co.uk/archie.html**. From there, you can select the ArchiePlex service, shown in Figure 8.12, nearest you.

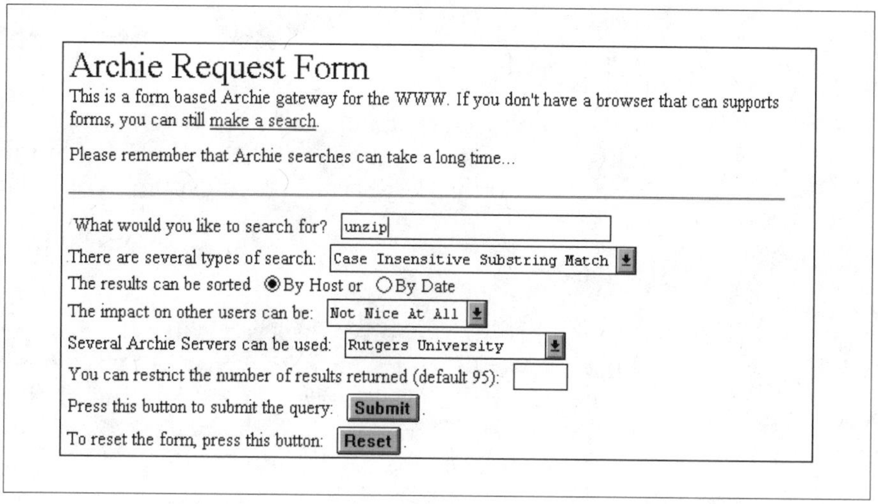

Figure 8.12:
ArchiePlex lets you query Archie servers around the world from your Web Browser.

Archie Request Form

This is a form based Archie gateway for the WWW. If you don't have a browser that can supports forms, you can still make a search.

Please remember that Archie searches can take a long time...

What would you like to search for? [unzip]

There are several types of search: [Case Insensitive Substring Match ▼]

The results can be sorted ⦿ By Host or ○ By Date

The impact on other users can be: [Not Nice At All ▼]

Several Archie Servers can be used: [Rutgers University ▼]

You can restrict the number of results returned (default 95): [   ]

Press this button to submit the query: [Submit]

To reset the form, press this button: [Reset]

Using ArchiePlex

To use ArchiePlex, do the following:

1. Enter the name, or part of the name, of the file you want to search for.

2. Select the type of search you want to perform: **Case Insensitive Substring Match**, **Exact Match**, **Case Sensitive Substring Match**, or **Regular Expression Match** (Regex). Unless you know the exact name of the file you want to search for, select **Case Insensitive Substring Match.**

3. Select whether you want the results sorted by Host (location) or by date.

4. Select the Impact on Other Users. The options range from **Not Nice at All** to **Nicest**. You might get your results faster with Not Nice at All, but you might also annoy people who are using the same Archie server.

5. Select the Archie server you want to use for your search from the list of servers.

6. Then, you can restrict the number of results from your search by entering a number in the box provided.

195

7. Finally, just click on the **Submit** button and wait for your search results.

The amount of time required to complete your search will depend on the complexity of your search, the number of results you get, and how busy the Archie server is when you submit your request.

WSArchie

WSArchie, by David Woakes, is a Winsock Archie client program that makes Archie servers incredibly easy. All you do is enter your search information, select your server, and WSArchie, shown in Figure 8.13, does the rest.

Figure 8.13:
WSArchie is a Winsock Archie program that makes Archie searches easier than ever.

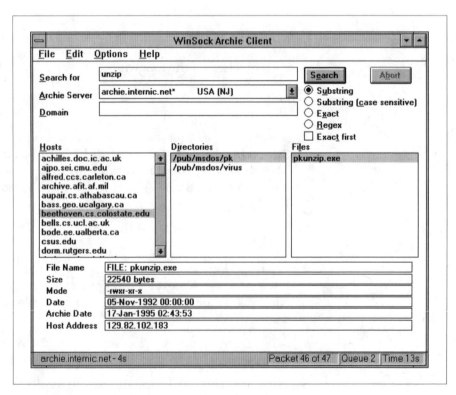

> You can get WSArchie from **ftp.demon.co.uk**, in the **/pub/ibmpc/winsock /apps/wsarchie** directory. The current version at the time of this writing is Alpha .07, and the filename is **wsarch07.zip**.

WSArchie is freeware, and there is no charge for non-commercial use.

 WSArchie was designed to work with WS-FTP (see Chapter 2). If you want, you can install WSArchie in the same directory as WS-FTP, and then you can automatically start up WS-FTP from WSArchie.

Installing WSArchie

To install WSArchie, do the following:

1. Create a **WSARCHIE** directory on your hard disk, or, if you want to use WSArchie with WS-FTP, skip this step.

2. Uncompress the zip file into either the \WSARCHIE directory or the \WS-FTP directory.

3. Create an icon for the **WSARCHIE.EXE** file on your Windows desktop.

Using WSArchie

To use WSArchie, do the following:

1. Start up WSArchie. The WSArchie screen appears.

2. Enter the name, or part of the name, of the file that you want to search for in the **Search for** field.

3. Select the Archie server you want to use from the **Archie Server** list box.

4. Click on one of the option buttons to select the type of search you want to perform: **Substring**, **Substring (case sensitive)**, **Exact**, or **Regex**. Unless you know the exact filename, use Substring.

Information   CH. 8

197

Regex mode lets you use special characters like wildcards, but the search language is different than most wildcard search languages you're probably used to. If you want to learn more about Regex searches, see the WSArchie help file.

5. Now click on **Search**. WSArchie will connect to the server. Once it's connected, you'll see some additional information in the bottom right corner of the WSArchie Window, including your place in the queue. If it seems like you're pretty far back in the queue, you can click on **Abort** and select a different Archie server to use.

6. When the search is complete, you'll see a list of hosts, directories, and filenames that Archie found. To see more information about a particular file, just click on it. You'll see information about the file at the bottom of the window, including the file size and date.

7. If you have installed WSArchie in the same directory as WS-FTP, you can now just double-click on the filename to have WSArchie automatically start up WS-FTP and take you to the FTP server and directory that the file is located in. You can then just use WS-FTP to easily download the file. See Chapter 2 for more information about WS-FTP.

If you want to save or print the list of the files and their locations, select Edit ➤ Copy Result and paste the results into the Windows Notepad. You can then save or print the results of your search.

Searching for People

Finding other people on the Internet can be rather difficult at times. There is no single place where all Internet users are cataloged. But there are several directories that you may be able to use to find the person you're looking for.

Although several "white pages" directories of Internet users have been planned, few have actually come into being.

Four11 Directory Services

The Four11 Directory is probably the closest you're going to come to a real white pages directory on the Internet. It's a Web server run by

SLED Corporation that collects user information from Usenet postings. So, if you've ever posted a message to a Usenet newsgroup, your name is probably in there already (see Figure 8.14).

The other way Four11 collects user information is by registration. If you want to use the service, you first have to register yourself in their database. Registration is free, and once you've registered, you can search the database all you want.

Figure 8.14:
If you have friends on the Internet, SLED's Four11 Directory Service can help you find them.

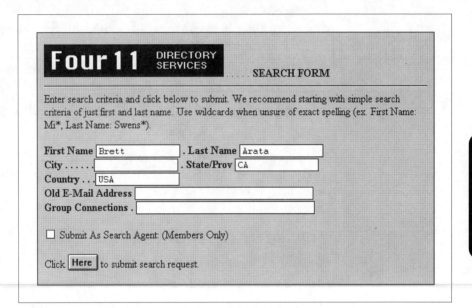

One very nice feature of Four11 is the fact that they don't sell their mailing list, so you won't have to worry about junk e-mail if you sign up.

SLED also offers a more advanced service for $20 per year. The advanced service gives you more advanced listings and the ability to create search agents, which will alert you if someone who you've been looking for signs up. Other advanced services include PGP (Pretty Good Privacy) public encryption key certification services, and the ability to create a link from your listing to a personal Web page, if you have one.

Registering With the Four11 Directory

To sign up and use the free Four11 service, do the following:

1. Set your Web browser to URL **http://www.Four11.com/**.

2. Click on **First Time Users Start Here**.

3. Enter your name, location, and e-mail address in the spaces provided. You can also include up to two additional e-mail addresses, and can even enter an old address that you may not be using anymore. There's also a field for you to enter group connections, for example, company or college affiliations that others can use to search for you.

4. Read the Acceptable Use Policy statement at the bottom of the screen.

5. Submit the registration form by clicking on the **Here** button.

You'll get back three messages, probably within a few minutes. These messages will confirm your listing, provide you with information about upgrading your membership, and give you your password to use when searching the database.

Using the Four11 Directory

To search for someone in the Four11 directory, do the following:

1. Once you have your password, go back to the Four11 home page and log into the server by giving your e-mail address and the password you received in the mail. Click on the **Here** button.

2. If your login is successful, you'll see the Search Form screen. To search for someone, enter as much information as you can about the person in the appropriate fields (First Name, Last Name, City, State, etc.).

3. Click on the **Here** button to submit your request.

4. If your search is successful, you'll see the person's listing. If not, click on the **Back** button on your Web browser and try a different set of search criteria. Sometimes narrowing or widening your search criteria will help.

If you want to change your listing or your password, send a message to change@Four11.com for information on how to change your password.

Directory Servers

Many organizations, such as corporations and universities offer online directories of their employees and students on the Internet. Most of these servers use one of several different directory service protocols: Ph (CSO), X.500, Whois, and Netfind. There are also directory servers that simply catalog the names and e-mail addresses of anyone who posts a message to a Usenet newsgroup.

But the protocol doesn't really matter. The important thing is being able to find the person you're looking for. The easiest way to find people in these directories is to go somewhere where all organizations using these servers are listed.

University of Minnesota Gopher

The University of Minnesota Gopher is the best place I've found to look for organizational directory servers. Just about every directory service on the Internet can be reached from there (see Figure 8.15).

Figure 8.15:

From the University of Minnesota Gopher, you can access directory servers all over the Internet.

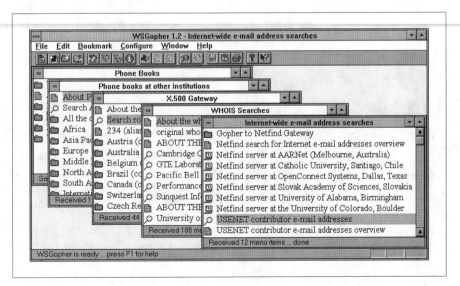

201

If you're looking for someone who might be listed in an organizational directory, or who may have posted a message to a Usenet newsgroup, you might be able to find that person using one of these directories. To use the University of Minnesota Gopher to find someone who is listed in a Netfind, X.500, Usenet postings, CSO (Ph) Nameserver, or Whois database, do the following:

1. Set your Gopher client to **gopher.tc.umn.edu**.

2. Select **Phone Books**. You'll see a list of all the phone book services available.

3. You'll probably have to poke around a bit to find the right one to help you find the person you're looking for. Here are a couple of suggestions for starting points that may help you in your search:

- **Phone Books at Other Institutions**, **X.500 Gateway**, and **WHOIS Searches** are good places to start if the person you're looking for is at a university or corporation.

- **Internet wide e-mail address searches** are the best options if you're not sure where to start. From there, you can do either a Netfind or Usenet contributor database search. Most Internet users will show up in one of these two databases.

4. When you find the right database, you'll be prompted to enter a name to search for. Your best bet is to search for the person's last name.

Depending on the database you're searching, you may only get the person's e-mail address, or, you may get a complete listing for that person, including phone number and (physical) address.

Finger

Well, now that you've found the person you're looking for, you might want to find out a little more about them. Finger lets you look up information about a person who has an account on a Unix server. When you finger someone, you get back information about that person—usually their e-mail address, real name, and the last time they logged on.

Finger also displays the contents of that person's *.plan* file. A .plan file is simply a text file that the user has put in their home directory. Most people who put up .plan files include information about themselves, or perhaps a quote, or sometimes useful or amusing information. (For a list of interesting and amusing finger locations, see **Fun Fingers** at the end of this section.)

There are several different ways to finger a person. I'll talk about three of them:

- Fingering from Unix
- Fingering from the Web
- Fingering from Windows

Fingering From Unix

To finger someone in Unix, just get to a Unix prompt and type **finger userid**. You'll get back information about that person:

```
% finger bertie
Login: bertie                          Name: Bertram Wooster
Directory: /home/bertie                Shell: /bin/ksh
Last login Sat Apr 1 13:24 (PST) on ttyt3 from tty-slow

I say, Jeeves, how do you work this bloody thing?
```

Finger returns back information about the userid, including the person's full name, and time of last login. Below that is displayed the information from the person's .plan file.

Some people do interesting or amusing things with their .plan files. And, still other people use .plan files to tell you about the soda machine down the hall, or to provide information about recent earthquakes or weather events. Unfortunately, .plan files are strictly a Unix beast. If you have an account that doesn't give you shell access, you won't be able to create your own .plan file. And, some systems don't even allow outside users to finger people on their servers.

Fingering From the Web

To finger someone from the Web, just set your Web browser to **http://www.dlr.de/cgi-greving/mfinger.** Then just enter - **username @location.org** in the field provided, and press Enter

203

(see Figure 8.16). You'll see the same information you'd see if you ran finger from Unix.

Winsock Finger

There are a number of finger programs for Windows. Winsock Finger, by Jim O'Brien, is my favorite. It's just about the best finger program for Windows available. Winsock Finger, shown in Figure 8.17, is easy to use, and can even function as a Whois gateway.

Figure 8.16:
Reach out and Finger someone from the World Wide Web.

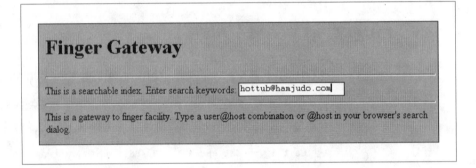

Figure 8.17:
Winsock Finger makes it easy to finger someone from Windows.

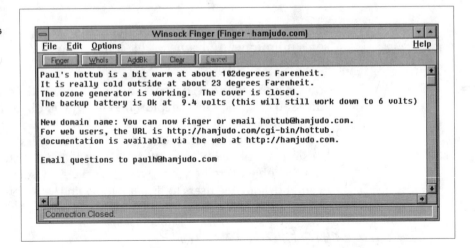

Fun Fingers

There are a bunch of user IDs out there on the Internet that were born to be fingered. Some of them belong to real human beings, while others are just there for the fun of it. Here are some of the more interesting and/or fun fingers out there:

Soda Machines. I don't know where the idea came from to connect soda machines up to the Internet, but I would imagine the idea was probably hatched by a computer science student pulling an all-nighter. Here's a list of some of the more popular ones:

coke@cs.cmu.edu (Carnegie Mellon University)

coke@xcf.berkeley.edu (UC Berkeley)

cocacola@cunix.cc.columbia.edu (Columbia University)

Earthquake Information. Hey, earthquakes aren't just for Californians anymore. Check out the recent earthquake info from one of these fingers:

quake@slueas.slu.edu (Midwest)

quake@andreas.wr.usgs.gov (Northern California)

quake@geophys.washington.edu (Pacific Northwest)

quake@scec2.gps.caltech.edu (Southern California)

quake@eqinfo.seis.utah.edu (Rocky Mountains)

spyder@dmc.iris.washington (World)

NASA and Space News. To find out what's going on at NASA, try fingering one of these spots:

nasanews@space.mit.edu

magliaco@pilot.njin.net

For more fun and interesting fingers, check out the hypertext version of Scott Yanoff's Fingerinfo script, which makes it easy to finger some of the more popular finger fun and information spots. Set your Web browser to URL **http://sundae.triumf.ca/fingerinfo.html.**

Information
CH. 8

You can get Winsock Finger via anonymous FTP from **sparky.umd.edu**, in the **/pub/winsock** directory. The current version at the time of this writing is 1.4, and the filename is **wsfngr14.zip**.

Winsock Finger is shareware, and costs $10 to register.

Installing Winsock Finger

To install Winsock Finger, do the following:

1. Create a **WSFINGER** directory on your hard disk.
2. Uncompress the zip file into that directory.
3. Create an icon on your Windows desktop for the **WSFINGER .EXE** file.

Using Winsock Finger

To use Winsock Finger, do the following:

1. Start up Winsock Finger. The Winsock Finger main screen is displayed.
2. Click on the **Finger** button. A popup box appears, with a field that you can enter a user ID in.
3. Enter the person or thing that you want to finger, and click on **OK**.

If there is finger information on that person, the results will appear in the Winsock Finger window.

Finger

Another good finger program is Finger, by Zoran Dukic. It allows you to save host names and user names separately, which can come in handy if you tend to finger different people at the same location. Finger, shown in Figure 8.18, also lets you run multiple fingers at the same time.

Figure 8.18:
Finger, by Zoran Dukic, is another excellent Finger program for Windows.

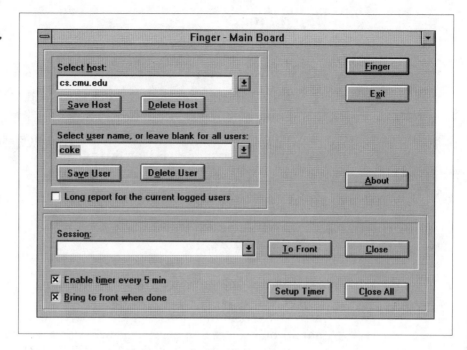

You can get Finger from **oak.oakland.edu**, in the **/SimTel/win3/winsock** directory. The current version at the time of this writing is 3.0, and the filename is **finger30.zip**.

Finger is free for non-commercial use.

Installing Finger

To install Finger, do the following:

1. Create a **FINGER** directory on your hard disk.

2. Uncompress the zip file into that directory.

3. Create an icon on your Windows desktop for the **FINGER.EXE** file.

Information
CH. 8

Using Finger

To use Finger, do the following:

1. Start up Finger. You'll see the Finger—Main Board window.

2. Enter the host name in the **Select Host** field. If you want to save the host name, click on **Save Host**.

3. Enter the user name in the **Select User** name field. If you want to save the user name, click on **Save User**.

4. Click on the **Finger** button to start fingering.

5. When you're done, click on **Close**.

6. To exit Finger, click on **Exit**.

The tools that are currently available for finding information on the Internet are incredibly helpful. And as more people get connected to the Internet, the demand for better search tools will grow. To meet this demand, you can bet that developers will continue to explore and refine ways of making information more accessible.

9

Making Sense
of Files

FILES CAN BE a problem. Not a major problem, but a problem nonetheless. I can pretty much guarantee that at some point on your journey through the Internet you're going to come across a file type you've never seen before, and you're not going to know what to do with it.

Here and in the next chapter, I'm going to talk about the different kinds of files you may find on the Internet, and the tools you'll need in order to get them to work on your PC. In this chapter, I'll talk about encoding and decoding files, as well as compressing and uncompressing them.

If you haven't already run across an encoded file, I'm sure you will eventually. If someone sends you a file that looks like it came from Mars, it's probably encoded.

Also, I'm sure at some point in your experience with PCs, you've run across .ZIP files. This book is chock full of them. But occasionally, you'll run into one of the other kinds of file archives, like .LZH, .ARC, or even .GZ. These kinds of archives require special tools to make the files they contain accessible to you, and it's these tools that I'll introduce to you in the upcoming sections.

Mail File Tools

Back in Chapters 2 and 4, I talked about the differences between ASCII and binary files, and how you can't send binary files via e-mail through the Internet. To send binary files via e-mail or to post them to a Usenet newsgroup, you first have to encode them as ASCII text, using one of the more popular encoding formats, such as UUEncode or MIME Base64.

If you have a mail program and newsreader that can both encode and decode using UUEncode and MIME Base64, you can skip this section. But if your mail program or newsreader only understands one of these formats and not the other, you should at least skim through it to see if there's a tool that fits your needs.

Which Format is Which?

There are currently several different formats for encoding binary files as ASCII, and, as you might expect, none of them are compatible with one another. The two most popular are *UUEncode* (Unix-to-Unix Encode) and *MIME* (Multipurpose Internet Mail Extensions), which uses the Base64 encoding format. A third format, BinHex, is very common among the Macintosh community, but rarely used by PC users.

For all practical purposes, UUEncode and MIME Base64 work pretty much the same way. The main difference is the tools you need to encode and decode the files.

Before you jump in and try to decode a file, you first need to be able to identify the difference between the two formats. Given just a casual glance, they look an awful lot alike (see Figure 9.1)

Figure 9.1:
A UUEncoded file. Notice the "begin" and "end" lines.


```
begin 644 argyle.bmp
M0DUU`@````````'8````H````(`````"``````!``0``````````"````````````
M`````````0```````````````@```@`````("```(``````"```(``@(````("`@`#`P,``
M``#_``#_`````___\`_P```/\`_P#__P```_____`$U$1$1$1$9$1$1$1$U$
MU$1$1$1L9$1$1$1$341$U$1$1$1&QL9$1$1$1-1$1$U$1$1$;&QL9$1$1$
MU$1$1$U$1$1L;&QL9$1$341$1$1$U$1&QL;&QL9$1-1$1$1$1$U$;&QL;&QL
M9$U$1$1$1$1$UL;&QL;&QL;41$1$1$1$1&UL;&QL;&QM9$1$1$1$1$;&UL;&
MQL;&UL9$1$1$1$1L;&UL;&QL;6QL9$1$1$1&QL;&UL;&QM;&QL9$1$1$;&QL
M;&UL;&UL;&QL9$1$1L;&QL;&UL;6QL;&QL9$1&QL;&QL;&UM;&QL;&QL9$;&
MQL;&QL;&UL;&QL;&QL9$;&QL;&QL;6UL;&QL;&QD1$;&QL;&QM;&UL;&QL;&
M1$1$;&QL;&UL;&UL;&QL9$1$1$;&QL;6QL;&UL;&QD1$1$1$;&QM;&QL;&UL
M;&1$1$1$1$;&UL;&QL;&UL9$1$1$1$1$;6QL;&QL;&UD1$1$1$1$1-;&QL;&
MQL;&U$1$1$1$1$U$;&QL;&QL9$U$1$1$1$341$;&QL;&QD1$U$1$1$1-1$1$
M;&QL;&1$1$U$1$1$U$1$1$;&QL9$1$1$U$1$341$1$1$;&QD1$1$1$U$1-1$
M1$1$1$;&1$1$1$1$U$U$1$1$1$1$9$1$1$1$1$W41$1$1$1$1$1$1$1$1$
`

end
```


A MIME Base64-encoded version of the same file. Notice the Content-Transfer-Encoding: Base64 line.


```
MIME-Version: 1.0
Content-Description: "Base64 encode of argyle.bmp"
Message-ID: <38635892073068_argyle.bmp>
Content-Type: image\X-bmp; name="argyle.bmp"
Content-Transfer-Encoding: Base64
Content-Disposition: attachment; filename="argyle.bmp"

Qk12AgAAAAAAAHYAAAAoAAAAIAAAACAAAAABAAQAAAAAAAACAAAAAAAAAAAAAAAAAAQAAAAAAAA
AAAAgAAAgAAAAICAAIAAAACAAIAAgIAAAICAgADAwMAAAAD/AAD/AAAA//8A/wAAAP8A/wD//wAA
////AE1EREREREREZEREREREE1E1ERERERERsZEREREETURE1EREREGxsZEREREERNRERE1ERE
REbGxsZERERE1ERERE1ERERsbGxsZERETURERERE1ERGxsbGxsZERNREREREE1EbGxsbGxsZE1E
RERERERE1sbGxsbGxsbURERERERERG1sbGxsbGxtZEREREREREbG1sbGxsbG1sZEREREREsbG1s
bGxsbWxsZEREREREGxsbG1sbGxtbGxsZEREREEbGxsbG1sbG1sbGxsZEREREsbGxsbG1sbWxsbGxsZE
RGxsbGxsbG1tbGxsbGxsZEbGxsbGxsbG1sbGxsbGxsZEbGxsbGxsbW1sbGxsbGxkREbGxsbGxtbG
1sbGxsbGREREbGxsbG1sbG1sbGxsZEREREbGxsbWxsbG1sbGxkRERERbGxtbGxsbG1sbGREREREE
REbG1sbGxsbG1sZEREREREEbWxsbGxsbG1kREREREREREREQNbGxsbGxsbG1EREREREREE1EbGxsbGxs
ZE1EREREREETUREbGxsbGxkRE1EREREREERNREREbGxsbGREREE1EREREE1EREREbGxsZEREREE1ERETURE
REREbGxkREREREE1ERNREREREREbGREREREREE1E1EREREREREZEREREREREE3UREREREREREREREREERE
RERE
```

Both files contain a similar collection of seemingly meaningless ASCII characters, but when you take a closer look, you'll see some subtle differences.

The biggest difference you'll notice is in the header lines. Because MIME supports additional mail capabilities, like the ability to enable appropriate viewers to automatically display the file, the file needs to carry with it the information needed for the MIME-aware client program to determine which viewer is needed to display the file.

Also, notice that in the UUEncoded file, every encoded line begins with a capital letter M, and the words "begin" and "end" mark the beginning and end of the encoded file.

Now that you can tell the difference between the two major types of encoding, you can determine which type of decoder to use if you run across a UUEncoded or MIME Base64-encoded file.

The MIME specification includes the ability to define as many different content types as are needed. One of these types is UUEncode format. Although most MIME client programs use the Base64 format for binary encoding, you may occasionally run into a MIME message that uses the UUEncode format. If this is the case, you'll see the MIME header lines, but the file will be in UUEncode format and the **Content-Transfer-Encoding:** *line will read* **X-uuencode.** *If you see this, you'll need to use UUDecode to decode the file.*

If you're going to be sending a binary file to someone over the Internet, it's a good idea to find out beforehand what kind of decoding program the person has before sending the file. For example, if you send a MIME Base64 encoded file to a friend who only has UUDecode, they'll probably call you back screaming that the file you sent was corrupted. But if you know before you encode the file that your friend only has UUDecode, you can use UUEncode to encode the file, and save them some excess grief.

UUEncoding and Decoding in Unix

If you need to encode or decode a file in Unix, UUENCODE and UUDECODE are the programs to use. These programs are very straightforward, and are available on most Unix systems.

No More UUEncoding?

Everyone agrees that sending binary files over the Internet is a pain. The problem is, when the mail system was originally written many years ago, no one thought that sending binary files would be necessary, since everyone had FTP servers. If you needed to get a file to someone, you'd just send them a message telling them to get the file from your anonymous FTP server.

It made sense at the time, when the only Internet users were at universities or other large institutions, and anyone who needed to could put their files on an anonymous FTP server. The problem is, these days, most Internet users don't have that kind of access to FTP servers.

So people had to resort to other means to transfer binary files across the Internet. UUEncode did the job just fine, for most users. But UUEncode doesn't work with all systems. Partly to resolve the compatibility problem, but mostly to add more functionality to the current Internet mail system, the *MIME* (Multipurpose Internet Mail Extensions) standard was written.

MIME is more than just an encoding standard. It defines the official Internet standard for sending *multipart* mail messages. A multipart mail message is any message that contains more than one kind of information.

So, for example, if you have a MIME-aware mail program, when you send "attachment" files along with your e-mail message, MIME automatically identifies each attachment, encodes it if necessary, and sends the whole thing off as a single, ASCII e-mail message.

In fact, the MIME standard also defines a way to "view" the files you receive. So, for example, if I send you a picture file in JPEG format (.JPG), your MIME-aware mail program will understand that a file with the extension .JPG is a picture, and can be viewed using the LView program you have installed on your system. So your mail program would then ask you "do you want to view the picture now?" and if you say "yes" your mail program will automatically start up LView and display the picture.

MIME also supports character sets other than American ASCII, which is great if you need to send messages in languages that can't be written using the standard ASCII character set, like Russian or Japanese.

Support for the MIME standard is growing every day. As new mail systems are being written and older systems are updated, many are including at least basic MIME support. Several of the mail programs discussed in Chapter 4 support the MIME standard for encoding and decoding binary files.

Using UUEncode in Unix

To encode a file in Unix with UUENCODE, type **uuencode file.bin file.bin >file.uue** at a Unix prompt, where **file.bin** is the binary file that you want converted and **file.uue** is the name of the encoded file. Note that you need to enter the filename twice—once to specify the file, and the second time to specify the name that is embedded in the UUEncoded version.

Using UUDecode in Unix

To decode a UUEncoded file in Unix, do the following:

1. If the file you want to decode is in a mail message or a Usenet posting, save the message to a file, using the appropriate command from your mail program or newsreader.

2. Type **uudecode filename** at a Unix prompt to decode the file. The original binary file will be saved in the same directory with its original name, which is embedded in the UUEncoded version.

Wincode

Encoding and decoding files is nasty business. But fortunately for Windows users, there's Wincode, by George Silva. Wincode is a nice little program that takes a lot of the hassle out of encoding and decoding files, in either UUEncode or MIME Base64 encoding format.

With Wincode, you can easily encode and decode any UUEncode or MIME Base64 encoded file with ease (see Figure 9.2). In fact, you can even drag and drop files from the Windows File Manager (Windows 3.1) or Windows Explorer (Windows 95).

Wincode is available from **ftp.cica.indiana.edu**, in the **/pub/pc/win3/util** directory. The current version at the time of this writing is 2.61 and the file-name is **wncode26.zip**.

Wincode is freeware, and can be freely distributed, but the author maintains the copyright to the source code and the application. A

Figure 9.2:
Wincode makes encoding and decoding files in Windows easy.

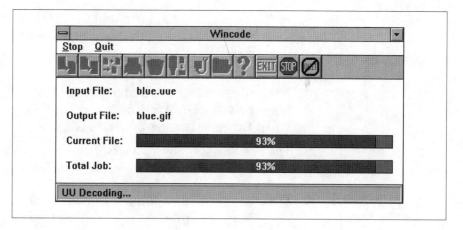

complete help file for the product, along with regular updates, are available for $5 from the author.

Installing Wincode

To install Wincode, do the following:

1. Uncompress the zip file into an empty directory.

2. Run the **INSTALL.EXE** program. Accept the defaults, if possible.

Using Wincode

The easiest way to use Wincode is to use it interactively with the Windows File Manager in Windows 3.1, or with the Windows Explorer in Windows 95.

Encoding Files With Wincode   To encode a file with Wincode using either UUEncode or MIME Base64 encoding format, do the following:

1. Start up Wincode.

2. Start up File Manager (Windows 3.1) by double-clicking on the icon or start up Windows Explorer (Windows 95) by selecting it from the Start menu.

215

3. In File Manager or Explorer, find the file that you want to encode. Using your mouse, drag the file that you want to encode over to the Wincode window, and drop it. The Interactive Drag & Drop window will appear.

4. Select the encoding method (**UUcode**, **BASE64 (MIME)**, etc.) from the **Wincode Method** list box and select **Encode** from the **Drop to:** options. Click on **OK** to continue.

5. The File: window now appears. This window allows you to select from a number of different MIME Content-types for the file. This is useful if you're going to be sending the file to someone with a MIME-aware mail program. Click on OK. If all goes well, you'll see a *filename* **encoded into # file(s)** message.

The file is then encoded. Wincode always puts encoded files in the \WINCODE\ENCODE directory. You can now insert the encoded file into your mail program or newsreader.

Decoding Files With Wincode To decode a UUEncoded or MIME Base64-encoded file with Wincode, do the following:

1. Start up Wincode.

2. Start up File Manager (Windows 3.1) by double-clicking on the icon or start up Windows Explorer (Windows 95) by selecting it from the Start menu.

3. In File Manager or Explorer, find the file that you want to decode. Using your mouse, drag the encoded file over to the Wincode window, and drop it. The Interactive Drag & Drop window will appear.

4. Select the decoding method (**UUcode**, **BASE64 (MIME)**, etc.) from the **Wincode Method** list box and **Decode** from the **Drop to:** options. Click on **OK** to continue.

5. The file will decode. If all goes well, you'll see a **File(s) decoded ok! message**. Click on **OK**.

Wincode always puts decoded files in the \WINCODE\DECODE directory.

XFERPro

XFERPro (Information Transfer Professional), by Sabasoft, is similar to Wincode, and allows interactive drag-and-drop encoding and decoding. XFERPro can use UUEncode and MIME Base64 formats (see Figure 9.3).

Figure 9.3:
XFERPro is a shareware encoding and decoding program for Windows.

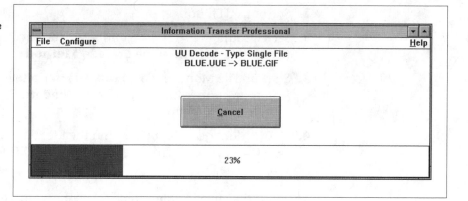

XFERPro is available from **ftp.cica.indiana.edu**, in the **/pub/pc/win3/util** directory. The current version at the time of this writing is 1.0 and the filename is **xferp100.zip**.

XFERPro is shareware, and costs $10 to register. The shareware version can be freely distributed provided that the program files are not altered.

Installing XFERPro

To install XFERPro, do the following:

1. Uncompress the zip file into an empty directory.

2. Run the **SETUP.EXE** program. Accept the defaults, if possible.

Using XFERPro

Like Wincode, the easiest way to use XFERPro is by enlisting the help of the Windows 3.1 File Manager or the Windows 95 Explorer.

Encoding Files With XFERPro To encode a file with XFERPro using either UUEncode or MIME Base64 encoding format, do the following:

1. Start up XFERPro.

2. Select Configure ➤ Encode and select the encoding method (UU, MIME, etc.) from the **Encode Method** options.

3. Start up File Manager (Windows 3.1) by double-clicking on the icon or start up Windows Explorer (Windows 95) by selecting it from the Start menu.

4. In File Manager or Explorer, find the file that you want to encode. Using your mouse, drag the file over to the XFERPro window, and drop it. The Encode Output To window will appear. Click on **OK**.

By default, the encoded file will be saved in the same directory as the original file.

Decoding Files With XFERPro To decode a UUEncoded or MIME Base64-encoded file with XFERPro, do the following:

1. Start up XFERPro.

2. Start up File Manager (Windows 3.1) by double-clicking on the icon or start up Windows Explorer (Windows 95) by selecting it from the Start menu.

3. In File Manager or Explorer, find the file that you want to decode. Using your mouse, drag the file over to the XFERPro window, and drop it.

4. The Decode Output To window will appear. Select the directory where you want to save the file.

UnMacIt

If you ever run across a BinHex encoded file (.HQX), UnMacIt can decode it. UnMacIt can also uncompress Mac SIT compressed files (.SIT), should you ever run across one. Of course, if the file you get is an executable, it won't run on a plain ol' PC, but if it's an image or word processing document file, you can usually view it on your PC without any problem.

UnMacIt is actually comprised of two files: UnHQX and UnSIT. It doesn't offer a real fancy interface, but it does the job (see Figure 9.4).

Figure 9.4:

UnMacIt's UnHQX isn't pretty, but it will un-BinHex any .HQX files you may run across. UnSIT, the companion program, can uncompress Mac SIT programs just as easily.

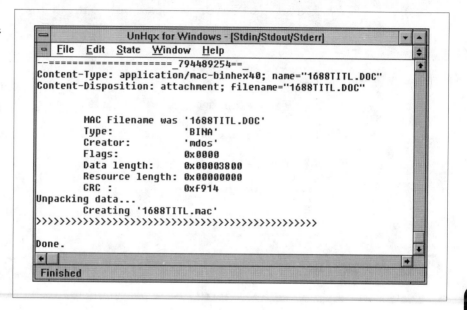

You can get UnMacIt via anonymous FTP from **ftp.cica.indiana.edu**, in the **/pub/pc/win3/util** directory. The filename is **unmacit.zip**.

UnMacIt is freeware, and may be freely distributed.

Installing UnMacIt

To install UnMacIt, do the following:

1. Create an **UNMACIT** directory on your hard disk.

2. Uncompress the zip file into that directory.

3. Run the **UNMACIT.EXE** self-extracting archive file to extract the UNNHQX.EXE and UNSIT.EXE files.

4. Create icons on your Windows desktop for the **UNNHQX.EXE** and **UNSIT.EXE** files.

Using UnMacIt

To use UnHQX to Un-BinHex a file, do the following:

1. Put the file you want to Un-BinHex into the UNMACIT directory.

2. Start up UnHQX.

3. Enter the name of the file you want to decode and press Enter. The file will decode into the same directory.

To use UnSIT to Uncompress a SIT file, do the following:

1. Put the file you want to Un-BinHex into the UNMACIT directory.

2. Start up UnSIT.

3. Enter the name of the file you want to uncompress and press Enter.

File Archive & Compression Utilities

File compression is a way of life on the Internet. If it wasn't for file compression and archive utilities, you'd spend a lot more time downloading files. Compression utilities for DOS have been around for many years, and have provided users and developers alike with an easy way to squeeze big files down to a manageable size.

The most commonly used compression format for DOS is the zip (.ZIP) format. Although you still see the occasional archive (.ARC) format file, which was popular in the 1980s, it has been almost completely replaced by the zip format. Another relatively common format is LHarc (.LZH).

But out there on the Internet, you'll also run into some Unix compression and archiving formats, primarily .Z (compression) and .tar (Tape Archive), and sometimes .tar.Z (Compressed Tape Archive). The concept of having separate archiving and compressing utilities is kind of alien to PC users who have grown accustomed to the zip format, which both compresses and archives.

Here's a quick guide to help you determine the right tool to use to uncompress and unarchive files that you may find out there on the Internet:

Extension	Tool Required
.ARC	WinZip
.GZ	GNUZip or WinZip
.LZH	LHA or WinZip
.SIT	UnMacIt
.TAR	ExTAR or WinZip
.tar.Z or .TAZ	GNUZip then ExTAR or WinZip
.ZIP	UnZip or WinZip

If you download a file with the Unix filename extension of .tar.Z, your FTP program will probably change it to a DOS filename, either .TAR or .Z, depending on how it parses long filenames. If you do download a file like this, make a note of the original filename extension, or better yet, rename the file to .TAZ, so you'll know that it's both TAR (archived) and Z (compressed).

GNUZip

If you find yourself looking at a Unix Z file (.gz, .z, or .Z), you'll need the GNUZip uncompression utility.

The difference between the Z compression format and many of the DOS compression formats is that Z only compresses files. Also, it doesn't archive multiple files into a single archive file. For that, you need TAR (Tape Archive), which archives but doesn't compress. That's why you see a lot of Unix files in .tar.Z format, which is simply a Z-compressed TAR archive file.

You can get GNUZip via anonymous FTP from **oak.oakland.edu,** in the **/SimTel/msdos/compress** directory. The current version at the time of this writing is 1.24 and the filename is **gzip124.zip**

GNUZip is freeware and can be freely distributed.

Installing GNUZip

To install GNUZip, do the following:

1. Create a **GZIP** directory on your hard disk.

2. Uncompress the zip file into that directory.

3. Either edit the PATH statement in your **AUTOEXEC.BAT** file to include the \GZIP directory or copy the GZIP.EXE file to a directory that's already in your path. To edit the PATH statement in your AUTOEXEC.BAT file, just open it up using a plain text editor like the Windows Notepad, and add the \GZIP directory to the end of the **PATH=** statement. If you don't want to mess with your AUTO-EXEC.BAT file, or if your PATH statement is already pretty long (if you have to scroll over a page or two to find the end of it), you can just put GZIP.EXE in a directory that's already in your PATH.

Using GNUZip

To use GNUZip, do the following:

1. Get to a DOS prompt, and change to the directory where the gzipped file resides.

2. Type **gzip -d *filename***, where *filename* is the file you want to uncompress. The file is uncompressed. Unlike other uncompress utilities, GNUZip deletes the compressed version of the file when you uncompress it.

Remember that if the file you're trying to extract is a Unix executable file, you'll need to have Unix to be able to run it. Most people tend to compress executable files in their native format. DOS and Windows executables usually aren't found archived in .tar.Z format. In general, if you see a file in .tar.Z format on a Unix server, and the readme file says something to the effect that this is a great program, chances are, it's a great Unix program. Non-executable files, for example Postscript documents, sound files, and images, are readable on your PC, with the right viewers and players. See the next chapter for information about the different viewers and players available.

LHA

LHA, by Haruyasu Yoshizaki, is one of the earlier compression archive tools for DOS. Although the LHarc (.LZH) archive format is not as common as other compression formats, it is still around.

> You can get LHA via anonymous FTP from **oak.oakland.edu**, in the **/SimTel/msdos/archiver** directory. The current version is 2.13, and the filename is **lha213.exe**, which is a self-extracting archive file.

LHA is freeware and may be freely distributed provided that the files are not altered.

Installing LHA

To install LHA, do the following:

1. Create an **LHA** directory on your hard disk.

2. Run the self-extracting archive file in this directory to uncompress the files.

3. Either edit the PATH statement in your **AUTOEXEC.BAT** file to include the \LHA directory or copy the LHZ.EXE file to a directory

223

that's already in your path. To edit the PATH statement in your AUTOEXEC.BAT file, just open it up using a plain text editor like the Windows Notepad, and add the \LHA directory to the end of the **PATH=** statement. If you don't want to mess with your AUTO-EXEC.BAT file, or if your PATH statement is already pretty long (if you have to scroll over a page or two to find the end of it), you can just put LHA.EXE in a directory that's already in your PATH.

Using LHA

To uncompress files using LHA, do the following:

1. Get to a DOS prompt, and change to the directory where the .LZH file resides.

2. Type **lha e *filename***, where *filename* is the file you want to uncompress. The file will then uncompress. The original .LZH file will remain in the directory along with the uncompressed files.

ExTAR

So, you got yourself a Unix TAR file. What you need is Gisbert W. Selke's ExTAR for DOS. ExTAR is just a very basic utility that un-TARs Unix Tape Archive files.

ExTAR isn't fancy, but it works quite well, and is smart enough to change Unix long filenames to more DOS-friendly ones, while retaining the filename extension (.txt, .doc, etc.)

> You can get ExTAR via anonymous FTP from **oak.oakland.edu**, in the **/SimTel/msdos/archiver** directory. The current version is 1.0, and the filename is **extar10.zip**.

ExTAR is freeware and can be freely distributed.

Installing ExTAR

To install ExTAR, do the following:

1. Create an **EXTAR** directory on your hard disk.
2. Uncompress the zip file into that directory.
3. Either edit the PATH statement in your **AUTOEXEC.BAT** file to include the EXTAR directory or copy the EXTAR.EXE file to a directory that's already in your path. To edit the PATH statement in your AUTOEXEC.BAT file, just open it up using a plain text editor like the Windows Notepad, and add the \EXTAR directory to the end of the **PATH=** statement. If you don't want to mess with your AUTOEXEC.BAT file, or if your PATH statement is already pretty long (if you have to scroll over a page or two to find the end of it), you can just put EXTAR.EXE in a directory that's already in your PATH.

Using ExTAR

To unarchive a TAR file, do the following:

1. Get to a DOS prompt, and change to the directory where the TAR'ed file resides.
2. Type **extar *filename***, where *filename* is the file you want to uncompress. The file is unarchived.

InfoZip

The best freeware DOS unzipping utility around is InfoZip's UnZip. UnZip can uncompress any .ZIP file easily and quickly. One thing I really appreciate about UnZip is it's ability to automatically create subdirectories when uncompressing a file, without the need for using an additional parameter.

If you like UnZip, you might also want to try its companion program, Zip.

> You can get InfoZip's UnZip via anonymous FTP from **oak.oakland.edu**, in the **/SimTel/msdos/zip** directory. The current version at the time of this writing is 5.12, and the filename is **unz512x3.exe**.
>
> InfoZip's Zip is also available via anonymous FTP from the SimTel archive at **oak .oakland.edu**, in the **/SimTel/msdos/zip** directory. The current version at the time of this writing is 2.0, and the filename is **zip20x.zip**.

InfoZip's UnZip is freeware and can be freely distributed provided that the files are not altered.

Installing InfoZip's UnZip

To install UnZip, do the following:

1. Create an **INFOZIP** directory on your hard disk.

2. Run the self-extracting archive file in this directory to uncompress the files.

3. If you downloaded the 386 version of UnZip, the executable name is UNZIP386.EXE. For simplicity's sake, rename this file to UN-ZIP.EXE.

4. Either edit the PATH statement in your **AUTOEXEC.BAT** file to include the \INFOZIP directory or copy the UNZIP.EXE file to a directory that's already in your path. To edit the PATH statement in your AUTOEXEC.BAT file, just open it up using a plain text editor like the Windows Notepad, and add the \INFOZIP directory to the end of the **PATH=** statement. If you don't want to mess with your AUTOEXEC.BAT file, or if your PATH statement is already pretty long (if you have to scroll over a page or two to find the end of it), you can just put UNZIP.EXE in a directory that's already in your PATH.

Using InfoZip's UnZip

To uncompress files using UnZip, do the following:

1. Go to the DOS prompt, and change to the directory where the zip file resides.

2. Type **unzip *filename***, where *filename* is the name of the file you want to uncompress. The zip file will then uncompress. The original .ZIP file will remain in the directory along with the uncompressed files.

Installing InfoZip's Zip

To install Zip, do the following:

1. Put the ZIP20X.ZIP file in the same INFOZIP directory where you installed UnZip

2. Uncompress the ZIP20X.ZIP file, using UnZip.

Using InfoZip's Zip

To use InfoZip's Zip to compress files, do the following:

1. Put all of the files you want to compress into an empty directory.

2. Open a DOS prompt, and change to the directory where these files are located.

3. Type **zip *zipfile* *.***, where *zipfile* is the name you want to give to the archive file.

*InfoZip's Zip offers a number of different archiving options. For more information, read the documentation files, or just type **zip** at a DOS prompt to see a quick list of commands.*

PKZip

Phil Katz's PKZip has become a defacto standard for zipping in the DOS world. With the 2.04g version, PKZip also adds the ability to add passwords to zip files, so that they cannot be extracted unless you have the right password.

You can get PKZip via anonymous FTP from **oak.oakland.edu**, in the **/SimTel/msdos/zip** directory. The current version at the time of this writing is 2.04g, and the filename is **pkz204g.exe**, which is a self-extracting archive file.

PKZip is shareware and costs $47 to register. Registration gets you a printed manual, the latest copy of the program, one free upgrade, and access to the support BBS.

Installing PKZip

To install PKZip, do the following:

1. Create a **PKZIP** directory on your hard disk.

2. Run the self-extracting archive file in this directory to uncompress the files.

3. Either edit the PATH statement in your **AUTOEXEC.BAT** file to include the PKZIP directory or copy the PKZIP.EXE and PKUNZIP.EXE files to a directory that's already in your path. To edit the PATH statement in your AUTOEXEC.BAT file, just open it up using a plain text editor like the Windows Notepad, and add the \PKZIP directory to the end of the **PATH=** statement. If you don't want to mess with your AUTOEXEC.BAT file, or if your PATH statement is already pretty long (if you have to scroll over a page or two to find the end of it), you can just put PKZIP.EXE and PKUNZIP.EXE in a directory that's already in your PATH.

Using PKUnzip

To uncompress files using PKUnzip, do the following:

1. Go to the DOS prompt, and change to the directory where the zip file resides.

2. Type **pkunzip -d *filename,*** where *filename* is the name of the file you want to uncompress. The zip file will then uncompress. The original .ZIP file will remain in the directory along with the uncompressed files. I recommend always using the **-d** option, since this ensures that any directories stored in the archive file will be automatically created when you extract the files.

Using PKZip

To use PKZip to archive files, do the following:

1. Place all of the files that you want to archive into an empty directory.

2. Open a DOS prompt and change to this directory.

3. Type **pkzip** *zipname* ***.***, where *zipname* is the name you want to give the archive file. The .ZIP file is created and the files you archived will remain in the directory, along with the .ZIP file.

WinZip

For easy compressing and uncompressing of files, you can't beat Niko Mak's WinZip. It's easy to use, supports drag-and-drop, and can even install itself as a menu option under File Manager in Windows 3.1 (see Figure 9.5).

Figure 9.5:
WinZip is (in this author's opinion) the best all-around compression utility for Windows.

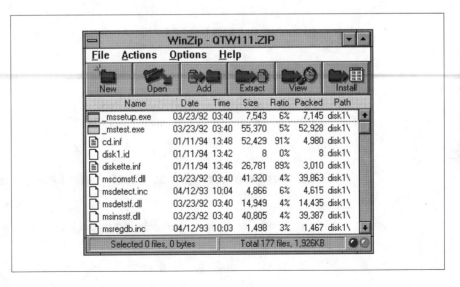

Making Sense of Files   CH. 9

WinZip supports all zip formats, plus arc and LHarc formats. And, starting with version 5.6, WinZip supports the Unix .tar, .Z, .gz, and even .tar.Z compression formats.

> You can get WinZip via anonymous FTP from **oak.oakland.edu**, in the **/SimTel/win3/archiver** directory. The current version at the time of this writing is 5.6, and the filename is **winzip56.exe**, which is a self-extracting archive file.

WinZip is shareware, and costs $29 to register. Registration gets you a copy of the program on disk, and support from the developer. The shareware version may be freely distributed provided that the files are not altered, or any fee is charged for the distribution.

Installing WinZip

To install WinZip, do the following:

1. Run the self-extracting archive file into an empty directory to uncompress the setup files.
2. Run the **SETUP.EXE** file. Accept the defaults, if possible.

Using WinZip

The easiest way to use WinZip is to use it interactively with the Windows File Manager in Windows 3.1, or with the Windows Explorer in Windows 95.

Uncompressing Files With WinZip To uncompress files, do the following:

1. Using File Manager (Windows 3.1) or Windows Explorer (Windows 95), find the file that you want to uncompress.
2. Double-click on the filename. As long as the filename extension is .ZIP, .ARC, .ARJ, .LZH, .TAR, .TAZ or .GZ, WinZip will start up, and display the zipped files.

3. To extract the files, just click on the **Extract** button.

4. The Extract window will appear. Select the directory that you want to uncompress the files to and click on **Extract**. The files will then uncompress.

If you want to open a .tar.Z file using WinZip, make sure you rename the file to filename.TAZ. WinZip recognizes that any file with an extension of .TAZ is a Unix .tar.Z file, and will uncompress and display the contents of the TAR file automatically.

Compressing Files with WinZip To compress files with WinZip, do the following:

1. Start WinZip.

2. Start up File Manager (Windows 3.1) by double-clicking on the icon or start up Windows Explorer (Windows 95) by selecting it from the Start menu.

3. Using File Manager or Explorer, find the files that you want to compress.

4. Using your mouse, drag the files over to WinZip, and drop them.

5. The Drag and Drop window will appear. Enter the path and file-name for the zip file you want to create in the **Add to Archive** field and click on the **Add** button.

If you want to configure WinZip as a client program viewer for .ZIP, .ARC, .GZ, .TAR, and .tar.Z files, point your client program to the WINZIP.EXE file for these application types: **application/zip, application/x-tar,** *and* **application/x-compressed.**

Now that you've got the tools you need for encoding, decoding, archiving, and unarchiving, you're ready to dip into the big wide world of multimedia. There are all kinds of sounds, images, and videos out there on the Internet for you to download and enjoy. In the next chapter, I'll talk about the tools you'll need to be able to view and play these files on your PC.

10

Viewers and
Players

MULTIMEDIA HAS BECOME integral to the Internet, especially on the World Wide Web. As you surf your way around the world, you'll probably run into a number of different sounds, images, and even movies.

The problem is, they all don't conform to a single standard. There are standards for Unix, and DOS/Windows, and Macs. There are even standards for specific types of sound cards. And you'll find at least one sample of each flavor if you look hard enough. That was the bad news. The good news is that most of these files can be played on your PC, provided that you have the right viewer or player handy.

For example, you may have run across a sound file with a name like *this.is.a.great.sound.au.* And, your first reaction might have been something like "How did they get all that text into a filename, and what does *.au* mean?" Well, first off, Unix allows long filenames, and secondly, .au is the most popular type of sound file for Unix computers.

But you don't have to let that stop you from hearing this great sound— you can change the name of the file when you download it to something more DOS-friendly, like *greatsnd.au*, and you can get a sound player, like Wham, that can play .au files.

That's what this chapter is about—how to recognize different sound, image, and video files, and know what to do with these files once you've downloaded them.

Images

There are a number of different image formats you're likely to run across. The two most popular are GIF (CompuServe's Graphics Interchange Format) and JPEG (Joint Photographic Experts Group), although occasionally you'll find a BMP (Bitmap) or TIFF (Tagged Image File Format) image as well.

LView and LView Pro: Viewing JPEGs, GIFs, BMPs, and TIFFs

LView and LView Pro, by Leonardo Haddad Loureiro, are good all-around viewers for JPEG, GIF, BMP, and Targa files, and either program makes an excellent viewer application for your favorite Gopher or Web browser (see Figure 10.1). They let you view and manipulate image

Figure 10.1:

LView lets you display JPEG and GIF files easily.

files with ease, although neither program lets you draw or edit pictures. In addition, LView Pro supports TIFF format files.

Another note of interest is that LView Pro is one of the only products on the market that supports "transparent" GIF files, which are becoming increasingly popular on Web pages. Transparent GIFs let you designate a particular color as a "background" color, which shows up as transparent when viewed in a Web browser. This allows you to create images that appear to have an irregular shape, or that just simply have the same background color as the background (see Figure 10.2).

This feature is only supported in the newer GIF format, GIF89a, which LView Pro supports. For more information about designing your own Web page, see Chapter 3.

Viewers and Players
CH. 10

235

Figure 10.2:
LView Pro lets you create "transparent" GIF files, which allows you to designate a background color that will appear transparent when viewed with certain Web browsers.

The transparent image shown above is displayed in Netscape below.

You can get LView via anonymous FTP from **ftp.cica.indiana.edu**, in the **/pub/pc/win3/desktop** directory. The current version is 3.1, and the file-name is **lview31.zip**.

You can get LView Pro via anonymous FTP from the SimTel archive at **oak.oakland.edu**, in the **/SimTel/win3/** directory. The current version at the time of this writing is 1a, and the filename is **lviewp1a.zip**.

LView is the freeware version, and may be freely distributed, provided that the files are not altered and no fee is charged for the program. LView pro is the shareware version, and costs $30 to register. With registration, you can optionally get the 32-bit version of LView Pro. Registration is required for commercial or work usage of LView Pro.

Installing LView

To install either LView or LView Pro, do the following:

1. Create an **LVIEW** or **LVIEWP** directory on your hard disk.

2. Uncompress the zip file into that directory.

3. Create an icon on your Windows desktop for the **LVIEW.EXE** or **LVIEWP.EXE** file.

4. Create an association for .JPG and >GIF files in Windows using File Manager (Windows 3.1) or Exploreer (Windows 95).

Using LView

To use LView or LView Pro, do the following:

1. Start up LView or LView Pro.

2. Select File ➤ Open to open a new graphic file.

3. By default, LView starts up looking for .JPG files. If you want to open a different kind of file, click on the **List Files of Type** list box to select a different file type.

Viewers and Players   CH. 10

237

If you want to configure LView or LView Pro as a client program viewer for .GIF and .JPG files, configure your client program to use the LVIEW.EXE or LVIEWP.EXE file for the **image/gif** *and* **image/jpeg** *application types.*

Where to Find JPEGs and GIFs

Here are just a few places to go looking for picture files on the Internet:

WUArchive Images Archive. Washington University in St. Louis, Missouri houses one of the biggest FTP archive sites on the Internet. Their multimedia and graphics archives are very extensive. Check out the **/multimedia/images** and **/graphics** directories at **wuarchive.wustl.edu**.

Artlink. Magellan Media has put together an incredible page full of links to museums and galleries around the world. From here you can visit the Louvre, the Andy Warhol museum, and the Vatican Museum, among others. To get there, set your Web browser to the following URL:

http://www.webcom.com/~magellan/artlink.html

Art Source. Another excellent resource for art lovers, Mary Molinaro at the University of Kentucky has put together a selective collection of links to Art resources the world over. To get there, set your Web browser to the following URL:

http://www.uky.edu/Artsource/artsourcehome.html

Binary Pictures Newsgroups. And, if you want to try out both your decoders and your viewers and players, there's no place like the *alt.binaries.pictures.** groups. Although the content can sometimes be, shall we say, a little racy, you'll find pictures to suit just about any taste. To get there, just point your newsreader to the following hierarchy on Usenet:

alt.binaries.pictures.*

Videos

There are a number of different standards for video images that you're likely to find on the Internet. MPEGs, Video for Windows™ files, Apple Quicktime™ movies, and even the occasional AutoDesk Flic file.

238

Naturally, these formats are all incompatible with one another, so you'll need several different viewers to be able to view them all. Fortunately, there are Windows viewers available for all of the standard formats.

VMPEG: Viewing MPEGs

MPEG stands for Moving Pictures Expert Group, and is one of several standards for displaying movies on your PC. VMPEG, by Stefan Eckart, is a 32-bit MPEG player for Windows, and is one of the better ones I've found (see Figure 10.3). It isn't as "jerky" as some of the others I've seen, and it doesn't have a 1MB size restriction like some other MPEG players do.

Figure 10.3:
VMPEG is an excellent 32-bit MPEG player for Windows.

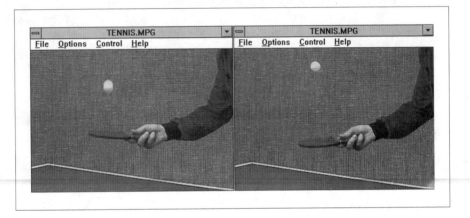

VMPEG also comes with a DOS version, and a WinG version, which optimizes the program for your display.

If you want to use the WinG version of VMPEG, you'll also have to get WinG and install it. It's available from **ftp.microsoft.com**, *in the* **/developer/drg /WinG** *directory. The current version at the time of this writing is 1.0, and the filename is* **WING10.ZIP**.

Most MPEG players you'll find are 32-bit, which means that if you're not running Windows 95 or Windows NT, you'll have to install the

239

Win32s 32-bit extensions for Windows. I wish I could recommend a 16-bit MPEG player to you, but I'm afraid I couldn't find one that worked reliably.

> You can get VMPEG via anonymous FTP from **ftp.cica.indiana.edu**, in the **/pub/pc/win3/desktop** directory. The current version at the time of this writing is 1.2a, and the filename is **vmpeg12a.zip**.

VMPEG is freeware and may be freely distributed provided that the files are not altered and no fee is charged for the program.

*If you're installing VMPEG on a Windows 3.1 system that doesn't already have Win32s installed, you'll need to get that as well. You can find the current version of Win32s at **ftp.ncsa.uiuc.edu**, in the **/Web/Mosaic/Windows** directory. The current version at the time of this writing is Version 1.25, and the filename is **W32SOLE.EXE**, which is a self-extracting archive file.*

Installing VMPEG

As I mentioned before, if you're using Windows 3.1, you first need to install Win32s before installing VMPEG. The following steps descsribe the installation procedure for Win32s. If you're running Windows 95 or Windows NT, you can skip these steps and start at the next set of steps.

1. Before you start, close all open applications.

2. Put the self-extracting archive file into an empty directory, and run it to expand the Win32s setup files.

3. Run the **INSTALL.BAT** file. This will expand all of the Win32s install files into their appropriate subdirectories.

4. Change to the **\DISK1** subdirectory and run the **SETUP.EXE** file. The Win32s files will install. Accept the defaults if possible. When it's done installing, the Setup program will reboot Windows.

5. Delete the setup files.

At this point, you're ready to install VMPEG.

1. Create a **VMPEG** directory on your hard disk.

2. Uncompress the zip file into that directory.

3. Create an icon for the **VMPEGNWG.EXE** file on your Windows desktop. (If you have WinG installed, you can use the **VMPEGWIN.EXE** file.)

4. If you're not going to need the DOS version, you can delete the VMPEG and GO32.EXE files, the entire \DRIVERS subdirectory and the VMPEG*.BAT batch files.

5. Create an association for VMPEG in Windows.

Using VMPEG

To use VMPEG, do the following:

1. Start up File Manager or the Windows Explorer and change to the directory where the .MPG file you want to play is located.

2. Double-click on the .MPG file to open it.

3. VMPEG starts up. Select Control ➤ Play to start the movie.

If you want to configure VMPEG as a client program viewer for .MPG files, configure your client program to use the VMPEGNWG.EXE for the **video/mpeg** *application type.*

Microsoft Video for Windows: Viewing AVIs

Microsoft's Video for Windows was supposed to take off as *the* standard format for Windows movies, but has never quite gained the foothold that Microsoft hoped it would. But it is a good and relatively popular format, and you may run across the occasional .AVI file on the Internet (see Figure 10.4).

Microsoft bundles the Video for Windows drivers with many other products, so you may already have it installed. To find out, open Control Panel ➤ Drivers, and see if there's a listing for **[MCI] Microsoft Video for Windows**. *If there is, you don't need to install the Video for Windows drivers. And, if you're running Windows 95, it's already installed.*

241

Figure 10.4:
The Video for Windows drivers let you use the Windows Media Player to play .AVI files.

You can get the Microsoft Video for Windows drivers from **ftp.microsoft.com** in the **/developer/drg/Multimedia** directory. The current version at the time of this writing is 1.1 and the filename is **WV1160.EXE**.

Installing Microsoft Video for Windows

To install Microsoft Video for Windows, do the following:

1. Uncompress the zip file into an empty directory.

2. Run the **SETUP.EXE** file. Accept the default settings, if possible.

Using Microsoft Video for Windows

The Video for Windows installation program creates an association in Windows, so that you can automatically start the Windows Media Player from File Manager or Windows Explorer.

To use Video for Windows, do the following:

1. Start up File Manager or the Windows Explorer and change to the directory where the .AVI file you want to play is located.

2. Double-click on the .AVI file to open it.

3. The Windows Media Player starts up. Click on the **Play** button at the bottom of the movie window to start the movie.

If you want to configure the Windows use Media Player as a client program viewer for .AVI files, configure your client program to use the MPLAYER.EXE file in your \ WINDOWS directory for the **video/x-msvideo** *application type.*

Apple Quicktime for Windows: Viewing MOVs

Apple's Quicktime format works on both Windows and Macintosh systems, making it the most popular format for movie files on the Internet. The Quicktime viewer for Windows, shown in Figure 10.5, is bundled with many commercial CD-ROMs, but it's also available on the Internet.

Figure 10.5:
The Apple Quicktime movie viewer lets you view .MOV files you find on the Internet.

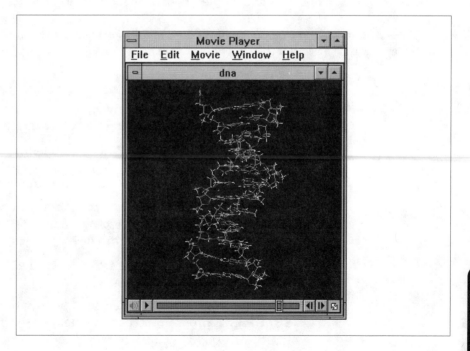

You can get Apple's Quicktime Viewer for Windows via anonymous ftp from **ftp.cuhk.hk** in the **/pub/mov** directory. The current freeware version is 1.11, and the filename is **qtw111.exe**, which is a self-extracting archive file.

Version 2.0 is available from CompuServe for a $9.95 license fee. Enter **Go QTIME** to order a copy.

There are two versions of the Quicktime Viewer for Windows. Version 1.11 is freeware. Version 2.0 is available from third-party products, such as CD-ROMs, and from CompuServe. For most .MOV files, however, you'll do just fine with version 1.11.

Installing Quicktime for Windows

To install Quicktime for Windows, do the following:

 The Quicktime for Windows installation requires two empty diskettes. You can't install it from your hard drive.

1. Run the self-extracting archive file in an empty directory to uncompress the **DISK1.ZIP** and **DISK2.ZIP** files.

2. Uncompress the **DISK1.ZIP** file into an empty directory. If you're using PKUnZip, make sure you use the **-d** option (**pkunzip disk1 -d**) to extract files into the right subdirectories.

3. Delete the DISK1.ZIP file and copy all of the remaining files and subdirectories to an empty diskette. Label it **QTW Disk 1**. Then delete these files from your hard disk.

4. Repeat steps 2 and 3 for the **DISK2.ZIP** file. Label the disk **QTW Disk 2**.

5. Insert the QTW Disk 1 into your floppy drive and run the **SETUP.EXE** program. Accept the default settings, if possible. Insert the QTW Disk 2 when prompted.

Using QuickTime for Windows

The QuickTime for Windows installation program creates an association in Windows for files with the .MOV extension, so that you can automatically start the QuickTime movie player from File Manager or Windows Explorer.

To use QuickTime for Windows, do the following:

1. Start up File Manager or the Windows Explorer and change to the directory where the .MOV file you want to play is located.

2. Double-click on the .MOV file to open it.

3. The QuickTime Movie Player starts up. Click on the Play button at the bottom of the movie window to start the movie.

You can control the sound volume by clicking on the speaker icon at the bottom of the movie window and adjusting the volume up or down.

If you want to configure the Quicktime Movie Player as a client program viewer for .MOV files, point your client program to use the \QTW\BIN\PLAYER.EXE *file for the* **video/quicktime** *application type.*

AAPlay: Viewing FLIs & FLCs

AutoDesk's Flic format is excellent for computer-generated animation, and provides a much cleaner-looking movie than MPEG. You'll usually find fractals and other computer-generated movies in .FLI or .FLC format. If you come across a file in either of these formats, you'll need AutoDesk's freeware AAPlay viewer to play it (see Figure 10.6).

> You can get AAPlay via anonymous FTP from **ftp.povray.org**, in the **/pub/povray/utilities** directory. The current version at the time of this writing is 1.1, and the filename is **aawin.zip**.

AAPlay is freeware, and may be freely distributed.

Viewers and Players CH. 10

Figure 10.6:
AAPlay lets you play Flic format files easily.

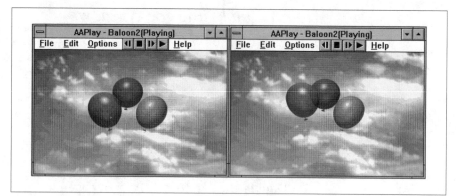

Installing AAPlay

To install AAPlay, do the following:

1. Uncompress the zip file in an empty directory.

2. Run the **AASETUP.EXE** file. Accept the defaults, if possible.

3. Create an association for AAPlay in Windows for files with the FLI and FLC extentions.

Using AAPlay

To use AAPlay, do the following:

1. Start up File Manager or the Windows Explorer and change to the directory where the .FLI or .FLC file you want to play is located.

2. Double-click on the .FLI or .FLC file to open it. AAPlay starts up.

3. Click on the **Play** button at the top of the window to start the movie.

If you want to configure AAPlay as a client program viewer for .FLI and .FLC files, configure your client program to use the AAWIN.EXE file for the **video/fli** *application type.*

246

Where to Find MPEGs, AVIs, FLIs, MOVs, and More

Wondering where all the movies are stored? Here are a few places where you can find movie files in various formats:

The Fractal Movie Archive. A part of the Fractal Archive at the Conservatoire National des Arts et Métiers, this is just about the biggest archive site for fractal animations on the Internet. Definitely worth checking out. To get there, set your Web browser to the following URL:

http://www.cnam.fr/fractals/anim.html.

Animations Index. Looking for links to animations and film clips? This is the place. Thant Nyo has compiled an extensive list of links to animations on the Web. A great place to take your movie viewers for a test drive. To get there, set your Web browser to the following URL:

http://mambo.ucsc.edu/psl/thant/thant.html.

The Yahoo Multimedia Directory: Movies. Check out Yahoo's directory when you just feel like surfing for links to movies. You're sure to find something interesting. To get there, set your Web browser to the following URL

http://www.yahoo.com/Computers/Multimedia/ Movies/.

Document Viewers

Although most people who tend to distribute text information on the Internet generally use plain ASCII text, you will occasionally find a document file in a different format. The two most popular formats both come from Adobe: Acrobat and Postscript.

Acrobat is the new kid on the block—it's only been available for the last couple of years or so. But Adobe's Postscript formatting language has been around almost since the first desktop computers. It's the most commonly found non-ASCII text document format you're likely to find out there on the Internet.

Adobe Acrobat Reader: Viewing PDFs

The Adobe Acrobat Reader allows you to read Adobe Acrobat files. Acrobat is a hypertext document format which is becoming a popular format for distributing online help files and documents (see Figure 10.7).

Figure 10.7:
Adobe Acrobat lets you read hypertext Acrobat documents.

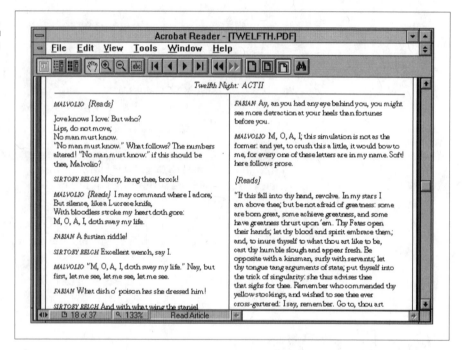

You can get the Adobe Acrobat Reader via anonymous FTP from **ftp.adobe.com**, in the **/pub/adobe/Applications/Acrobat/Windows** directory. The current version at the time of this writing is 2.0, and the filename is **acroread.exe**.

The Adobe Acrobat reader is distributed free of charge by Adobe.

Installing Adobe Acrobat

To install the Adobe Acrobat Reader, do the following:

1. Close all open applications.

2. Run **ACROREAD.EXE**. The Acrobat Reader Installer screen appears, displaying the licensing agreement for Adobe Acrobat.

3. Read the license agreement, and click on **Accept**. Follow the directions on screen to install the program.

4. When Acrobat is done installing, it will restart Windows.

Using Adobe Acrobat

To use Adobe Acrobat, do the following:

1. Start up File Manager or the Windows Explorer and change to the directory where the .PDF file you want to play is located.

2. Double-click on the .PDF file to open it. The Adobe Acrobat Reader starts up.

The Acrobat reader is quite easy to use. Here are some things to remember when running Adobe Acrobat:

To move around the page, click on the hand button if it isn't already selected. If the cursor is a hand with a down pointing arrow, just click anywhere on the page to move down to the next screenful of text. Otherwise, you can just hold down the left mouse button to grab the page, and move it up or down.

To move forward a page, click on the forward button (right pointing triangle).

To move back a page, click on the backward button (left pointing triangle).

To move to the end of the document, click on the fast forward button (two right pointing triangles).

To move to the beginning of the document, click on the rewind button (two left pointing triangles).

To find text, select Tools ➤ Find or click on the binoculars button. Enter the text you want to search for and click on Find.

To zoom in, click on the + magnifying glass button, and click on the area that you want to zoom in on.

To zoom out, click on the – magnifying glass button, and click anywhere on the page.

To select text, click on the abc button and select the text. You can then copy the text to some other application.

Ghostscript and GhostView: Viewing Postscript PS Files

Ghostscript is a great program for interpreting files in Adobe's Postscript format. The Postscript standard is quite heavily used on Macintosh and Unix platforms for displaying formatted text documents. But it never really gained a foothold in the PC market, which is why you need a program like Ghostscript to be able to interpret these files. Ghostscript is the Postscript interpreter program. It reads in any .PS file, and translates it into a format that can be read. GhostView is the accompanying viewer for Windows. It reads the output from Ghostscript, and displays it on your screen. GhostView also lets you print Postscript files easily, even on a non-postscript printer (see Figure 10.8).

> You can get Ghostscript via anonymous FTP from **ftp.cica.indiana.edu**, in the **/pub/pc/win3/util** directory. The current version as of the time of this writing is 2.61, and the filenames are **gs261exe.zip** and **gsview10.zip**. You should also get the **gs260fnt.zip** file, as this contains a number of fonts that you'll need.

Ghostscript and GhostView are freeware and can be freely distributed.

Installing Ghostscript

To install Ghostscript and the Ghostscript viewer, do the following:

1. Create a **GS** directory on your hard disk.

2. Uncompress the **GS261EXE.ZIP**, **GS260FNT.ZIP**, and **GSVIEW261.ZIP** files into that directory.

Figure 10.8:
The Ghostscript
Interpreter and Viewer
let you display and print
Postscript format files.

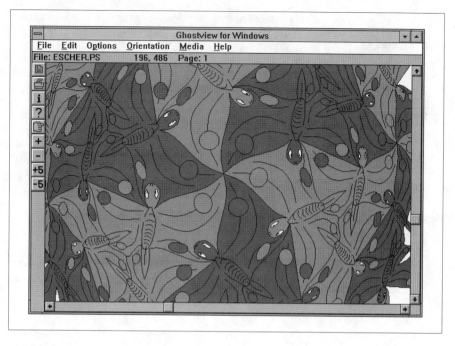

3. Create an icon on your Windows desktop for the **GSVIEW.EXE** file. Make sure that the Working directory for the icon points to the \GS directory.

4. Create an association in Windows for Ghostscript.

Using Ghostscript

To use the Ghostscript viewer, do the following:

1. Ghostscript requires that the .PS file you want to view is in the \GS directory. So, you'll have to move the file there, if it isn't there already.

2. Open GSView by double-clicking on the icon.

3. Select File ➤ Open and select the .PS file you want to view.

4. After a few seconds, the file should display.

If you want to configure Ghostscript as a client program viewer for .PS files, configure your client program to use the GSVIEW.EXE file for the **application/postscript** *application type.*

Sound Players

Once again, there are several different formats for sounds, and (repeat after me) none of them are compatible with one another. But, there are sound players available that will play most of the sounds you'll encounter out there on the big old Internet.

Wham

Wham (Waveform Hold and Modify) by Andrew Bulhak, is a good all-around sound player for Windows. It's easy to use, and it lets you see the sounds as you play them (see Figure 10.9).

You can get Wham via anonymous FTP from **ftp.cica.indiana.edu**, in the **/pub/pc/win3/sounds** directory. The current version at the time of this writing is 1.33, and the filename is **wham133.zip**.

Wham is shareware, but may be freely distributed. The developer asks that if you find it useful, you send him a $25-$30 donation.

Installing Wham

To install Wham, do the following:

1. Create a **WHAM** directory on your hard disk.

2. Uncompress the zip file into that directory.

3. Create an icon on your Windows desktop for the **WHAM.EXE** file.

4. Using File Manager (Windows 3.1) or Explorer (Windows 95), create an association for Wham in Windows for files with the following extensions: **WAV, AU, IFF, VOC, AIF.**

Figure 10.9:

Wham lets you see, as well as play sounds that you find on the Internet.

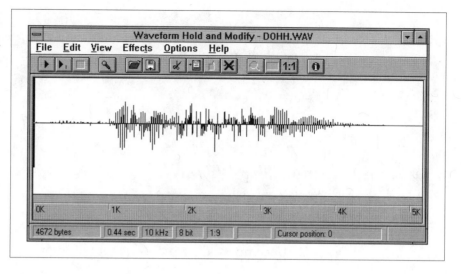

Using Wham

To use Wham, do the following:

1. Start up File Manager or the Windows Explorer and change to the directory where the .WAV, .AU, .IFF, .VOC, or .AIF file you want to play is located.

2. Double-click on the file to open it.

3. Wham starts up. Click on the **Play** button at the top of the window to start the sound.

*If you want to configure Wham as a client program viewer for .WAV, .AU, .IFF, .VOC, or .AIF files, configure your client program to use the WHAM.EXE file for the **audio/basic**, **audio/x-wav**, and **audio/x-aiff** application types.*

WPlany

WPlany, by Bill Neisius, is the most unobtrusive sound player you can find for Windows. No buttons to push, no annoying screens—all it does is play sounds. Which makes it the perfect sound player for your Gopher and Web browser client programs. WPlany plays .VOC, .AU, .WAV, .SND, and .IFF format sound files.

253

You can get WPlany via anonymous FTP from **ftp.cica.indiana.edu**, in the **/pub/pc/win3/sounds** directory. The current version at the time of this writing is 1.1, and the filename is **wplny11.zip**.

WPlany is freeware, and can be freely distributed.

Installing WPlany

To install WPlany, do the following:

1. Create a **WPLANY** directory on your hard disk.

2. Uncompress the zip file into that directory.

3. Create an association for WPlany in Windows for files with the following extentions: **WAV**, **AU**, **IFF**, **VOC**, **SND**.

Finding Sounds on the Internet

There are a number of sound archives on the Internet. Here are a couple of good starting points:

The Yahoo Multimedia Directory: Sounds. The Yahoo directory is always a good place to start searching. To get there, set your Web browser to the following URL:

> http://www.yahoo.com/yahoo/Computers/Multimedia/ Sound/.

Binary Sounds Newsgroups. Although not quite as extensive a selection as the *alt.binaries.pictures.** groups, you can find a number of different sounds here. To get there, just point your newsreader to the following hierarchy on Usenet:

> alt.binaries.sounds.*

Using WPlany

To use WPlany, do the following:

1. Start up File Manager or the Windows Explorer and change to the directory where the .WAV, .AU, .IFF, .VOC, or .SND file you want to play is located.

2. Double-click on the file to play it.

If you want to configure WPlany as a client program viewer for .WAV, .AU, .IFF, .VOC, or .SND files, configure your client program to use the WPLANY.EXE file for the **audio/basic**, **audio/x-wav**, *and* **audio/x-aiff** *application types.*

Now you have the tools you need to deal with just about any kind of file you're likely to encounter on your journeys through the Internet. I know some of this stuff may seem complicated, but once you have everything set up, you don't have to think about it any more.

Now, we'll move on to some of the other fun things you can do on the Internet, like chatting, talking, and playing games.

Communicating
with Netfolk

WHILE MANY THINGS you do on the Internet involve interacting with other people around the world, most of the time, you're actually communicating with a computer that someone else has communicated with previously. Very few things on the Internet involve real-time communication. Things are looking up in this area, however, and that's what this chapter is about. Live interactive communication—text, voice, and even video and games—are all available to you on the Internet, if you have the right tools.

While at this point the aim of most of these applications and services are strictly recreational, there are some real possibilities here for serious business-related purposes. Internet-based audio and video conferencing, for instance, would allow you to share ideas with colleagues from all over the world.

Internet Relay Chat

IRC, or Internet Relay Chat, has become one of the most popular things to do on the Internet. Originally written by Jarkko Oikarinen of Finland, the IRC protocol allows clients to communicate on what amount to text-based CB-channels.

There are IRC servers all over the world, and hundreds of different channels. Some channels are strictly talk-oriented, while others offer online games, and even interview sessions with famous or interesting people.

All IRC users go by a nickname. Your nickname is just what other folks online use to refer to you. Your nickname can be your actual name, a favorite word, or just something distinctive. Remember, the more common your nickname, the more likely it is that someone else is already using it. There's no law that says you can't use the same nickname as another user, it just might not be the best idea, especially if you happen to pick the same nickname used by someone who's well-known (perhaps for all the wrong reasons) on IRC.

Channel operators are people who are trusted to maintain the channel, and are usually folks who are regular visitors to that channel. If someone gets obnoxious, a channel operator can kick them out. Sometimes, you'll see channels where most of the participants are operators, while other times you'll see channels with only one or two operators. It all depends on the social atmosphere of that particular channel. Only a channel operator can designate someone to be a co-operator.

There are currently two major IRC networks: IRC and IRC Undernet. They're similar, although the general atmosphere and etiquette are slightly different. For more information about either of these networks, check out the FAQs in the RTFM anonymous FTP archive at **rtfm.mit.edu**, in the **/pub/usenet-by-group/alt.irc** directory.

List of IRC Servers

Here is just a brief list of IRC servers:

irc.bu.edu (Massachusetts)

irc.colorado.edu (Colorado)

tramp.cc.utexas.edu (Texas)

jello.qabc.uq.oz.au (Australia)

bim.itc.univie.ac.at (Austria)

irc.funet.fi (Finland)

cismhp.univ-lyon1.fr (France)

sokrates.informatik.uni-kl.de (Germany)

endo.wide.ad.jp (Japan)

irc.ethz.ch (Switzerland)

irc.nada.kth.se (Sweden)

The list of servers changes frequently. You can get a complete, up-to-date list of IRC servers via anonymous FTP from **cs-ftp.bu.edu**, in the **/irc/support/** directory. The filename is **servers.***yymmdd* (where *yymmdd* is the date).

*When you're first getting started on IRC you should try one of the channels that is geared toward new users. There are usually folks there who can help you out with commands, etiquette, and pointers to channels that you might be interested in. If you're on IRC, the help channel is **#irchelp**, and if you're on the IRC Undernet, the help channel is **#wasteland**.*

IRC Commands

When you first visit IRC, it can be pretty overwhelming. There are often people talking all at once on the popular channels, and it's easy to feel lost. So, I've put together a list of the basic IRC commands that you'll need to get around.

You can use these commands on all IRC servers. It doesn't matter how you get to an IRC server, whether from a Unix shell account, via a Telnet session, or from a Windows front-end, the commands are all the same.

If you're logging in from a Unix session, just type **irc *nickname***, where *nickname* is the name that you want to go by on IRC. If you're logging in using one of the Windows front ends, see the sections later in this chapter for information about how to log into an IRC server using these IRC clients.

Once you're logged in, you'll see a bunch of information rush by the screen. Most of it is a welcome banner.

The IRCII screen, shown in Figure 11.1, is displayed. You enter commands on the single line at the bottom of the screen, and the conversation and informational messages appear at the top. The status line just

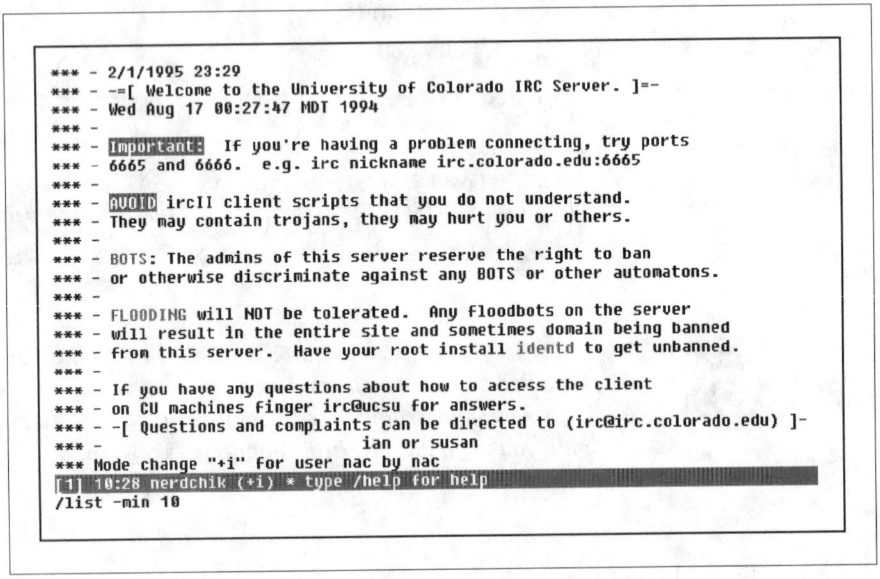

Figure 11.1:
IRCII is the most popular IRC client program for Unix.

```
*** - 2/1/1995 23:29
*** - -=[ Welcome to the University of Colorado IRC Server. ]=-
*** - Wed Aug 17 00:27:47 MDT 1994
*** -
*** - Important: If you're having a problem connecting, try ports
*** - 6665 and 6666.  e.g. irc nickname irc.colorado.edu:6665
*** -
*** - AVOID ircII client scripts that you do not understand.
*** - They may contain trojans, they may hurt you or others.
*** -
*** - BOTS: The admins of this server reserve the right to ban
*** - or otherwise discriminate against any BOTS or other automatons.
*** -
*** - FLOODING will NOT be tolerated.  Any floodbots on the server
*** - will result in the entire site and sometimes domain being banned
*** - from this server.  Have your root install identd to get unbanned.
*** -
*** - If you have any questions about how to access the client
*** - on CU machines finger irc@ucsu for answers.
*** - -[ Questions and complaints can be directed to (irc@irc.colorado.edu) ]-
*** -                          ian or susan
*** Mode change "+i" for user nac by nac
[1] 10:28 nerdchik (+i) * type /help for help
/list -min 10
```

above the input line shows your current nickname, the time, and the modes set for you and the channel that you're on. (For a list of the different modes, type **/help mode** in IRC.)

All IRC commands begin with a forward slash (/). If you forget the slash, your command will just be displayed as a message.

Commands for Starting Off

/nick *nickname* — Changes your nickname to the one you specify.

/list -min *n* **-wide** — Displays a list of channels. If you only want to see the ones with a minimum number of participants, use the **-min *n*** option, where ***n*** is the minimum number. To display the list so that they won't scroll off the top of your screen, use the **-wide** option.

/names -min *n* — Like **/list**, except this shows you all the nicknames of the people currently on each channel.

/join *#channel* — Lets you enter the channel you specify. Channel names always begin with the pound sign (#). Each channel is like a room—when you're in a channel, you can see the messages from everyone else who's in that particular channel.

/server *server-name* 6667 — Lets you jump to a different IRC server. The port number is usually 6667, although sometimes you'll see 6665 or 6666. You might want to change servers if the server you're on is too busy. Or, you might want to change to a server on a different IRC network.

IRC Commands When You're in a Channel

/away message Alerts everyone in the channel that you're going to leave your keyboard for a few minutes. The *message* is just an informational note to let people know why you're away, for example "gone to get a soda." When you return, just type **/away** again to return, and everyone on the channel will be alerted that you're back.

/ignore nickname Lets you ignore messages from a particular person. Messages from this person are not displayed on your screen.

/me action Sends a message to the channel telling everyone something that you're doing or thinking. Kind of like referring to yourself in the third person. For example, if John wants to tell everyone about the music he's listening to, he could type **/me is listening to the Beatles,** and everyone on the channel would see *[ACTION] John is listening to the Beatles.*

/invite nickname #channel Sends an invitation message to another user on IRC to come join the channel you specify.

/kick nickname Kicks someone out of the current channel. This option is only available to channel operators.

/leave or **/part** Allows you to leave the channel you're currently on. Either of these commands takes you out of the channel and leaves a message for the other users letting them know that you're leaving.

General IRC Commands

/clear	Clears your screen.
/lastlog	Displays the most recent messages that have come across the channel.
/notify *nickname*	Lets you know if the person you specify logs in to or out of IRC while you're there.
/msg *nickname message*	Lets you send a private message to someone.
/query *nickname*	Lets you initiate a private conversation with someone.
/quit or **/bye** or **/exit** or **/signoff**	Ends your IRC session.

Informational IRC Commands

/help *command*	Displays help on the command you specify.
/who *#channel*	Displays a list of the users on the channel you specify.
/whois *nickname*	Displays information about the person whose nickname you specify.
/whowas *nickname*	Displays information about someone who has recently left the IRC server.
/admin	Displays information about the IRC server.
/date or **/time**	Displays the date and time.
/motd	Displays the IRC server message of the day. This is the same message you see when you first log in.
/stats	Displays IRC server statistics.
/users	Displays a list of the users on the IRC server.

▶ *For a good overview and introduction to IRC, read the IRC Primer and IRC FAQ, available via anonymous FTP from* **cs-ftp.bu.edu**, *in the* **/irc/support** *directory.*

About Bots

One of the first things you'll probably notice when you log into an IRC server is some kind of warning about '*bots*. What is a 'bot? Well, it's short for robot, and is a script or program that can be put on an IRC channel and set to perform some sort of interactive function.

A 'bot may look at first like a real person, and, if programmed well, may even be able to pass for one. But, for the most part, 'bots are usually found performing a specific function, such as running a game.

But aspiring 'bot programmers occasionally let loose a 'bot on IRC that can cause problems for others, such as flooding a channel with useless drivel. For this reason, many IRC server administrators do not allow 'bots of any kind, and actively search for and remove them if found.

Most authorized 'bots usually have "'bot" in their names, for example, "GameBot."

For more information about 'bots, and IRC in general, check out the *alt.irc.** newsgroups on Usenet.

IRCII For Windows

IRCII For Windows, by Troy Rollo, is a very basic IRC client for Windows. Nothing fancy, but if you're used to using IRCII, the most popular IRC software for Unix, you'll appreciate its familiar look and feel (see Figure 11.2.).

You can get IRCII For Windows via anonymous FTP from **cs-ftp.bu.edu**, in the **/irc/clients/pc/windows** directory. The current version at the time of this writing is 2.6, and the filename is **ircii2_6.zip**.

Figure 11.2:

IRCII for Windows offers the familiarity of the Unix IRCII software with the convenience of a Windows front-end.

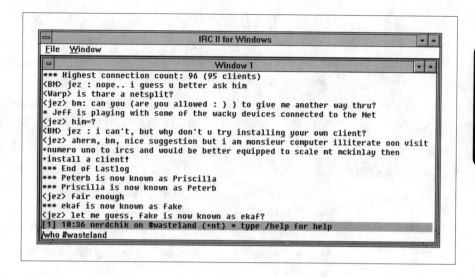

```
                         IRC II for Windows                    ▼ ▲
 File  Window
                            Window 1                           ▼ ▲
*** Highest connection count: 96 (95 clients)
<BM> jez : nope.. i guess u better ask him
<Warp> is thare a netsplit?
<jez> bm: can you (are you allowed : ) ) to give me another way thru?
* Jeff is playing with some of the wacky devices connected to the Net
<jez> him=?
<BM> jez : i can't, but why don't u try installing your own client?
<jez> aherm, bm, nice suggestion but i am monsieur computer illiterate oon visit
+numero uno to ircs and would be better equipped to scale mt mckinlay then
+install a client!
*** End of Lastlog
*** Peterb is now known as Priscilla
*** Priscilla is now known as Peterb
<jez> fair enough
*** ekaf is now known as fake
<jez> let me guess, fake is now known as ekaf?
[1] 10:36 nerdchik on #wasteland (+nt) * type /help for help
/who #wasteland
```

IRCII for Windows is freeware, and may be freely distributed.

Installing IRCII For Windows

To install IRCII For Windows, do the following:

1. Create an **IRCII** directory on your hard disk.

2. Uncompress the zip file in this directory, using the **-d** option, so that the files are extracted in the appropriate subdirectories. (Note that both UnZip and WinZip both default to use the -d option.)

3. Create an icon on your Windows desktop for the **IRC.EXE** file.

To configure IRCII for Windows, do the following:

1. Open the **IRCII.INI** file, using the Windows Notepad or any text editor program.

2. Change the entry under **[RealNames]** to your name, the **Server=** to the name of an IRC server near you, and the **Nick=** to your default nickname.

3. Move the IRCII.INI file to your WINDOWS directory.

Using IRCII for Windows

Using IRCII for Windows is amazingly similar to using IRCII on a Unix system. See the *IRC Commands* section earlier in this chapter for an overview of IRCII commands.

You type your commands at the bottom of the screen, and they, along with the comments and messages, appear on the top half of the screen.

WSIRC

WSIRC, by Caesar M. Samsi, is the Cadillac of IRC clients for Windows (see Figure 11.3). It's easy to use, and lets you execute many of the more commonly used IRC commands just by clicking on a button.

WSIRC makes it easy for even a novice to get up and running on IRC without stumbling.

Figure 11.3:
WSIRC is the best, and easiest to use IRC client for Windows.

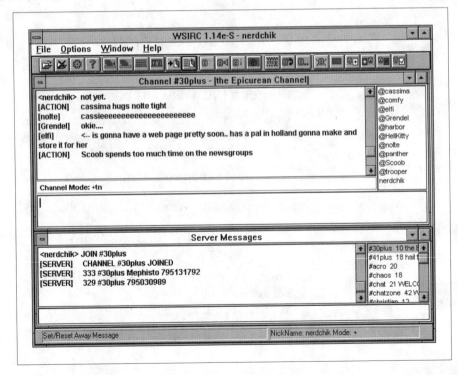

WSIRC is available via anonymous FTP from **cs-ftp.bu.edu**, in the **/irc/ clients/pc/windows** directory. The current version at the time of this writing is 1.14e-S, and the filename is **wsirc14e.zip**.

The WSIRC distribution zip file contains both shareware and freeware versions. The shareware version costs $39 to register, and offers additional features not included in the freeware version.

Installing WSIRC

To install WSIRC, do the following:

1. Create a **WSIRC** directory on your hard disk.

2. Uncompress the zip file in that directory.

3. Create an icon for the **WSIRCG.EXE** file on your hard disk.

To configure WSIRC, do the following:

1. Start WSIRC. A message box will appear asking you to complete the server options. The help file also appears.

2. Minimize the help file for now, and click on the **WS-IRC Setup Options** dialog box. Enter the IRC server that you want to use, your nickname, username, e-mail address, and PC name in the appropriate fields. When you're done, click on **OK.** A message will appear reminding you that the changes will take effect on your next connect.

3. Select File ➤ Connect. You will be connected to the server of your choice. When you first log on, you'll see a series of welcome messages scroll by.

Using WSIRC

When you start up WS-IRC, it will connect you to the server you specified when you configured it.

You can use all of the same commands shown in the *IRC Commands* section earlier in this chapter. You can also enter many of them automatically by clicking on the buttons at the top of your window. Here are just a few of the commands you can access from the button bar:

To find out what the function of each button is, wave your mouse cursor over each of the buttons. The description is displayed at the bottom of your window.

To get help, click on the Help Contents icon.

To list the available channels, click on the List Channels button.

To join a channel, click on the Join a Channel button.

To mark yourself as being away, click on the Set/Reset Away Message button, enter a message and click on OK. To mark yourself as being back, click on it again, and click on OK.

To do an action within a channel, click on the Action in Channel button.

Sending Messages on the Internet

If you have other friends on the Internet, and you'd like to send messages or have real-time text conversations with them when you're on-line, you can! There are several programs available which allow you to exchange text messages with other users, in both Unix and Windows.

Talking in Unix

The Unix Talk program provides a convenient way to converse with someone else on the Internet. When you open a Talk channel with a friend, you'll see a split screen, like the one shown in Figure 11.4, with your friend's words displayed on the bottom half, and your words displayed on the top.

Talk is available on most Unix systems. If it's not available on your system, contact your system administrator to find out if they can install it.

Figure 11.4:
With the Unix Talk program, you can have a real-time text conversation with other users from around the world.

```
[Connection established]
I'm fine -- how are you?




------------------------------------------------------------------------
Hi!  How are you doing?



```

Using Talk

To use Talk, do the following:

1. Type **talk *username@hostname*** at a Unix prompt. You'll see a message telling you that Talk is waiting for your party to respond.

If the person you want to talk to is on a SLIP or PPP connection, you need to use the complete hostname. For more information, see Finding the **Right Hostname** *later on in this chapter.*

2. When the person responds, you'll see a message telling you that the connection is established. Now, start typing, and your words will be seen on both computers, as will your friend's.

3. When you're done talking, press Ctrl+C to end the call.

WinTalk

WinTalk, by Glen Daniels, is a Windows version of the Unix Talk program. It uses the same protocol as the Unix version of Talk, so you can use it to open a Talk channel with anyone who's on a system that has a version of Talk installed.

269

WinTalk is similar to the Unix version of Talk, in that it allows you to see both your words and your friends in a split-screen (see Figure 11.5). But it also adds some additional features, like the ability to keep an address book of other users, so you can open a talk session with someone just by clicking on their name.

Figure 11.5:
With WinTalk, you can have real-time conversations with friends on the Internet.

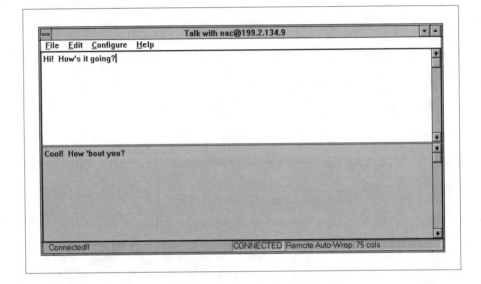

You can get WinTalk via anonymous FTP from **ftp.elf.com**, in the **/pub/ wintalk** directory. The current version at the time of this writing is 1.21, and the filename is **wtalk121.zip**.

WinTalk is freeware, and may be freely distributed. There is also a commercial version available, WinTalk Pro, which adds the ability to do call screening, and automatic call answering. WinTalk Pro currently costs $20.

Installing WinTalk

To install WinTalk, do the following:

1. Create a **WINTALK** directory on your hard disk.

2. Uncompress the zip file into that directory.

3. Move the .DLL file to your WINDOWS\SYSTEM subdirectory.

4. Create an icon on your Windows desktop for the **WINTALK.EXE** file.

To configure WinTalk, do the following:

1. Start WinTalk.

2. You'll see a message telling you that WinTalk requires at least one local username. Click on **OK**.

3. The Local usernames dialog box appears. Enter your user name in the box and click on **Add**. Then click on **OK**. WinTalk is then ready to run—you'll see the WinTalk icon minimized at the bottom of your screen.

Using WinTalk

To open a WinTalk Session with someone, do the following:

1. Click once on the WinTalk icon with your left mouse button (Windows 3.1) or right mouse button (Windows 95). A menu of options appears.

2. Select **Talk**. The Open Talk Connection dialog box appears.

3. Enter the address of the person you want to talk with in the **To (user@host)** field, using the person's user ID and hostname. If the person you want to call is on a SLIP or PPP connection, you need to enter the *full* hostname. For more information, see *Finding the Right Hostname* below.

Sticky

Sticky, by Harry Feroka, Kent Fitch, and John Dovey, is a fun and at times useful little program that lets you send short messages to another

Finding the Right Hostname

Figuring out someone's full hostname can be a little tricky, because it isn't always obvious what hostname they're using. Here are some guidelines to help you find the right hostname:

- If the person you want to talk with is on a Unix system, their address should just be *username@hostname*. For example, joe@host.com.

- If the person you want to talk to is on a SLIP or PPP account, their address is *username@IPname.hostname*. The tricky part here is figuring out what the IP name is.

The *IP name* is the name of the connection, and is different depending on the system. It may be slip123.host.com, or it might be 123.host.com, or 123.slip.host.com, or it might be something totally different. If the person you want to talk to doesn't know what their IP Name is, ask them to open a Telnet or FTP session to another host, and see if their full hostname, which includes the IP Name is displayed. If they can telnet to a Unix system on which they have an account, they can type **w myusername**, to display the full hostname.

Alternately, most of these programs will let you substitute the IP address for a full hostname. But if you're on a system that uses dynamic IP addressing, the address changes every time you log in. But you can find out what your current IP address is by checking your Winsock dialer. Both Trumpet Winsock and Chameleon Sampler display this information. See Appendix B for information about how to look up your IP address using either of these packages.

Also, if you know your IP address, but don't know what your IP name is, you can use the NSLookup program discussed in Chapter 12 to look up your IP name.

Sticky user. When you send a sticky to someone, it pops up on their screen, like a system message. It's sort of the Internet equivalent of passing little notes back and forth (see Figure 11.6).

Figure 11.6:
Sticky lets you and
your friends send little
notes to each other

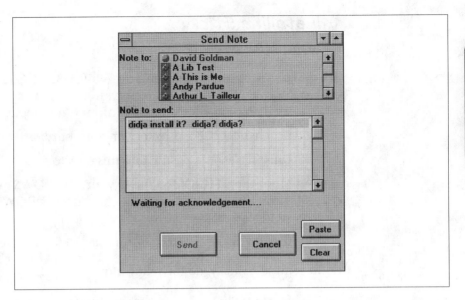

> You can get Sticky via anonymous FTP from the SimTel archive at **oak
> .oakland.edu**, in the **/SimTel/win3/winsock** directory. The current ver-
> sion at the time of this writing is .8, and the filename is **sticky08.zip**.

Sticky is guiltware—it's free, but if you feel guilty about using it, the developer would appreciate it if you make a donation to the Common-
wealth Scientific and Industrial Research Organization (CSIRO), which
is the organization that sponsored Sticky's development. It can be
freely distributed, provided that it is not resold.

*This program does not come with the VBRUN300.DLL file, which is the runtime
library file required for all applications written in Microsoft Visual Basic™ 3.0.
Check your WINDOWS\SYSTEM directory to see if you already have it installed.
If not, you can get it from the SimTel archives at* **oak.oakland.edu**, *in the*
/SimTel/win3/dll *directory. The filename is* **vbrun300.zip**.

Installing Sticky

To install Sticky, do the following:

1. Check to make sure you have VBRUN300.DLL installed in your WINDOWS\SYSTEM directory. If not, get a copy of it and install it there. (See previous note for information about obtaining this file.)

2. Create a **STICKY** directory on your hard disk.

3. Uncompress the zip file into this directory.

4. Move the **STICKY.INI** file to your WINDOWS directory, and move the .DLL and .VBX files to your WINDOWS\SYSTEM subdirectory.

5. Create an icon on your Windows desktop for the **STICKY.EXE** file.

To configure Sticky, do the following:

1. Start up Sticky. The program starts up minimized, so maximize it now.

2. Select Configure ➤ Other Sticky's. Enter your name in the **Your friendly name** field.

3. Select Configure ➤ Auto Response. Enter your automatic response message in the box provided. This is the message that will be sent if you have Auto Message turned on. It's a good idea to set this if you plan to be away from your computer for a little while.

Using Sticky

Now you're ready to send a test sticky to the developer. Do the following:

1. Select **Send Sticky**.

2. Select the **A This is me** address, and enter your message below. Enter your name, e-mail address, whether you want to be included in his published list of Sticky users, and what times you're logged in (relative to GMT). Click on **Send** to send the sticky.

3. You'll get a response back, which lets you if there have been any updates to your version, and how to get the latest patch.

As you can see, using Sticky is pretty straightforward. Here are a couple of other options you might want to try with Sticky:

To include the address of someone who's sent you a sticky, click on the Add Address button.

To add a new address to your list, select Configure ➤ Other Sticky's. Enter the person's name in the Friendly Name field, and their hostname address in the Machine Address field. When you're done, click on the Add button. Click on OK.

To edit an entry in your list of Sticky Hosts, select Configure ➤ Other Sticky's, select the entry you want to edit, and click on the Modify button. Click on OK.

To sort the entries in your list of Sticky Hosts, select Configure ➤ Other Sticky's, and click on Sort. Click on OK.

To include a message you've received in your response, click on the Copy to Clipboard button. Then click on the Reply button, and click on Paste to insert the original message.

Voice of the Internet

I suspect that voice applications are going to be the next big boom on the Internet. At the time I write this, there are only a couple available, but if their extreme popularity is any indication, there will be many more products appearing shortly. Although I tested a couple, Internet Phone is currently the only product that's ready for prime time, but there are others following close behind. Stay tuned...

Internet Phone

Internet Phone, by Vocaltec, represents a whole new concept in Internet communication. It's kind of a cross between IRC and Ham radio. Internet Phone requires that you have a sound card installed in your system, with speakers and a microphone.

When you start up Internet Phone and connect to an Internet Phone IRC server, you can connect with any of the users available, and start up a live voice conversation with them (see Figure 11.7).

Figure 11.7:
Internet Phone lets you talk with other users on the Internet, using your sound card, microphone, and speakers.

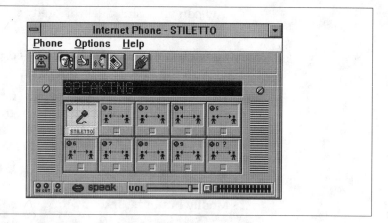

You can get Internet Phone via anonymous FTP from **ftp.vocaltec.com**, in the **/pub** directory. The current version at the time of this writing is 2.5, build 6a, and the filename is **iphone6a.exe**, which is a self-extracting archive file.

Internet Phone is shareware and costs $49 to register. You can try out the demo version for 30 days. The demo version is fully functional, but only allows you to speak for 1 minute per session.

Installing Internet Phone

To install Internet Phone, do the following:

1. Create an **IPHONE** directory on your hard disk.

2. Uncompress the self-extracting archive file into that directory.

3. Run the **ADDICONS.EXE** file to automatically create the Internet Phone icons on your Windows desktop.

To configure Internet Phone, do the following:

1. Start Internet Phone.

2. You'll see a message asking you to enter your personal informa-tion. Click on **OK**. The User Information dialog box then appears.

3. Enter your user information. Click on **OK**.

4. The license agreement is displayed. Read it and click on **Accept**.

5. Now you'll see a message reminding you that this is an evaluation copy, and can only be used for 30 days and only allows you to talk for 60 seconds at a time.

6. The next message informs you that Internet Phone needs to test your system performance. Click on **OK**. If your system scores less than 50, you cannot run Internet phone.

7. Then you'll be asked if you want to run the Quick Tour. If you're new to Internet Phone, you should take a look through the Quick Tour. It explains how to use Internet Phone and gives you some good tips.

Using Internet Phone

To use Internet Phone, do the following:

1. Connect to an Internet Phone IRC server by clicking on the electrical plug button on the button bar.

2. Select one of the servers from the list box and click on OK. The two primary servers are **irc.vocaltec.com** and **irc.pulver.com**. It really doesn't matter which server you select, because they're all on the same network.

3. At the Connect to IRC dialog box, click on **OK**.

Once you're connected, here are a few options available to you:

To see a list of people on the server, click on the one of the ten connection buttons displayed in the middle of the window. When you click on one of these buttons, a pop-up menu appears. Click on Set Button option. The Set Button dialog box appears.

To select someone to call, select the name at the left side of the Set Button dialog box, and double-click on it. If they're available, and accept the call, you'll be connected. Internet Phone is voice activated, so you just need to speak to talk. But remember, you can't both talk at the same time. Once one person starts talking, the other person cannot speak.

To change the voice activation level, click on the green and red control bar at the bottom left hand corner. When you speak, the volume level of your voice is shown as a light green bar moving from left to right, just like a sound level meter on a stereo system. The knob shows the microphone activation level. If your voice isn't loud enough to reach this knob, the voice activation won't kick in, and the other person won't be able to hear you. Try setting this level low enough that you'll be able to talk, but not so low that the noise of your computer will activate it.

To change the volume, move the volume knob (VOL) left (down) or right (up).

To disconnect from a conversation, click on the connection button (1 through 10) with your right mouse button and select Disconnect.

To clear the connection button, click on the connection button (1 through 10) with your right mouse button, and select Clear Button from the pop-up menu.

To disconnect from the Internet Phone IRC server, select Phone ➤ IRC Disconnect.

 For more information about Internet Phone, check out the Internet Phone home page at **http://www.vocaltec.com**.

Sesame

Sesame, by Ubique, is an audio and text conversation extension to your Netscape or Mosaic Web browser, and is part of Ubique's "Virtual Places" concept. It allows you to connect to Web pages, and talk to people there, either by text or by voice. It's a fascinating concept that opens up a lot of possibilities, for example, the ability to hold classes, demonstrations, or conferences long-distance, without the need for any special equipment, other than an Internet connection, sound card, and microphone (see Figure 11.8).

The version I tried is still in Alpha testing, and the documentation is pretty sparse, but this product is in heavy development and should be completed by the time you read this.

Figure 11.8:

Sesame is a voice and text conversation extension for Netscape and Mosaic—with it, you can converse with other people who are visiting the same Web page as you.

You can get the Sesame client program via anonymous FTP from **ftp.ubique.com**, in the **/pub/outgoing/pc** directory. The current version at the time of this writing is 0.9.8A, and the filename is **install.exe**, which is a

Sesame is a demo version of the Virtual Places client program, and does not include audio support. The full-featured client program is a commercial product, and costs $49 per copy.

Installing Sesame

Sesame requires that you have either Netscape or NCSA Mosaic installed on your system. For more information on Netscape and Mosaic, see Chapter 7.

Sesame also requires that you have Win32s installed. For more information about getting and installing Win32s, see the *NCSA Mosaic* section in Chapter 7.

To install Sesame, do the following:

1. Run the self-extracting archive file in an empty directory to uncompress the setup files.

2. Run the **SETUP.EXE** file. Accept the default settings, if possible.

To configure Sesame, do the following:

1. Start Sesame, using the Open Sesame icon.

2. The Welcome screen is displayed. Read the instructions for completing your personal business card, and click on **OK**.

3. The Sesame—Personal Business Card screen is displayed. Enter your personal information in the spaces provided (name, e-mail address, address, home page, address) and click on **Save**. Then click on **OK**.

4. Sesame will then start up. First, Sesame loads itself, and then it starts up your Web browser.

5. If you have a little .GIF file that you want to use for your personal "face," you can configure it by selecting Options ➤ Preferences. Click on the **Browse** button in the icons section to select your .GIF file. The file must be 48x64 pixels wide. If you don't have a face, you can get a cartoon face from Ubique's server (more on this later).

Using Sesame

You need to connect to a server that runs Ubique's Doors server software to be able to use Sesame. The best place to start is Ubique's home page at URL **http://www.ubique.com/**. If other users are online, you'll see their pictures.

To get around using Sesame, you only need to know a few things:

To see someone's business card, click your right mouse button over the person's face, then select Show Business Card. You'll see the information that this person has entered in their business card info.

To start a conversation with someone, click your right mouse button over the person's face, then select Start Conversation. If you're both audio-enabled, you can talk voice, otherwise you can send text messages to one another using the Sesame screen.

To talk (voice), click on the speak button at the lower right corner of the Sesame screen. The button changes to a microphone. Now you can talk into your microphone. When you're done speaking, click on this button again.

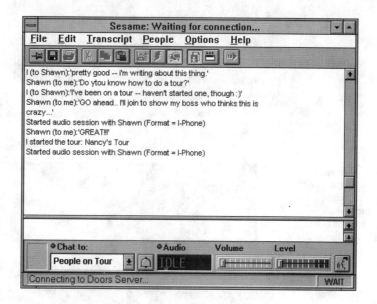

To type a message, just type in the field at the bottom of the Sesame screen.

To say something to everyone on the page, select People in Place from the Chat to: list box.

To find out who else is in the same place as you, select Transcript ➤ Who's in this Place.

To find out who else is on the same server as you, select Transcript ➤ Who's in this Server.

To save a copy of a text conversation you've had with someone, select File ➤ Save Transcript.

To join a tour, click with your right mouse button on a an existing tour, and select Join Tour. When you join a tour, the "driver" can take you to anywhere on the Web.

To start your own Tour, select People ➤ Start Tour. Select the type of tour: Virtual Places tour or Web (non-Virtual Places) tour, for either two or ten people. When you start a tour, you are in the driver's seat—anywhere you go, your passengers go as well.

To leave a tour, select People ➤ Stop/Leave Tour.

CU-SeeMe

CU-SeeMe, from the Cornell University Information Technology department, is a real-time video conferencing utility that runs on the Internet. It was originally developed for the Macintosh platform, but the Windows version is currently in active development (see Figure 11.9).

Figure 11.9:
With CU-SeeMe, you can participate in, or just watch video conferences with people from all over the world.

To use the Windows version of CU-SeeMe to view, all you need is a PC running Windows. If you want to be able to transmit, however, you need a video camera and a video digitizing card in your computer. Sound requires a compatible sound card, and a high-speed connection—the recommended minimum is 32kpbs, which you can't get with a modem connection, unless you have ISDN.

With CU-SeeMe, you can have one-on-one conversations with someone, or you can participate in a conference with multiple people, with the use of a "Reflector" server, which redirects the video output to multiple locations. The Reflector server software only runs on Unix systems.

But despite the heavy hardware requirements, CU-SeeMe is still pretty darned cool, even running in view only mode on a PC.

> You can get CUSeeMe via anonymous FTP from **cuseeme.cornell.edu**, in the **/pub/CU-SeeMe** directory. The current version at the time of this writing is 0.34, Beta 4, and the filename is **cuseeme.zip**. This program is in heavy development, so there will probably be a newer version there by the time you read this.

CU-SeeMe is freeware, and may be freely distributed.

Installing CU-SeeMe

To install CU-SeeMe, do the following:

1. Create a **CUSEEME** directory on your hard disk.

2. Uncompress the zip file into this directory.

3. Create an icon on your Windows desktop for the **CUSEEME.EXE** file.

To configure CU-SeeMe, do the following:

1. Start up CU-SeeMe.

2. Select File ➤ Preferences.

3. Enter your name in the **Your Name** field.

4. You can also set the maximum number of video windows or the maximum or minimum transmission settings (in KB/sec.) if you'd like, although the default settings will work just find in most cases.

Using CU-SeeMe

To use CU-SeeMe, do the following:

1. To connect to a server, select Connection ➤ Connect. If you don't have a video card and drivers installed, the **I Will Send Video** option will be grayed out. If you do, you'll be able to send as well as receive video.

2. A list of public reflector sites is listed in the drop-down list box. Try selecting one.

3. If the server you select is running, you'll probably see a connection message of the day, and you'll start seeing faces pop up on your screen. If not, you'll get a *No Response* message.

 For more information about CU-SeeMe, including pointers to some really cool CU-SeeMe sites, check out the CU-SeeMe page at the State University of New York, Plattsburgh, **http://bio444.beaumont.plattsburgh.edu/CUSeeMe.html.**

MUD Clients

MUDs, MUSHes, MOOs, and MUSEs, are all very popular gathering places on the Internet. All of them evolved from the original dungeon games of the early 1980s, but have grown and matured quite a bit since then.

Although all MUDs and MUD-like games and environments were designed primarily to be accessed via a standard Telnet session, several Windows utilities have appeared recently to help you get around your MUD of choice. These utilities let you execute commands with just a click of a mouse button, letting you navigate with ease.

MUDMan

MUDMan makes MUDding easy. It gives you point-and-click access to all the basic movement commands you'll need (see Figure 11.10), plus the ability to program your own macro buttons, so you can issue more complicated commands, just by clicking a button.

What's a MUD? A MUSH? A MUSE?

MUDs, or Multi-User Dimensions, are an experiment in virtual reality, which originated with the early online dungeon games of the early 1980s. A MUD can be a lot of things. Some MUDs are dungeon-like games, where each user assumes a character on a quest, and there's lots of dragon slaying and pillaging going on, while others are more social, allowing users to interact, chat, and gossip. It all depends on the MUD.

Other variants are MUSHes, Multi-User Simulated Hallucinations, which are similar to MUDs, but allow more creativity and freedom among the users.

MUSEs, or Multi-User Simulated Environments, are primarily for educational purposes, the best-known of which is the MicroMUSE at MIT, which lets users play around in a simulated world of the future.

For more information, you should check out Lydia Leong's MUD Information Page on the Web, which provides an extensive collection of information and links to resources all over the Internet. To get there, set your Web browser to the following URL:

http://www.cis.upenn.edu/~lwl/mudinfo.html.

Figure 11.10:
MUDMan is an easy-to-use and easy-to-configure MUD navigational tool.

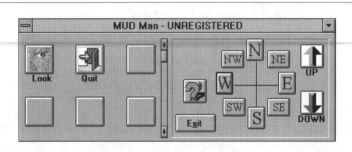

You can get MUDMan via anonymous FTP from **ftp.cica.indiana.edu**, in the **/pub/pc/win3/misc** directory. The current version at the time of this writing is 1.2 and the filename is **mudman12.zip**.

MUDMan is shareware, and costs $9 to register. Registration gets you additional and enhanced macro buttons, more button graphics, and program updates.

 *This program does not come with the VBRUN300.DLL file, which is the runtime library file required for all applications written in Microsoft Visual Basic 3.0. Check your WINDOWS\ SYSTEM directory to see if you already have it installed. If not, you can get it from the SimTel archives at **oak.oakland.edu**, in the **/SimTel/win3/dll** directory. The filename is **vbrun300.zip**.*

Installing MUDMan

To install MUDMan, do the following:

1. Check to make sure you have VBRUN300.DLL installed in your WINDOWS\SYSTEM directory. If you don't, get a copy of it and install it there.

2. Create a **MUDMAN** directory on your hard disk.

2. Uncompress the zip file in that directory.

3. Create an icon on your Windows Desktop for the **MUDMAN.EXE** file.

Using MUDMan

To use MUDMan, do the following:

1. Start up MUDMan. You'll see a reminder that this program is shareware. Click on **OK**.

2. You'll be prompted to start up your communications program and enter the desired MUD. Using your telnet client application, connect to the MUD you want to participate in. Then click on **OK**.

3. You'll be prompted to select your communications program from the list box. Select your telnet application and click on **OK**.

Now MUDMan starts up, and the floating toolbar appears on top of your Windows desktop. It has all the directional commands you need, so you don't need to type them in by hand.

To issue a command, just click a button, and the command is issued automatically.

To customize the toolbar buttons, click on the button with your right mouse button. A Customize MUD Man Toolbar dialog box appears. Enter your description for the button and the actual command you want it to issue in the appropriate fields. You can then select one of the pre-configured button graphics by moving the sliding bar right or left.

MUDWin

MUDWin, by Sam Denton, is another MUD client for Windows that is currently under development (see Figure 11.11). It allows you to make connections from within MUDWin, and lets you save configuration information for all the MUDs you visit. It offers customizable buttons, and all the basic commands you'll need to get around.

Figure 11.11:
MUDWin is a MUD client application and MUD toolbar all in one.

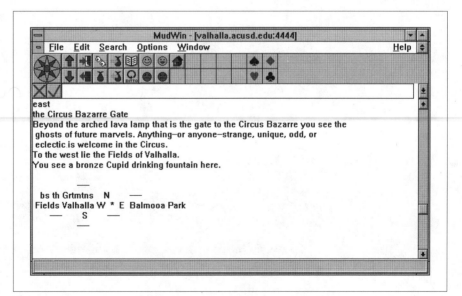

> You can get MUDWin from **ftp.microserve.com** in the **/pub/msdos/win-sock** directory. The current version at the time of this writing is 1.06, and the filename is **mudwin.zip**.

MUDWin is currently freeware, but the developer retains the copyright to the program.

Installing MUDWin

To install MUDWin, do the following:

1. Create a **MUDWIN** directory on your hard disk.

2. Uncompress the zip file into this directory.

3. Create an icon on your Windows desktop for the **MUDWIN.EXE** file.

Using MUDWin

To use MUDWin, do the following:

1. Start MUDWin.

2. Select File ➤ New to enter a new MUD location. The New Connection dialog box appears. Enter the host name and port number in the appropriate fields and click **OK**. You'll then be connected to your host.

Once you're connected to your MUD, you can enter commands in the text entry line at the top of the window. Here are some other things you can do with MUDWin:

To execute one of the button commands, click on the button.

To send movement commands, click on the appropriate portion of the compass.

To turn off echoing of commands, select Options ➤ Local Echo.

To change the font, select Options ➤ Font.

Games

There are all kinds of games you can play on the Internet with other folks, like backgammon, chess, and even Chinese chess, just to name a few.

These games have been available to telnet users for years. But just recently, developers have written programs that allow you to play these real-time games with others, and use a real Windows graphical interface. Here are just a few of these programs.

FIBS for Windows

If you're a backgammon fiend, you'll absolutely love FIBS for Windows (First International Backgammon Server for Windows) by Robin Davies. Well, maybe you'll hate it, because it's very addictive. FIBS for Windows lets you access the First International Backgammon Server, using a Windows front-end (see Figure 11.12). FIBS for Windows connects you to FIBS, then lets you log into the server and play all you want.

Figure 11.12:
FIBS for Windows lets you play backgammon with players from all over the world.

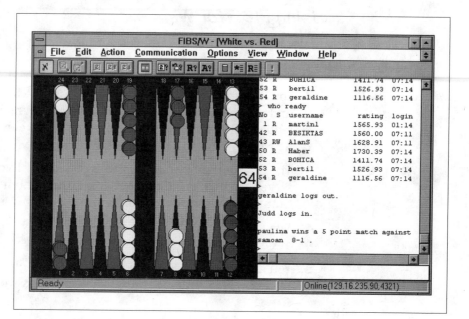

You can get FIBS/W via anonymous FTP from **resudox.net** in the **/pub/pc/windows/games/fibsw** directory. The current version at the time of this writing is 1.32, and the filename is **fibsw132.zip**.

FIBS for Windows is shareware and costs $40 to register. You may use the product for free for a 10-day evaluation period before you need to register it. After that, you will see a 30-second message pop up on the screen whenever you start the program reminding you to register the program.

Installing FIBS for Windows

To install FIBS for Windows, do the following:

1. Create a **FIBSW** directory on your hard disk.

2. Uncompress the zip file in this directory.

3. Create an icon on your Windows desktop for the **FIBSW.EXE** file.

Using FIBS for Windows

To use FIBS for Windows, do the following:

1. Start FIBS for Windows.

2. You'll see a message notifying you about the license agreement, and reminding you that this is shareware. When you are done reading the license agreement, close the window and click on **Agree**.

3. The Backgammon main screen is displayed. To connect to the server, click on the **Connect/Disconnect** button, or select Communication ➤ Connect.

4. The Port Settings dialog box appears. Select Winsock from the list of ports, and click on **OK**.

5. You'll then see the FIBS logon screen. If you already have an account on FIBS, enter your username and password, if not, enter **Guest**.

Now that you're connected, here are a few options available to you when using FIBS for Windows:

To see what each of the buttons does, wave the mouse cursor over the buttons. A description of the button's function will appear at the bottom of the window.

To see a list of everyone who's logged into the server, click on the Show All Players button.

To see a list of all the players who are ready to play, click on the Show Players Ready to Play button.

To signal other players that you're ready to play, click on the R? button.

To signal other players that you're away from your keyboard, click on the A? button.

To disconnect from the server, click on the Connect/Disconnect button.

To see a complete list of FIBS commands, type /help in the command window at the bottom right corner of the window.

SLICS

SLICS, by Don Fong, is a nice Windows interface for the many public chess servers on the Internet (see Figure 11.13). It allows you to connect with the server, log in, and start playing right away.

You can get SLICS via anonymous FTP from **ics.onenet.net**, in the **/pub/chess/Win3** directory. The current version at the time of this writing is 2.0g, and the filename is **slics20g.exe**, which is a self-extracting archive file.

SLICS is shareware. Registration costs around $5, and gets you regular updates from the developer.

Figure 11.13:
SLICS is a Windows front end that connects you to the many chess servers on the Internet.

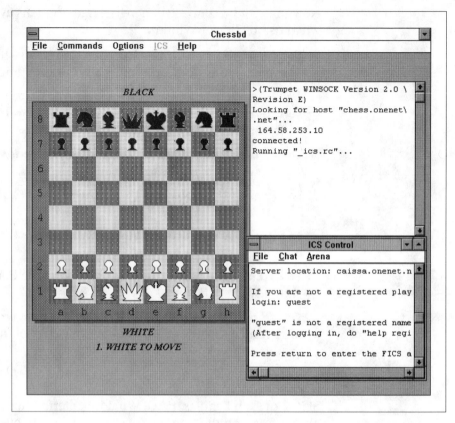

There are several chess servers on the Internet, and most of them are free. See Internet Chess Servers at the end of this section for a list of servers.

Installing SLICS

To install SLICS, do the following:

1. Create a **SLICS** directory on your hard disk.

2. Run the self-extracting archive file in this directory to uncompress the files.

3. Create an icon on your Windows desktop that points to the **CHESSBD.EXE** file.

To configure SLICS for use with a Chess server, do the following:

1. Copy the **EX_ICS.RC** file to **_ICS.RC**.

2. Using a text editor, like the Windows Notepad, open this file.

3. Change the `%icsoutput dfong\n` entry to reflect your login name on the chess server. For example, if you want to log in as guest, you'd change this entry to `%icsoutput guest\n`.

4. Change the `%icssend Diana` entry to reflect your password (unless your password is Diana). If you're logging in as **guest**, you can just delete the password.

Using SLICS

To use SLICS to connect to an Internet chess server, do the following:

1. Start SLICS.

2. Select ICS from the menu bar. The ICS dialog box appears.

3. Enter the address of the server in the ICS host field, and the Port number (usually 5000), in the port field.

4. Make sure the ICS login script field points to the configuration file that you created when you configured SLICS. If it does, then click on **OK**. SLICS then contacts the server, and logs you in.

Internet Chess Servers

There are several chess servers on the Internet. However, this is one of those things on the Internet that tends to change. To keep up to date on the comings and goings of chess servers on the Internet, check out the **rec.games.chess** newsgroup on Usenet.

Internet Chess Club. (Formerly Internet Chess Server) This is the most popular chess site on the Internet, although at the time I'm writing this, they have just announced a $49/per year registration fee, which could put a big dent in their popularity. In spite of this, ICC is the most respected chess server on the Internet, offering ratings for registered players, and drawing from all levels of expertise, from beginner on up to Grandmaster level. To get there, use **chess.lm.com**, Port **5000**.

FICS Servers. These servers run a different version of the server software, Free Internet Chess Server, and are located at several spots around the globe. To get to one of the FICS servers, use one of these addresses:

ics.onenet.net, Port **5000**

chess.pitt.edu, Port **5000**

rogue.coe.ohio-state.edu, Port **5000**

dds.hactic.nl, Port **5000** (Holland)

helium.daimi.aau.dk, Port **5000** (Germany)

lux.latrob.edu.au, Port **5000** (Australia)

 ▶ *For more information about chess server commands, type* **help** *at the chess server prompt when you get connected.*

Winsock Chess

Winsock Chess, by Donald Munro, was originally based on the Unix GNU Chess program. It allows two players to play chess over the Internet (see Figure 11.14).

You can get Winsock Chess from **ics.onenet.net**, in the **/pub/chess/Win3** directory. The current version at the time of this writing is beta 1, and the filename is **wschesb1.zip**.

Winsock Chess is freeware, and may be freely distributed in accordance with the Free Software Foundation guidelines.

Figure 11.14:
Winsock Chess lets you play chess with a friend over the Internet.

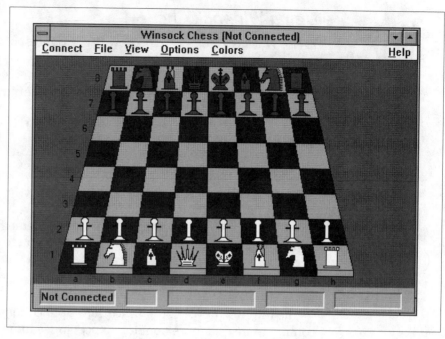

Installing Winsock Chess

To install Winsock Chess, do the following:

1. Create a **WSCHESS** directory on your hard disk.

2. Uncompress the zip file into this directory.

3. Create an icon on your Windows desktop for the **WSCHESS.EXE** file.

To configure Winsock Chess, do the following:

1. Start Winsock Chess.

2. Select Connect ➤ Communication Type.

3. Click on the **Windows Sockets** button, then click on **OK**.

Using Winsock Chess

To use WSChess, you need to know the IP address of the person you want to play with. Remember, if the service provider uses dynamic IP addressing, the IP address changes every time you log in. See *Finding the Right Hostname* earlier in this chapter for information about how to find your IP address.

> **To play Winsock Chess in Host mode**, where another player contacts you to start a game, select Connect ➤ Host. Then Winsock Chess will listen for someone to call.

> **To connect to someone else**, select Connect ➤ Connect to Host. Enter the person's IP address in the space provided, and click on OK. Winsock Chess will then establish contact. Remember that the other person has to be running in host mode for you to be able to contact them.

As the Internet grows, communications applications like these are becoming more and more popular. Expect to see many more Winsock communications applications appearing in the next couple of years.

Also, as data compression and digital transmission technologies become more sophisticated and more widespread, we'll begin to see more real-time Internet applications that incorporate voice, graphics, and even video. This looks to be the most exciting area of Internet communications yet to come. Stay tuned....

12

Getting Deeper into Winsock

IF YOU'RE THE sort of person who likes rolling up your sleeves and digging into configuration settings, or just have a driving need for speed, this is the chapter for you. Here I'll be covering tools for getting the most out of your Winsock experience, as well as tools that can be a real help when things don't go exactly right.

Some of these tools, like time accounting programs, provide you with a constant reminder of how much time (and money) you're spending online. Other tools will help you to improve the performance of your Winsock and SLIP or PPP connection.

Still other tools can help you figure out what's going on when things don't work right. The most common problems you're likely to experience are due to bad communications. There may be problems with your configuration, or your provider may just have too many people using their connection to the rest of the Internet, or it could just be that some guy out in Bakersfield drove a pickax through a fiber optic link. But with the right diagnostic tools, you can get a better idea about what's gone wrong.

Dialing and Time Accounting Tools

Dialing and time accounting tools are designed to help you better manage your SLIP or PPP account. Dialing programs can provide more flexibility than the dialers that come with your Winsock package. A good dialing program, for instance, will automatically redial when the line is busy, and even launch applications automatically after you're connected.

If you have an account on a system that charges you by the hour, or if you have a limit on the number of hours you can use each month before getting charged extra, you should check these programs out.

NetDial

NetDial, by James A. Sanders, is the best alternative dialer program you can find. It's easy to configure and use, and it takes a lot of the hassle out of complicated dialing procedures.

NetDial (see Figure 12.1) can automatically redial if the line is busy, and keep redialing until you're connected. NetDial also supports multiple configurations, so you can set up specific dialing configurations for specific needs.

Figure 12.1:
NetDial is a complete dialing program for any Winsock package.

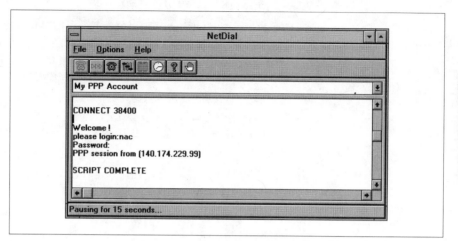

> You can get NetDial via anonymous FTP from the SimTel archive at **oak. oakland.edu**, in the **/SimTel/win3/winsock** directory. The current version at the time of this writing is 2.5, and the filename is **nd250s.zip**.

NetDial is shareware, and costs $20 to register. Registration gets rid of the nag/guilt popup box, and gets you unlimited technical support, and discounts on future versions.

Installing NetDial

To install NetDial, do the following:

1. Uncompress the zip file into an empty directory.

2. Run the **SETUP.EXE** program.

To configure NetDial, do the following:

1. Start NetDial.

2. Select the **Undefined** configuration from the list box in the Net-Dial main screen and select Options ➤ Configure. The NetDial Configuration screen is displayed.

3. Click on the **Modem Options** tab. The Modem Options page is displayed. Check to make sure these options are correct for your modem. If you're not sure, leave these options at their defaults. If you have problems with the initialization string, try using the basic **ATZ** instead.

4. Click on the **Call Settings** tab. The Call Settings page is displayed. Enter a name for the connection in the **Connection Name** field.

5. If you'd like NetDial to continue dialing until you're connected, check the **Cycle Dial Entry** box.

6. Enter your provider's dial-in phone number in the **Phone Number** field.

7. Select the correct COM Port, Baud rate, and communications settings from the appropriate list boxes.

8. Now, click on the **Login Script** tab. The Login Script page is displayed.

9. In the **Wait:** field, enter **ogin:** (you leave out the first letter, because it may be **L** or **l**), and in the **Send:** field, enter your user name. Click on the **Add** button.

10. Next, in the **Wait:** field, enter **assword:** (you leave out the first letter, because it may be **P** or **p**), and in the **Send:** field enter your password. Click on the **Add** button.

11. If there are any additional commands you know of that are required to start up your connection, enter these after your login name and password.

12. If your provider uses dynamic IP addressing, make sure the last entry in this list of commands is **[PARSEIP]**, which is one of the selections in the **Wait:** list box. Also make sure that your Winsock dialer application has the IP address set to **0.0.0.0**. The PARSEIP

command is needed to retrieve your IP address, and pass it on to your regular Winsock dialer program.

13. Click on the **Startup Programs** tab. The Startup Programs page is displayed. Click on the Select button to select your Winsock application.

14. Add other applications you want to start up afterwards, if desired. If you want these applications to automatically shut down when you exit NetDial, check the **Close on disconnect** box.

15. Click on the **Add** button.

16. Click on **OK** to save your configuration.

Using NetDial

To use NetDial, do the following:

1. Select the connection name from the list box in the NetDial main screen.

2. Click on the dial (phone symbol) button.

SLIP db

SLIP db, by Derrick R. Webber, is a nice time accounting program. It can be installed so that it is automatically started whenever you log in, and stopped whenever you log out. It keeps a detailed listing of all of your login times, the amount of time you spend online, and how much money you've spent (see Figure 12.2).

You can get SLIP db via anonymous FTP from **ollc.mta.ca**, in the **/pub/slip** directory. The current version at the time of this writing is 1.01, and the file-name is **slipdb10.zip**.

SLIP db is shareware, and costs $30 (Canadian) to register.

Figure 12.2:
SLIP db helps you to
keep your online costs
down by letting you
know how much time
you're spending online.

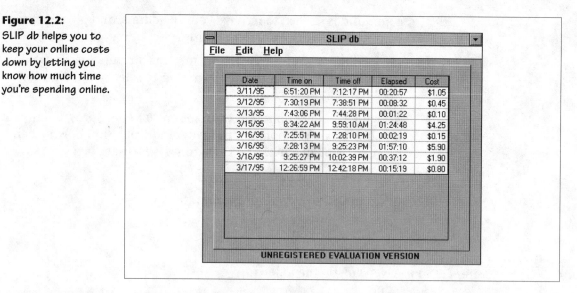

Installing SLIP db

To install SLIP db, do the following:

1. Uncompress the zip file into an empty directory.

2. Run the **SETUP.EXE** program.

3. When the setup is complete, you'll see a message telling you that you'll need to edit your dialing scripts to run SLIP db. Click on **OK**.

To configure SLIP db, do the following:

1. Start SLIP db. You'll see a message telling you that it can't find the SLIPDB.INI file. Click on **OK**.

2. Then you'll see a message telling you to specify your initial settings. Click on **OK**. The SLIP db Setup dialog box appears.

3. In the **Rates** portion of the SLIP db Setup dialog box, enter the different rates your service provider charges for different times of the day by entering the starting times, ending times, and the corresponding cost per minute in the appropriate fields.

4. Enter the starting day of your billing month in the **Billing day of the month** field.

5. Select additional configuration options at the bottom of the screen, if desired.

6. Click on **Save**. The unregistered shareware message appears telling you that you may evaluate this program for 30 days before registering it. Click on **Okay**.

To add SLIP db to your dialer's login script so that SLIP db starts automatically when you log in, do the following:

1. Make a backup copy of the login and logout scripts for your dialer. If you're using Trumpet Winsock, the filenames are LOGIN.CMD and BYE.CMD. If you're using Chameleon Sampler, you cannot edit your login script manually. You need to enter changes from within Chameleon itself. For more information about Chameleon, see Appendix B. If you're using a different Winsock dialer, see the documentation that came with your dialer to find out how to add commands to the login and logout scripts.

2. Using a text editor like the Windows Notepad, open your login script file. Search for the line that loads your password, and enter the following line after this:

```
exec "c:\slipdb\slipdb.exe on"
```

3. Save the file.

4. Now open your logout script. Add the following line to the end of this file:

```
exec "c:\slip\slipdb.exe off"
```

Different Winsock dialers use different scripting languages, although most of them use similar commands. Check with the documentation that came with your dialer to find out how to execute Windows applications from within the login and logout scripts.

Alternately, if you want to manually start and stop SLIP db, do the following:

1. Make a copy of the SLIP db icon, by dragging it from Program Manager in Windows 3.1 or Windows Explorer in Windows 95, and name the copy SLIP db ON.

2. Edit the properties for the icon, by pressing Alt + Enter in Windows 3.1, or clicking the right mouse button in Windows 95, to add the ON command to the Command line option (Windows 3.1) or the Shortcut Target option (Windows 95), so that it reads like this:

```
c:\slipdb\slipdb.exe on
```

3. Make a copy of the SLIP db icon, and name the copy SLIP db OFF.

4. Edit the properties for the icon by pressing Alt + Enter in Windows 3.1, or clicking the right mouse button in Windows 95, to add the OFF command to the Command line option (Windows 3.1) or the Shortcut Target option (Windows 95), so that it reads like this:

```
c:\slipdb\slipdb.exe off
```

5. When you want to start the timer, just start SLIP db from the SLIP db ON icon, and stop the timer from the SLIP db OFF icon.

Using SLIP db

SLIP db keeps a running tab on your account for the entire month. Some of the options available include:

To see your usage to date, start SLIP db. Your total usage is displayed.

To copy the data to another program, such as a spreadsheet, select the cells that you want to copy, and select Edit ➤ Copy.

To print out a report of your usage, select File ➤ Print.

WS-Timer

WS-Timer, by Louis Aube, is a simple little time accounting program that you can use with your Winsock dialer (see Figure 12.3). For your sickly curious side, it also keeps a lifetime accumulation count of the time you spend online.

You can get WS-Timer via anonymous FTP from **ftp.sentex.net**, in the **/pub/winsock/apps** directory. The current version as of the time of this writing is 2.02, and the filename is **wstmr2.20.zip**.

Figure 12.3:
WS-Timer helps you keep track of how much time you spend online.

WS-Timer is freeware, and may be freely distributed provided that the files are distributed intact.

> *This program does not come with the VBRUN300.DLL file, which is the runtime library file required for all applications written in Microsoft Visual Basic™ 3.0. Check your WINDOWS\ SYSTEM directory to see if you already have it installed. If not, you can get it from the SimTel archives at **oak.oakland.edu**, in the **/SimTel/win3/dll** directory. The filename is **vbrun300.zip**.*

Installing WS-Timer

To install WS-Timer, do the following:

1. Uncompress the zip file into an empty directory.

2. Run the **SETUP.EXE** program.

3. Add the **SET WSTIMER=C:\WSTIMER** line to your AUTOEXEC.BAT file. (If you installed it in a directory other than C:\WSTIMER, use that directory name instead.)

If you want WS-Timer to start automatically when you log in, do the following:

1. Make a backup copy of the login and logout scripts for your dialer. If you're using Trumpet Winsock, the filenames are LOGIN.CMD and BYE.CMD. If you're using Chameleon Sampler, you cannot edit your login script manually. You need to enter changes from within

305

Chameleon itself. For more information about Chameleon, see Appendix B. If you're using a different Winsock dialer, see the documentation that came with your dialer to find out how to add commands to the login and logout scripts.

2. Using a text editor like the Windows Notepad, open your login script file. Search for the line that loads your password, and enter the following line after this:

```
exec "c:\wstimer\wstimer.exe on a"
```

3. Save the file.

4. Now open your logout script. Add the following line to the end of this file:

```
exec "c:\wstimer\endtimer.exe"
```

Different Winsock dialers use different scripting languages, although most of them use similar commands. Check with the documentation that came with your dialer to find out how to execute Windows applications from within the login and logout scripts.

If you want to be able to start and stop WS-Timer from an icon on your Windows desktop, you need to edit the Properties for the WS-Timer icon, to add the **ON A** option to the **WSTIMER.EXE** command line. For more information about Icon properties, refer to your Windows documentation.

Using WS-Timer

Using WS-Timer is very easy. You start it up, and it runs. It automatically starts minimized, although you can maximize it at any time. In addition, a little *This Call* window is always visible on your desktop, letting you know how long you've been online.

Nullsock

For those times when you can't get connected to your network, but you just gotta show someone that cool Internet application you found, a nullsock is indispensable.

A nullsock is basically just a brain-dead WINSOCK.DLL file. It tricks your Winsock applications into thinking that you've got Winsock loaded and you're online, when we all know you're not.

I think a nullsock is a must for anyone who needs to give Web browser presentations. (Your audience will never know the difference.)

Mozock

This nullsock is brought to you by Netscape Communications Corporation, the makers of Netscape. It's unsupported, but it's free, and it does the job quite well.

Deeper into Winsock CH. 12

> You can get Mozock via anonymous FTP from **ftp.netscape.com**, in the **/unsupported/windows** directory. The filename is **mozock.dll**. You should also pick up the **mozock.txt** file while you're there.

Installing Mozock

To install Mozock, do the following:

1. Make a copy of your real **WINSOCK.DLL** in your WINDOWS \SYSTEM directory and put it in a safe place.

2. Rename your real WINSOCK.DLL file in your WINDOWS\SYSTEM directory to something different, like **REALSOCK.DLL**.

3. Copy the **MOZOCK.DLL** to your WINDOWS\SYSTEM directory.

4. Using a text editor, like the Windows Notepad, create a new batch file called **MOZOCK.BAT**. Put the following line in it:

```
copy mozock.dll winsock.dll
```

5. Save the file in your WINDOWS\SYSTEM subdirectory.

6. Now, create another batch file, this time called **REALSOCK.BAT**. Put the following line in it:

```
copy realsock.dll winsock.dll
```

7. Save the file in your WINDOWS\SYSTEM subdirectory.

8. Create icons for the **MOZOCK.BAT** and **REALSOCK.BAT** batch files on your Windows desktop.

Running Mozock

Now, all you need to do is run the appropriate batch file to make the switch.

To start up Mozock, just run the MOZOCK.BAT file. You can now run most (if not all) of your Winsock applications just as if you had the real thing loaded.

To return to your original Winsock, just run the REALSOCK .BAT file.

DNS Lookup and Route Tracing Tools

A good DNS lookup program is an essential part of your Internet toolkit. These programs can talk directly to your DNS (Domain Name Server), and get information from the server's database of information.

For example, if I wanted to look up the real IP address of, say, the White House, a DNS lookup tool could tell me that it's IP address is 198.137.241.30. Similarly, if someone gives me a mysterious IP address, I could look up what that IP address points to.

Route tracing programs show you the route that packets take between you and a remote machine. Why is this information useful? Well, if you're experiencing slow response time from a remote server, using a route tracer might tell you that your packets going from San Francisco to Los Angeles are taking a detour through Detroit. And a route tracer helps you to understand a little more about how the Internet is connected. You may be surprised by some of the things you find out.

NSLookup

NSLookup, by Ashmount Research, Ltd., is as good an all-around DNS lookup program as you'll find. It lets you look up IP names and IP addresses, and gives you information about all the name records associated with that name or address (see Figure 12.4).

Figure 12.4:
Ashmount Research's NSLookup program lets you look up any IP address or hostname with ease.

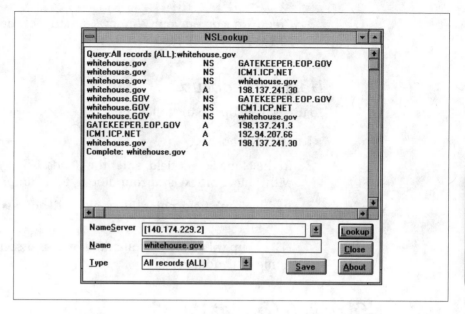

▶ *This application may not work with all versions of Winsock.*

You can get NSLookup via anonymous FTP from **disabuse.demon.co.uk**, in the **/pub/trumphurst/nslookup** directory. The current version at the time of this writing is 1.1, and the filename is **nslookup.zip**.

NSLookup is freeware, but Ashmount reserves the copyright for the program.

Installing NSLookup

To install NSLookup, do the following:

1. Create an **NSLOOKUP** directory on your hard disk.

2. Uncompress the zip file into this directory.

309

3. Create an icon on your Windows desktop for the **NSLOOKUP.EXE** file.

Using NSLookup

To use NSLookup, do the following:

1. Start NSLookup.

2. In the NameServer field, enter the IP address of your local DNS, with square brackets surrounding it, for example, [198.41.0.4].

3. In the **Name** field, enter the name or IP address that you want to look up, and press **Enter**.

4. NSLookup will show you all of the records associated with that name or IP address.

NSLookup (32-bit)

This is a DNS lookup program by John Junod, that is written specifically for Windows NT and Windows 95. It is a command-line program, and isn't real fancy, but it does the job quite well, and it's the only DNS lookup program I've found that works with Windows 95 (see Figure 12.5).

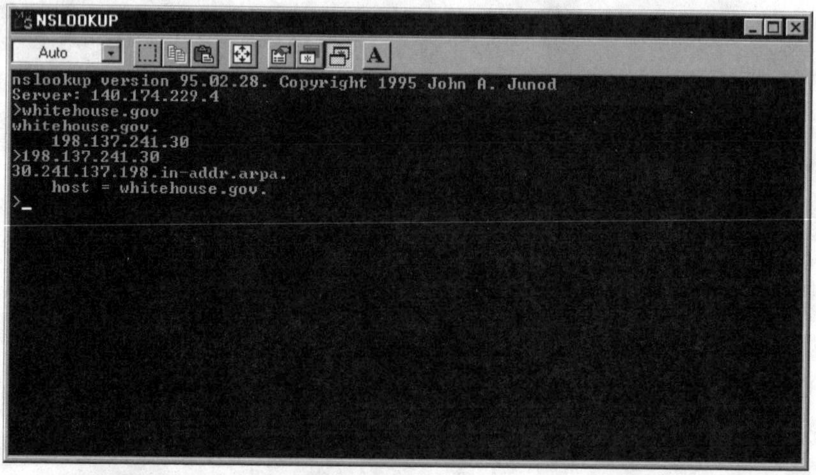

Figure 12.5:
John Junod's 32-bit NSLookup program lets you lookup IP addresses and hostnames in Windows NT and Windows 95.

▶ *Do not attempt to use this program in Windows 3.1. It is a 32-bit command-line program. Because of this, Windows 3.1 will attempt to run it in DOS, which will subsequently lock up your system, forcing you to perform a cold reboot.*

You can get John Junod's 32-bit NSLookup program via anonymous FTP from **ftp.usma.edu**, in the **/pub/msdos/winsock.files** directory. The current version at the time of this writing is 95.02.28, and the filename is **nslookup.zip**.

Installing NSLookup (32-bit)

To install NSLookup in Windows 95, do the following:

1. Create a **NSLOOK32** directory on your hard disk.

2. Uncompress the zip file into this directory.

3. Create an icon on your Windows desktop for the **NSLOOKUP.EXE** file.

Using NSLookup (32-bit)

To use NSLookup, do the following:

1. Start NSLookup.

2. If you'd like to see a detailed listing for each hostname, type **set d2** at the prompt and press **Enter**.

3. Enter the name or IP address you want to look up. The information is displayed.

4. When you're done, type **quit**.

For more information about NSLookup, type **help** at the NSLookup prompt.

311

WS Host

WS Host, by Andy H Coates, is a very simple little utility that lets you look up hostnames using an IP address or IP addresses using a hostname (see Figure 12.6).

Figure 12.6:
WS Host lets you look up an IP address if you know the hostname and vice versa.

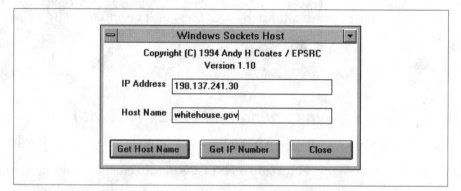

You can get WS Host via anonymous FTP from **ftp.cica.indiana.edu**, in the **/pub/pc/win3/winsock** directory. The current version at the time of this writing is 1.1, and the filename is **wshost11.zip**.

WS Host is postcardware—if you like it, send Andy a postcard with a nice view on the front and your name and e-mail address on the back. WS Host may be freely distributed.

Installing WS Host

To install WS Host, do the following:

1. Create a **WSHOST** directory on your hard disk.

2. Uncompress the zip file into this directory.

3. Create an icon on your Windows desktop for the **WSHOST.EXE** file.

Using WS Host

As I mentioned above, there are really only two options available with WS Host:

To find out the IP address of a hostname, enter the hostname in the Host Name field, and press Enter.

To find the hostname associated with an IP address, enter the IP address in the IP Address field, and press Enter.

Trumpet Hopcheck

Hopcheck, by Peter Tattam, is included in the WINAPPS2.ZIP file that comes along with Trumpet Winsock (see Appendix B for more on Trumpet Winsock). Most of the other programs that come in Winapps are very basic programs, and, although they all work quite well, they are not as sophisticated as similar programs I've discussed in more detail throughout this book.

Hopcheck, however, really stands out. It's sort of like a Ping utility, except it tells you all of the steps taken on the journey from you to your target (see Figure 12.7).

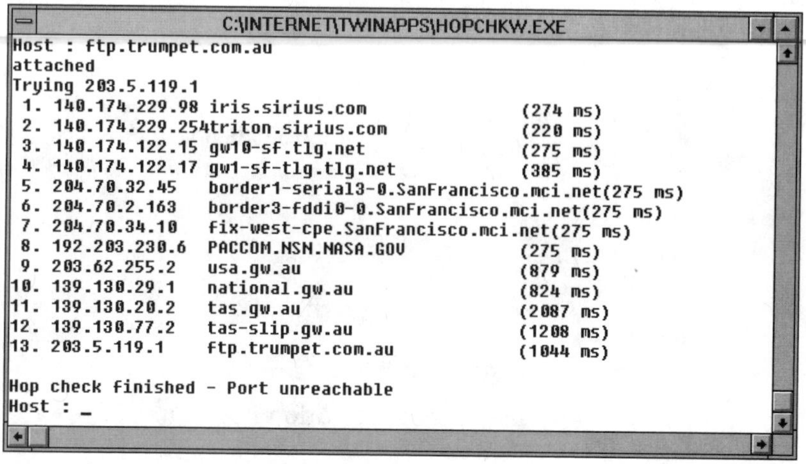

Figure 12.7:

Peter Tattam's Hopcheck lets Trumpet Winsock users find out how many hops it takes for a packet to reach its destination.

```
                    C:\INTERNET\TWINAPPS\HOPCHKW.EXE
Host : ftp.trumpet.com.au
attached
Trying 203.5.119.1
 1. 140.174.229.98  iris.sirius.com                 (274 ms)
 2. 140.174.229.254triton.sirius.com                (220 ms)
 3. 140.174.122.15  gw10-sf.tlg.net                 (275 ms)
 4. 140.174.122.17  gw1-sf-tlg.tlg.net              (385 ms)
 5. 204.70.32.45    border1-serial3-0.SanFrancisco.mci.net(275 ms)
 6. 204.70.2.163    border3-fddi0-0.SanFrancisco.mci.net(275 ms)
 7. 204.70.34.10    fix-west-cpe.SanFrancisco.mci.net(275 ms)
 8. 192.203.230.6   PACCOM.NSN.NASA.GOV             (275 ms)
 9. 203.62.255.2    usa.gw.au                       (879 ms)
10. 139.130.29.1    national.gw.au                  (824 ms)
11. 139.130.20.2    tas.gw.au                       (2087 ms)
12. 139.130.77.2    tas-slip.gw.au                  (1208 ms)
13. 203.5.119.1     ftp.trumpet.com.au             (1044 ms)

Hop check finished - Port unreachable
Host : _
```

Hopcheck is designed specifically for use with Trumpet Winsock. It probably will not work with other Winsock packages.

You can get Winapps via anonymous FTP from **ftp.trumpet.com.au**, in the **/ftp/pub/winsock** directory. The current version at the time of this writing is 2.0, and the filename is **winapps2.zip**.

Winapps is part of the Trumpet Winsock package, which is shareware. Other programs in Winapps include Chat, Ping, DNS lookup, Telnet, Archie, and a text viewer.

Installing Hopcheck

To install Hopcheck (and, optionally, the other applications in Winapps) do the following:

1. Create a **TWINAPPS** directory on your hard disk.

2. Uncompress the zip file into this directory.

3. Create an icon for the **HOPCHKW.EXE** file on your Windows desktop.

Neither Hopcheck nor most of the other programs in Winapps come with icons. But there are a number of icons that come with Windows. If you'd like, you can change the icon associated with any of these files. See your Windows documentation for more information about using the icons that come with Windows.

Using Hopcheck

To use Hopcheck, do the following:

1. Start Hopcheck.

2. Enter the destination host name at the **Host:** prompt and press **Enter**.

3. If you get back an attached message, but no data, that means you need to be more specific about the host name. For example, you may not get back any data for *trumpet.com.au*, but you do for *ftp.trumpet.com.au*.

Diagnostic Tools

When something isn't working right, a good diagnostic tool can help you to figure out what the problem is. Once you've done that, you can start thinking of ways to fix it. For example, say you can't connect to your mail server all of a sudden. It could just be a simple case of your provider's DNS entry being down, or you may just have something configured wrong. With a good diagnostic tool, you'll be better equipped to figure out what the root cause of the problem is.

TracePlus

TracePlus, formerly called X-Ray Winsock, by Systems Software Technology, is a handy diagnostic utility that lets you record in detail all Winsock API calls made by your Winsock applications. You can start and stop it like a tape recorder. Once you've recorded a Winsock trace, you can view each call in detail, and even reference the Winsock API documentation to get more information about a particular API call. (see Figure 12.8)

Deeper into Winsock
CH. 12

Figure 12.8:

TracePlus lets you see detailed information about each Winsock call.

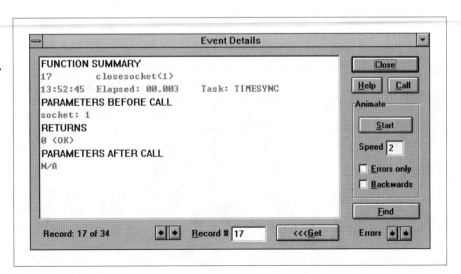

315

> You can get TracePlus via anonymous FTP from **ftp.netcom.com**, in the **/pub/ss/sstinc** directory. The current version at the time of this writing is 1.2 and the filename is **tpwins.zip**.

TracePlus is a demo version of the complete commercial product, and may be freely distributed. The commercial version costs $79.95, and includes additional functions.

*TracePlus is designed to work with the Winsock 1.1 specification help file. You can get this file via anonymous FTP from **ftp.microsoft.com**, in the **/bussys/WinSock/spec11** directory. The filename is **WINSOCK.HLP**.*

Installing TracePlus

To install TracePlus, do the following:

1. Create a **TRACEP** directory on your hard disk.

2. Uncompress the zip file into this directory.

3. Create an icon on your Windows desktop for the **XRAWINS.EXE** file.

To configure TracePlus, do the following:

1. Start TracePlus.

2. The first time you start TracePlus, you'll be prompted to enter the location of the WINSOCK.HLP file. If you have this file on your hard disk, click on **OK** and specify the location. If not, click on **Cancel**.

Using TracePlus

If you're having problems connecting to something, and particularly if you're getting Winsock error messages, just start up TracePlus, and repeat the procedure that generated the error. If the problem is a failed Winsock call, the failed call will appear in red. If you study that call, you may be able to figure out what went wrong.

Here are some options available to you when using TracePlus.

To start tracing, click on the solid right-pointing triangle button.

To stop tracing, click on the square button.

To pause tracing, click on the outline right-pointing triangle button.

To view event details for a specific event, double-click on the event name. The Event Details window is displayed.

To see information about a particular API call from the Event Details Window, if you have the WINSOCK.HLP file installed, click on the Call button to see information on that event from the Winsock Specification Help file.

Performance Tuning Tools

This section is for you speed jockeys out there. These are the tools that will help you to test and tune your Winsock so that you get the best performance possible.

Properly tuning your Winsock and your modem communications devices can help to increase your throughput by a considerable margin. If you're using Trumpet Winsock, you can tune your Winsock communications parameters to best meet your specific needs.

If you're running that Winsock over a SLIP or PPP connection, and you're using a high-speed modem, you've already won half the battle. But there's more to it than just upgrading your modem. You also need to consider your COM port itself, and how Windows manages that COM port.

Socket Wrencher

Socket Wrencher is a demo product from NetManage, Inc., the makers of Chameleon. Although it was designed primarily for Winsock network users, you can use it to check out your Winsock SLIP or PPP connection as well (see Figure 12.9).

Figure 12.9:
NetManage's Socket Wrencher lets you run diagnostic tests on your Winsock.

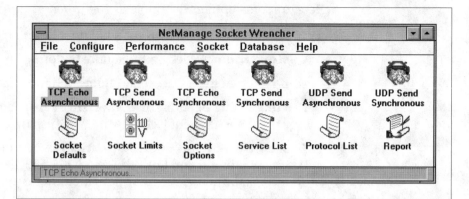

You can get SocketWrencher via anonymous FTP from **ftp.netmanage.com**, in the **/pub/demos/sockwrench** directory. The current version at the time of this writing is 1.0 and the filename is **socketw.exe**, which is a self-extracting archive file.

SocketWrencher is freeware and may be freely distributed. In fact, Net-Manage encourages users and developers alike to copy and distribute it unchanged free of charge, in hopes that distributing a good testing tool will lead to better quality products.

Installing Socket Wrencher

To install Socket Wrencher, do the following:

1. Create a **SOCKETW** directory on your hard disk.

2. Run the self-extracting archive file in this directory to uncompress the files.

3. Create an icon on your Windows desktop for the **SOCKWRC.EXE** file.

To configure Socket Wrencher, do the following:

1. Start Socket Wrencher. You'll see a number of different icons, one for each test.

2. Select Configure. The Configure dialog box appears.

3. Enter a host name in the **Host:** field. You should enter your provider's name or server name, as this will test your connection to the server.

4. The **Transmit Bytes** section lets you select from one of four options: 1KB, 64KB, 128KB, and 1MB. I recommend starting with the smallest size, 1KB, and working your way up, since the other sizes make for very long tests.

Using Socket Wrencher

Socket Wrencher includes a number of different tests. Here's an overview of each test:

TCP Echo Performance (Asynchronous/Synchronous) tests how long it takes to send data using TCP, with echoing (acknowledgment) on both ends enabled. In the asynchronous test, a Windows message is used to notify Socket Wrencher that more data can be sent, and in the synchronous test, Socket Wrencher just keeps looping data.

TCP Send Performance (Asynchronous/Synchronous) is the same as the TCP Echo Performance test, except without the echoing.

UDP Send Performance (Asynchronous/Synchronous) tests how long it takes to send data using UDP.

Socket Wrencher also provides several informational options:

Socket Defaults tells you the default settings for TCP and UDP sockets.

Socket Limits tells you the number of default maximum number of sockets.

Socket Options tests your socket options configuration.

Service List tells you which ports are enabled, and which protocols use them.

Protocol List tells you which protocols are supported.

Report lets you view, copy, or print a report of your test results.

When you're running the tests over a normal, non-ISDN SLIP or PPP connection, don't be dismayed by the comparison between your system's performance and the benchmark displayed. The benchmark reflects a system on a network, using a fast network card, talking to a fast server, over a 10 megabit per second connection. Naturally, your 14.4 or 28.8 kilobit per second connection will not provide such grand throughput.

Tweaking Your Trumpet

If you're a Trumpet Winsock user, you can make manual adjustments to change the way that Winsock transfers packets, which can boost your performance. The three options that you can adjust are:

MTU (*The Maximum Transmission Unit*). This is the maximum size for a single transmission unit, in bytes, including overhead (minimum of about 44 bytes).

TCP RWIN (*TCP Receive Window*). The largest amount of data you can receive in any one transmission, in bytes. This should be about four times the Maximum Sequence Size, which means you can receive four segments at a time.

TCP MSS (*TCP Maximum Segment Size*). The largest single transmission that you can receive, in bytes, not counting overhead.

Many users mistakenly believe that the higher the setting, the better. But setting these values too high can cause problems, especially if you're connecting to the Internet using a 14.4 modem.

First, if the size of the transmission is too large, your connection may time out before the packet is received, which means that the packet gets resent. If it times out the second time, it gets resent again, and so on. The end result is you never receive the packet.

Second, if there's an error in the packet, it gets resent. The smaller the packet, the less likely it is that an error will be encountered.

According to Peter Tattam, the author of Trumpet Winsock, the two most important values are TCP MSS and TCP RWIN. As his general rule of thumb, he suggests using TCP MSS=212/TCP RWIN=848 for users running CSLIP, or CPPP (SLIP or PPP with VJ Compression), and TCP MSS=512/TCP RWIN=2048 for users running normal SLIP or PPP. He also says that you can experiment with using these settings and raising the MTU as high as your provider will allow, but no higher than 1500.

If you'd like to experiment, start with lower values, then raise them a bit at a time, only after you make sure you aren't experiencing problems. Here are some sample settings to try:

MTU	TCP RWIN	MSS
256	848	212
512	1872	468
768	2896	724
1024	3920	980

Start out with 256/848/212, and see how things go for awhile. Run some performance tests, download a bunch of files, try out different applications. Once you're satisfied, try the next bunch of settings, and so on. If you get to a point where large file transfers start to bog down, you've gone too far.

TCPMeter

TCPMeter is a performance measurement application for Trumpet Winsock. It measures the throughput of your Winsock connection, in terms of incoming and outgoing data. (see Figure 12.10)

Figure 12.10:
TCPMeter lets Trumpet Winsock users measure performance.

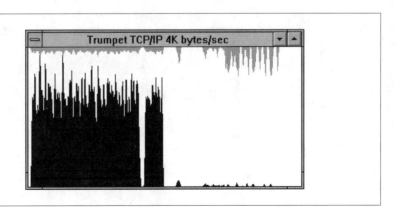

TCPMeter will not work with any other Winsock besides Trumpet (see Appendix B for more on Trumpet Winsock).

You can get TCPMeter via anonymous FTP from **ftp.trumpet.com.au**, in the **/ftp/pub/beta/tcpmeter** directory. The filename is **tcpmeter.exe**, which is the actual, uncompressed executable file.

TCPMeter is freeware, but is only useful if you have the shareware Trumpet Winsock .

Installing TCPMeter

To install TCPMeter, do the following:

1. If you'd like to keep TCPMeter in a directory by itself, create a **TCPMETER** directory on your hard disk.

2. Either put the **TCPMETER.EXE** file in the **TCPMETER** directory, or put it in the same directory where you have Trumpet Winsock installed.

3. Create an icon on your Windows desktop for the **TCPMETER.EXE** file.

TCPMeter does not come with its own icon. There are a number of icons that come with Windows. If you'd like, you can change the icon associated with TCPMeter. See your Windows documentation for more information about using the icons that come with Windows.

Using TCPMeter

To use TCPMeter, just start it up. The default setting is to measure incoming and outgoing traffic in 1KB/per second (kbps) increments.

There are two options available when using TCPMeter:

To change the metering up, click on the TCPMeter window with your left mouse button. The options are 2kbps, 4kbps, 8kbps, etc., on up to 262,144kbps.

To change the metering down, click on the TCPMeter window with your right mouse button. The options are 512bps, 256bps, 128bps, etc., on down to 1bps.

Of UART Chips and FIFO Buffers

The single leading cause of lousy SLIP and PPP performance is the bottleneck that occurs between the modem and the PC itself. This bottleneck is sort of like the toll plaza on a bridge or freeway during rush hour. The same thing happens in your PC. The toll booth, in this case, is your PC's UART chip and its FIFO (First-In, First-Out) buffer.

The problem occurs with the COM ports installed in older PCs, usually those built before 1994, which use the older versions of the UART chip, the 8000 series (8250, 8550). The problem with the UART 8550 is that it only has a 1 byte FIFO buffer. Which means, in practical terms that it can't handle modem speeds past 9600bps.

The newer version of the UART chip, the 16550 has a 16-byte adjustable FIFO buffer, which gives you up to *16 times* the buffering capability of the 8550. Depending on the application, you can increase your modem performance considerably, just by changing UART chips.

First, you should find out if you need to change chips. Run the MSD.EXE program in your DOS or windows directory. This is the Microsoft Diagnostics program, and it will tell you what kind of UART chip you have. Type **C** to see information about your COM ports. Look at the last line. If you see an 8000 series UART chip listed on the COM port used by your modem, its time to upgrade.

You have two options:

- Get an internal 14.4 or faster modem, which avoids the internal COM ports altogether.

■ If you already have a fast *external* modem, go out and buy a serial card that uses the 16550 UART chip, which, when installed, takes the place of your internal COM ports. These cards are pretty inexpensive—usually $25 to $50.

Now, after you've installed the new modem or serial card, you need to make some adjustments to Windows so that it will be able to use the new FIFO buffer. Open your Windows SYSTEM.INI file and look for the [386Enh] section. You need to add these lines anywhere in this section:

```
com1FIFO=true
com1buffer=1024
comboosttime=8
```

If your modem is connected to a COM port other than COM1, change the above lines to reflect the correct COM port.

CyberComm

Okay, you got your 16550 UART chip and you have Windows tuned to use that great big FIFO buffer. What more can you do to speed performance? Use a high-speed COMM driver. These drivers take the place of the standard Windows COMM.DRV driver, which can only take advantage of the 16550's larger FIFO buffer for receiving. These drivers enable the FIFO buffer for both receiving *and* transmitting.

The most widely used and tested alternative COMM driver is Cyber-Comm, by CyberSoft Corporation, Pty. Ltd.

You can get CyberComm via anonymous FTP from the SimTel archive at **oak.oakland.edu**, in the **/SimTel/win3/commprog** directory. The current version at the time of this writing is V1.1.0.0P, and the filename is **cybercom.zip**.

CyberComm is freeware, and may be freely distributed for non-commercial purposes.

Installing the CyberComm Driver

To install CyberComm, do the following:

1. Uncompress the zip file into an empty directory.

2. Move the **CYBERCOM.DRV** file to your WINDOWS\SYSTEM directory.

3. Open your **SYSTEM.INI** file, and search for the `comm.drv=comm.drv` line.

4. Comment out this line by putting a semicolon (;) in front of it, and entering the `comm.drv=cybercomm.drv` line.

5. Start or restart Windows.

Time Synchronizers

I don't know about you, but my PC clock is never right. It's usually off by anywhere from one minute to five minutes, which can get to be really annoying.

Time Synchronizers eliminate this annoyance. They check the time on reliable time servers on the Internet, report the time back to you, and reset your PC clock to match the real time.

Tardis

Tardis, by H. C. Mingham-Smith, is a nice little time-synchronization utility that works with Winsock. Tardis lets you get the time from any time server, and automatically resets your PC's clock to match the current time. It can be easily configured for your time zone, and even accounts for daylight savings time (see Figure 12.11).

> You can get Tardis via anonymous FTP from **ftp.cica.indiana.edu**, in the **/pub/pc/win3/winsock** directory. The current version at the time of this writing is 2.0a, and the filename is **tardis2a.zip**.

Tardis is shareware, and costs $20 to register.

Deeper into Winsock
CH. 12

325

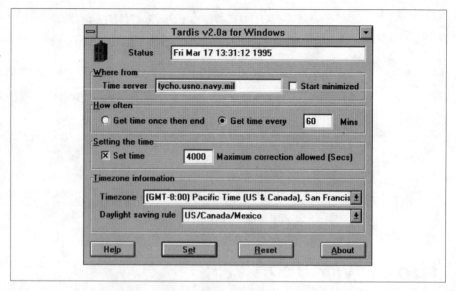

Figure 12.11:
Tardis lets you use a
reliable Internet time
server to automatically
set your PC clock to
the right time.

Installing Tardis

To install Tardis, do the following:

1. Create a **TARDIS** directory on your hard disk.

2. Uncompress the zip file into this directory.

3. Create an icon on your Windows desktop for the **TARDIS.EXE**
file.

To configure Tardis, do the following:

1. Start Tardis.

2. Select your time zone from the **Timezone** list box.

3. Select the appropriate daylight savings time from the Daylight
Savings Rule list box.

4. Enter your preferred time server in the **Time server** field. If
you don't want to use the default, which is in the UK, the documentation suggests using either **tycho.usno.navy.mil** (US Naval
Observatory) or **time-A.timefreq.bldrdoc.gov** (NIST in
Boulder, Colorado).

Using Tardis

To have Tardis automatically update your PC's clock, do the following:

1. Make sure you have Winsock running and you're logged into your Internet account.

2. Start Tardis.

3. After the time is set, you can close Tardis.

TimeSync

TimeSync, by Brad Greer, is a simple time synchronization utility for Winsock. It automatically connects to the time server you specify, checks the time, and resets your PC clock to the right time (see Figure 12.12).

Figure 12.12:

TimeSync lets you get the correct time from an Internet Time server and set your PC's clock automatically.

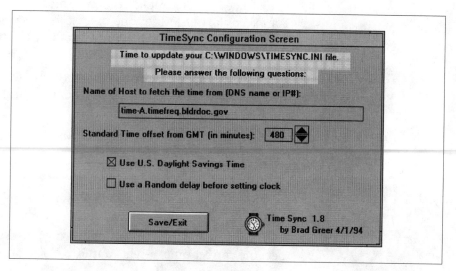

You can get TimeSync via anonymous FTP from **ftp.cac.washington.edu**, in the **/pub/winsock** directory. The current version at the time of this writing is 1.8, and the filename is **tsync1_8.zip**.

327

TimeSync is public domain software, and may be freely distributed.

Installing TimeSync

To install TimeSync, do the following:

1. Uncompress the zip file into an empty directory.
2. Run the **SETUP.EXE** file.

To configure TimeSync, do the following:

1. Start TimeSync. The TimeSync Configuration Screen appears.
2. Enter your preferred time server in the field provided. You can use either **tycho.usno.navy.mil** (US Naval Observatory) or **time-A .timefreq.bldrdoc.gov** (NIST in Boulder, Colorado).
3. Enter your time offset from GMT in minutes. Note that this application goes the opposite direction of most time zone indicators. For example, most time zone indicators consider Pacific Standard Time to be -8:00 from GMT, but with this application, it's +8:00, or 480 minutes. (I guess it all depends on your perspective.)
4. When you're done, click on **Save/Exit**. TimeSync starts up, connects with the time server, checks the time, and resets your clock.

Using TimeSync

To reset your PC's clock with TimeSync, do the following:

1. Make sure you have Winsock running and you're logged into your Internet account.
2. Start TimeSync. TimeSync automatically checks the time server, gets the correct time, resets your PC's clock, and shuts down.

Hopefully, you won't encounter too many roadblocks or traffic jams on the Internet, but if you do, at least now you know where to turn for roadside assistance.

13

Staking Your Claim on the Web

MORE AND MORE people are putting up their own Web pages, either for their own personal use, or for artistic or commercial purposes. It's a fun, and relatively easy way to disseminate or gather information, advertise, let people know what you *really* look like, tell them about your favorite hobbies, point them to your favorite Web links, and just generally express yourself.

Anyone can put up a Web page. You just need to have a Web server to put it on. While at first this may seem to be a difficult task, don't worry. You don't need to go out and buy a $10,000 Unix server to do it. There are several alternatives, and most of them won't cost you much, if anything at all.

Some of the ways you might be able to get access to a Web server include:

- Service providers who offer their customers a designated Web server space;

- Service providers who offer their customers publicly-accessible disk space (such as an anonymous FTP server) where customers can upload publicly-accessible files;

- Employers or schools that have a Web server that employees or students can use for personal (or business) reasons;

- A LAN that uses the TCP/IP protocol that can be accessed from the outside (i.e., one that's not behind a firewall);

- A dedicated SLIP or PPP connection (i.e., one that's up 24-hours a day), and a PC that can be dedicated as a Web server.

In the case of Internet service providers, a growing number are offering their customers Web server space. They may charge an extra fee for this service, perhaps $5 to $10 a month or more, usually depending on how much disk space you need. In some cases, you'll be able to maintain your own pages in your directory on the Web server. In other cases, you'll have to submit them to a system administrator for posting.

There are versions of the Web server software available for PCs. If you want to try to run a Web server from your PC, you need to load the server software, which, surprisingly, is very easy to install and run.

Keep in mind that, while you can run a Web server from your home computer on a dial-up SLIP or PPP connection, this is not recommended. If you can't leave the computer on and connected 24 hours a day, it won't necessarily be available to outside users when they try to access it. And, if you're on a system that uses dynamic IP addressing, remember that the address of your Web server will change every time you log in.

For information about setting up your own Web Server under Windows, Windows NT, or any one of a number of operating systems, check out the Web Server software home page at **http://www.w3.org/hypertext/WWW/Daemon /Overview.html.**

HTML Editors

Once you've found your Web server space, you need to put together your Web page. For that, you need an HTML (HyperText Markup Language) editor. HTML is the coding language used for Web pages, and HTML editors make it easy for you to design and edit Web pages. If you're wondering what HTML looks like, try looking at the document source option on your Web browser. You'll probably see something like this:

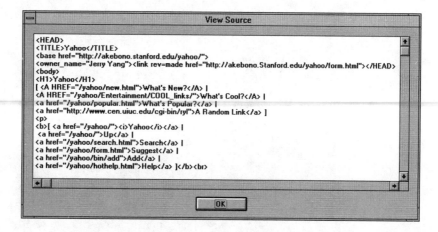

Each of the codes encased in <angle brackets> are formatting codes or links to other pages or images. **<B>** turns **Bold** on, and **</B>** turns it off. Links to other Web pages look like this:

```
<A HREF="http://www.yahoo.com">Yahoo</A><BR>
```

and pointers to image files look like this:

```
<IMG SRC="VGSTARRY.JPG" alt="[IMAGE]">.
```

While HTML is simpler than most other text-based coding languages (believe it or not), it's still rather difficult for a beginner to work with. Fortunately, there are some great tools out there that make editing and learning about HTML documents easy. Some of them are stand-alone tools, while others require that you use a word processing program, usually Microsoft Word for Windows™. Some hide the inner workings of HTML from you, while others display all of the codes. Some let you do whatever you want, while others constantly check to make sure you're using the codes correctly. Although I recommend that anyone who plans to write Web pages at least understand the basics of HTML coding, you should choose the tool that best fits your personal needs.

Deciphering HTML Codes

At first, figuring out all those HTML codes can be pretty intimidating. Fortunately, there are plenty of folks out there on the Internet who understand your problem, and they understand HTML as well. Here are some excellent resources for the beginning HTML writer:

A Beginner's Guide to HTML. This is an excellent tutorial for the HTML newbie, written by Marc Andreesen. It offers basic information about HTML coding, and offers real examples of codes and their results. To get there, set your Web browser to the following URL:

http://www.ncsa.uiuc.edu/demoweb/html-primer.html

HTML Documents: A Mosaic Tutorial. This is an excellent tutorial written by Wm. Dennis Horn of Clarkson University, which provides a number of exercises and examples to help you learn HTML coding. To get there, set your Web browser to the following URL:

http://fire.clarkson.edu/doc/html/htut.html

A Crash Course on Writing Documents for the Web. This is another good tutorial, written by Eamonn Sullivan. It's well-written, well-organized, and cuts to the chase quickly. To get there, set your Web browser to the following URL:

http://www.ziff.com/~eamonn/crash_course.html

HTML: The Complete Guide. Can't remember which code to use? Check out this extensive reference guide. To get there, set your Web browser to the following URL:

http://www.chem.emory.edu/html/html.html

The Elements of HTML Style. A quick checklist of style dos and don'ts for the Web Page writer written by J.K. Cohen. To get there, set your Web browser to the following URL:

http://bookweb.cwis.uci.edu:8042/Staff/StyleGuide.html

A Style Guide for Web Pages. Written by Tim Berners-Lee, the father of the Web, this extensive guide gives HTML writers and server administrators alike a set of guidelines for presenting and organizing information on Web pages. To get there, set your Web browser to the following URL:

http://info.cern.ch/hypertext/WWW/Provider/Style/Overview.html

Yahoo's HTML References. HTML is a hot topic, so you ought to check out the most complete and current source of reference information available—the Yahoo directory. To get to the HTML page in the directory, set your Web browser to the following URL:

http://www.yahoo.com/Computers/World_Wide_Web/HTML/

All of the HTML editors that follow have their own built-in editing programs. No additional software is required.

If you're a Word for Windows user, you should check out the Word for Windows HTML editors discussed later in this chapter.

WEB Wizard

WEB Wizard, by ARTA Software Group and David Geller, is the best get-started-quick HTML tool I've found. WEB Wizard prompts you to answer a few questions, after which it automatically creates a very basic home page for you, with all the right HTML codes (see Figure 13.1).

333

Figure 13.1:
WEB Wizard prompts
you through the
process of creating
your first home page.

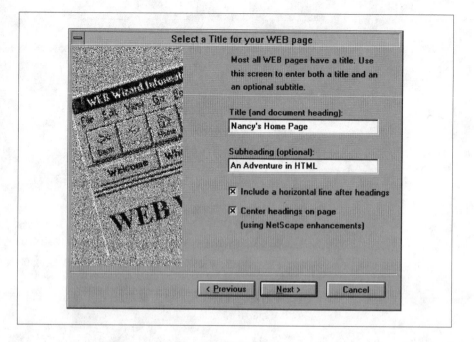

With WEB Wizard, you can create your first home page in just a few minutes. If you want to edit it later, you can use one of the HTML editors discussed later in this chapter.

You can get WEB Wizard via anonymous FTP from **ftp.halcyon.com**, in the **/local/webwizard** directory. The current version is 1.0. The 16-bit version is called **webwiz16.exe** and the 32-bit version is called **webwiz32.exe**. You can also get the files by using your Web browser and going to URL **http://www. halcyon.com/webwizard/welcome.html**. The files are uncompressed executables.

WEB Wizard comes in both 16-bit (Windows 3.1) and 32-bit (Windows NT and Windows 95) versions. WEB Wizard is freeware, and may be freely distributed, but ARTA Software Group and David Geller retain the copyright to the program.

Installing WEB Wizard

To install WEB Wizard, do the following:

1. Create a **WEBWIZ** directory on your hard disk.

2. Copy the **WEBWIZ16.EXE** or **WEBWIZ32.EXE** file to that directory.

3. Create an icon on your Windows desktop for the WEBWIZ16.EXE or WEBWIZ32.EXE file.

Using WEB Wizard

To use WEB Wizard, do the following:

1. Start WEB Wizard.

2. You'll see the opening screen. Click on **Begin >**.

3. The Welcome screen is displayed. This screen tells you a little about WEB Wizard. Click on **Next >** to get started.

4. The succeeding screens will ask you to enter a Title, an optional picture (.GIF or .JPG) file, a paragraph of text, some links to other Web pages, and a filename for the file. Simply follow the directions on each page.

When you're done, you'll see the name and location of your .HTM file and any associated picture files. If you associated a picture with the file, it will remind you that the file must be in the same directory as the .HTM file.

WEB Wizard will save the file either in the directory where WEB Wizard is located, or, if you entered a picture file, in the directory where the picture file is located.

Now that you have your basic Web page set up, you can use one of the other HTML Editors covered in this chapter to edit your new page.

For more information about WEB Wizard, check out **http://www.halcyon. com/webwizard/welcome.html**.

HoTMetaL

HoTMetaL, by SoftQuad, is one of the most popular HTML editors around. It offers extensive code checking, which prevents you from making a mistake. For example, if your cursor is in a bullet (unordered) list, the only HTML element you're allowed to enter is a new bullet. And, if you try to enter text where text is not allowed, HoTMetaL gives you a virtual whack on the knuckles and refuses to let you type anything there (see Figure 13.2).

Figure 13.2:
SoftQuad's HoTMetaL is a sophisticated HTML editor that won't let you break the rules.

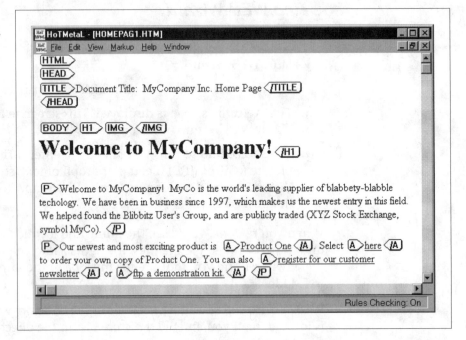

HoTMetaL also comes with a number of pre-formatted templates. The available templates include: a customer registration form, a definition list, simple heading (outline) documents, a personal home page, image documents, a simple paragraph document, a readme document, and list documents.

> You can get HoTMetaL via anonymous FTP from **ftp.ncsa.uiuc.edu**, in the **/Web/html/hotmetal/Windows** directory. The current version is 1.0+, release 50p1, and the filename is **hotm1new.exe**.

HoTMetaL is a demo version of the full commercial product. The full-featured, fully supported commercial version, HoTMetaL PRO, is available from SoftQuad for $195.

Installing HoTMetaL

To install HoTMetaL, do the following:

1. Run the **HOTM1NEW.EXE** file in an empty directory to uncompress the setup files.

2. Run the **HMINST.EXE** file to install HoTMetaL. Accept the default values if possible.

To configure HoTMetaL, do the following:

1. Using a text editor, like the Windows Notepad, open the **SQHM.INI** file in the **SQHM** directory that was created when you installed HoTMetaL.

2. Look for the following lines:

```
#html_browser    = mosaic.exe
#view_gif        = psp.exe
#view_bmp        = pbrush.exe
#view_jpg        = lview.exe
```

Edit these lines to reflect the helper applications that you normally use, including their full directory names. For each entry you edit, make sure you delete the pound sign (#) at the beginning of the line.

3. If you want to be able to use the Netscape extensions to the HTML specification, also find the **rules file=** line and change it to read **rules_file=html-net.mtl**.

4. Save the file and exit.

► *If you have a Postscript printer, or if you have the Ghostscript program discussed in Chapter 10, you can print out the HoTMetaL documentation. The documentation files are in the DOC subdirectory, and the manual filename is HOT-METAL.PS.*

Using HoTMetaL

HoTMetaL is a very powerful and sophisticated program, one that can be very intimidating for the beginner. If you're new to HTML coding, I recommend familiarizing yourself with HTML structure before you jump in and use HoTMetaL.

Here are some things to remember when using HoTMetaL:

To turn Rules Checking off, select Markup ➤ Turn Rules Checking Off.

To insert an HTML element, such as a header tag, select Markup ➤ Insert Element.

To mark existing text using an HTML element, such as a header tag, select Markup ➤ Surround.

To use one of the pre-formatted templates, select File ➤ Open Template and select one of the template files. Save the file under a new name, and begin editing it with your own information.

To insert an image, select Markup ➤ Insert Element, and select IMG. You'll then be prompted to enter information about the image.

 ► *For more information about HoTMetaL, check out* **http://www.sq.com**.

HTML Assistant

HTML Assistant, by Howard Harawitz, is a very straightforward, easy to use HTML editor. You can enter the text you want on your page, and then use the button bars to insert the appropriate coding (see Figure 13.3).

Figure 13.3:
With HTML Assistant, you can automatically insert HTML codes with a push of a button.

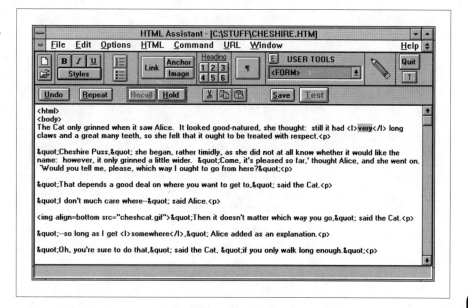

You can get HTML Assistant via anonymous FTP from **ftp.cs.dal.ca**, in the **/htmlasst** directory. The current version at the time of this writing is 1.4 and the filename is **htmlasst.zip**.

HTML Assistant is freeware, and may be freely distributed, provided that the files are distributed intact. The author retains the copyright to the program. A commercial version, HTML Assistant Pro, is also available, and costs $99.95. It offers printed documentation, an automatic page creating wizard, filters for removing HTML codes, and the ability to load files larger than 32KB.

Installing HTML Assistant

To install HTML Assistant, do the following:

1. Create an **HTMLASST** directory on your hard disk.
2. Uncompress the zip file into this directory.

339

3. Move all of the .DLL and .VBX files to your WINDOWS\SYSTEM subdirectory.

4. Create an icon on your Windows desktop for the **HTMLASST.EXE** file.

To configure HTML Assistant, do the following:

1. Start up HTML Assistant. The HTML Assistant welcome screen is displayed. Click on **OK**.

2. Select File ➤ Set test program name. Use the File Find window to select your favorite Web browser to use as a test program. Click on **OK**.

3. You'll be asked to confirm that you want to save this as your permanent test program. Click on **Yes**.

4. Now select Options ➤ Autosave file before test. Since you can't test the link without saving the file first, this ensures that you will always save your work before testing.

5. To change the default screen font, select Options ➤ Default Font. Select your preferred font and click on **OK**.

Using HTML Assistant

When you first start HTML Assistant, you only see part of the menu options. To see all of the menu options, open a new or existing file using either File ➤ New or File ➤ Open.

I recommend entering all of your text first, and then entering the appropriate codes. In fact, if you want, you can just create the text of your page in your favorite word processing program, save the file as plain text, open it in HTML Assistant and enter all of the HTML codes there.

Here are some handy commands to remember when using HTML Assistant:

To automatically insert paragraph marks, highlight the text, and select Command ➤ Autoinsert paragraph markings.

To mark text as a heading level or as a particular style, highlight the text, and select one of the heading levels from the

Heading buttons (1, 2, 3, etc.), or clicking the Styles button and selecting a style.

To mark lines as a numbered or bulleted list, highlight the text, and click on either the numbered or bulleted list button.

To insert a special character, such as quote marks, ampersands, and other characters that require a special code, position the cursor where you want the character to appear, and select HTML ➤ and the character you want to insert.

To repeat the previous command, press Ctrl+R. This comes in really handy when you're inserting repetitive things, like quotes or bullets.

To insert a URL, anchor, or image, position the cursor where you want it to appear and click on the Link, Anchor, or Image button.

To undo the last action, click on the Undo button.

To test your page using your Web browser, click on the Test button.

For more information about HTML Assistant, check out the HTML Assistant Frequently Asked Questions list at **ftp.cs.dal.ca***, in the* **/htmlasst** *directory. The filename is* **htmlafaq.html***.*

HTMLed

HTMLed, by Peter Crawshaw, is an impressive little package. It offers floating toolbars from which you can select a number of different styles and text elements. It even lets you design a custom toolbar that contains the tags and elements that you use most often (see Figure 13.4).

You can get HTMLed via anonymous FTP from **pringle.mta.ca** in the **/pub/HTMLed** directory. The current version at the time of this writing is 1.2e, and the filename is **htmled12.zip**.

HTMLed is shareware, and costs $39 to register. You may use if for evaluation purposes for 30 days before registration is required.

Figure 13.4:
HTMLed lets you select tag elements quickly from its floating toolbars.

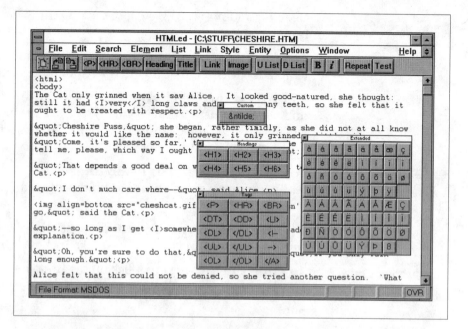

Creating Transparent Images

Okay, I know what you're thinking—"What's the point of having an image if you can't see it?" Well, there are several reasons why you might want to have a transparent, or more likely, a partially transparent image. By changing the background color of an image from, say, white to transparent, the images will appear to jump right out of the background. You can also use transparent images as spacers between other visible images, so that they'll format just the way you want them to on your page. And, transparent images load faster in Web browsers because the browser doesn't have to display the portion of the image that's transparent.

The ability to designate a particular color as transparent is relatively new. It's part of the specification for the GIF89a image format. It doesn't work if the image is saved in the older GIF87a format. Right now, the only shareware image manipulation program I know of that supports both GIF89a images and the transparent color option is LViewPro, version 1.9 and higher. The current version at the time of this writing, which I discussed in Chapter 10, is 1.a.

To create an image with a transparent color, do the following:

1. First you have to make sure that the area you want to make transparent is all one color. Multiple shades of the same color won't cut it. You can fix this by using an image editing program. Unfortunately, LViewPro doesn't offer this capability, so you'll have to use something like the Windows Paintbrush to make the background color a single color.

2. When you're done, open the file in LViewPro.

3. Select Options ➤ Background Color.

4. First, make sure the **Mask Selection Using** option is checked. If the color you selected is a light color, click on the **Black** button. If it's a dark color, click on the **White** button. Masking covers up everything *except* the color you want.

5. Now, select the color that you want to make transparent from the colors displayed at the top of the dialog box. Make sure that the masking covers up everything *except* that color.

6. Click on **OK**.

7. Now, save the file in GIF89a format.

And that's it—the color you designated as the Background color is now transparent. If you have a Web browser that lets you change the background color, such as NCSA Mosaic, you can check it out for yourself. The background, or transparent color will always be the same color as the background.

Installing HTMLed

To install HTMLed, do the following:

1. Create an **HTMLED** directory on your hard disk.

2. Uncompress the zip file into this directory.

3. Create an icon on your Windows desktop for the **HTMLED.EXE** file.

To configure HTMLed, do the following:

1. Start up HTMLed. The About HTMLed screen is displayed. Click on **OK**.

2. Select Options ➤ Setup. Check the boxes so that the four floating toolbars will be displayed on startup.

3. Click on the Browse button to select the Web browser that you want to use for testing documents. Click on **OK**.

4. To change the default font, select Options ➤ Font. Select your preferred font and click on **OK**.

To add your own tags to the Custom floating toolbar, do the following:

1. Select Options ➤ Configure Custom ToolBar.

2. Click on **New** to enter a new button, then enter the name for the new button. Click on **OK**.

3. Then, enter the tag text in the **First tag** box.

4. If the tag requires a beginning and an end code, click on the **Compound option** button and enter the ending code in the **Second tag** field.

5. Click on **Update**, then **OK**.

6. Exit and restart HTMLed so that your change takes effect.

Using HTMLed

When you first start up HTMLed, select File ➤ New to open a new file. You can select which of the standard codes to enter: **<HTML>**, **<BODY>**, **<HEAD>**, and author comments. This is rather nice, since it makes sure that you enter these codes. Here are some handy things to remember when using HTMLed:

To mark text as a heading level, highlight the text, and select one of the heading levels from the Headings floating toolbar.

To mark text as a particular style, highlight the text, and then select Style ➤ and the style that you want to use.

To enter a bulleted, numbered, definition, menu, or directory list, place the cursor where you want the list to appear and select List ➤ and the type of list that you want to insert. Then, to enter each bullet, click on the <LI> tag in the Tags floating toolbar.

To repeat the previous command, press Ctrl+R.

To "intelligently" insert tags, select Search ➤ Intelligent Tag Insert. Enter a particular text string to search for, and enter beginning and ending tags that you want to appear on every line that contains that search string.

To insert a URL or image, position the cursor where you want it to appear and click on the Link or Image button.

To undo the last action, select Edit ➤ Undo.

To test your page using your Web browser, click on the **Test** button.

 ▶

For more information about using HTMLed, see the HELP.TXT and README.TXT files in the HTMLED directory.

HTML Writer

HTML Writer, by Kris Nosack, is a very well-designed HTML editor. It lets you select just about any HTML code you'll ever need to insert from the menu, with the most commonly used tags available from the button bar (see Figure 13.5). The help file even includes a brief tutorial on HTML coding.

> You can get HTML Writer via anonymous FTP from **lal.cs.byu.edu**, in the **/pub/www/tools/** directory. The current version at the time of this writing is 0.9, Beta 4, and the filename is **hw9b4all.zip**.

Figure 13.5:
HTML Writer is a
well-designed,
easy-to-use HTML
Editor.

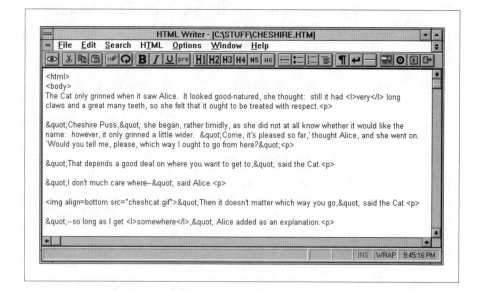

HTML Writer is donationware. If you use it and you think it's worth $10 (suggested donation), send it to the author to help fund the program's development.

*This program does not come with the VBRUN300.DLL file, which is the runtime library file required for all applications written in Microsoft Visual Basic™ 3.0. Check your WINDOWS\ SYSTEM directory to see if you already have it installed. If not, you can get it from the SimTel archives at **oak.oakland.edu**, in the /**SimTel/win3/dll** directory. The filename is **vbrun300.zip**.*

Installing HTML Writer

To install HTML Writer, do the following:

1. Create an **HTMLWRIT** directory on your hard disk.

2. Uncompress the zip file into this directory.

3. Move the .VBX and .DLL files to your WINDOWS\SYSTEM directory.

4. Create an icon on your Windows desktop for the **HTMLWRIT.EXE** file.

346

To configure HTML Writer, do the following:

1. Start HTML Writer.

2. To select the Web browser that you want to use to test your HTML pages, select Options ➤ Test using. Then select either Cello, Mosaic, or Netscape from the list.

3. To change the screen font, select Options ➤ Screen Font and select your preferred font.

Using HTML Writer

You can either import an existing text document into HTML Writer or do all of your composing in HTML Writer. Here are some handy commands to remember when using HTML Writer:

To mark text as a heading level, highlight the text, and select one of the heading levels from button bar.

To mark text as a particular style, highlight the text, and then select the style that you want to use from the button bar.

To enter a bulleted, numbered, or definition list, enter the list, then select all lines and click on the appropriate list style from the button bar.

To repeat the previous command, click on the Repeat Command button.

To insert a URL or image, position the cursor where you want it to appear and click on the Image or Hyperlink Target button on the button bar.

To undo the last action, select Edit ➤ Undo.

To test your page using your Web browser, click on the Test (eye) button. The first time you select this option, you'll be prompted to enter the path to your Web browser.

For more information about HTML Writer, check out the HTML Writer Home Page at **http://lal.cs.byu.edu/people/nosack/index.html**. *For help about using HTML Writer, press the F1 key at any time when using HTML Writer.*

Staking Your Claim   CH. 13

HTML Advanced Topics

Once you've mastered HTML, you might be ready to move on to the more sophisticated aspects of HTML design. Some of the things you can do include forms, graphical interface maps, and even more sophisticated formatting techniques. For more information about these aspects of HTML design, check out these information resources:

How to Create High-Impact Documents. From Netscape Communications, this guide can help you to take advantage of some of the more sophisticated HTML tricks. To get there, set your Web browser to the following URL:

http://www.netscape.com/home/services_docs/impact_docs/

Graphical Information Map Tutorial. Ever wonder how to embed hypertext links into an image? This tutorial will tell you how it's done. To get there, set your Web browser to the following URL:

http://wintermute.ncsa.uiuc.edu:8080/map-tutorial/ image-maps.html

MapEdit. MapEdit is a tool that lets you edit Graphical Information Maps in Windows. You can get it via anonymous FTP from **sunsite. unc.edu**, in the **/pub/packages/infosystems/WWW/tools/mapedit**. The filename is **mapedit.zip**.

The Common Gateway Interface (CGI). If you've got an urge to create forms on your Web page, you should familiarize yourself with the CGI scripting language. This page will give you an overview of CGI, and provide you with pointers to examples and other good reference information. To get there, set your Web browser to the following URL:

http://hoohoo.ncsa.uiuc.edu/cgi/

HyperText Markup Language. This is the ultimate resource point at CERN. Here you can find information on the HTML specification, and pointers to other information sources all over the world. To get there, set your Web browser to the following URL:

http://www.w3.org/hypertext/WWW/MarkUp/MarkUp.html

Word for Windows HTML Editors

All three of these HTML Editors require that you have Microsoft Word for Windows installed on your computer. They are all based on Word templates, which contain WordBasic macros that do all of the HTML coding for you.

If you're a Word user, you'll definitely want to check these editors out, because you have ready access to all of your favorite Word features.

CU-HTML

CU-HTML, by Kenneth Wong and Anton Lam of the Chinese University of Hong Kong, was one of the first HTML editors available. It's comprised of a set of WordBasic™ macros that run in Word for Windows, allowing you to create and edit HTML documents in a familiar environment. There are versions for both Microsoft Word 2.0 and 6.0, and each comes with plenty of documentation and examples (see Figure 13.6).

Figure 13.6:
CU-HTML lets you create and edit Web pages in Microsoft Word for Windows. Notice the additional toolbar added by CU-HTML underneath your normal toolbars.

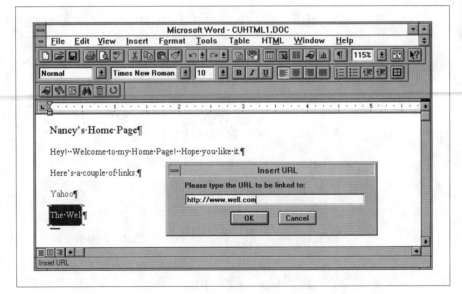

You can get CU-HTML via anonymous FTP from **ftp.cuhk.hk**, in the **/pub/www/windows/util** directory. The current version at the time of this writing is 1.5.3, and the filename is **cu_html.zip**.

CU-HTML is freeware and may be freely distributed, provided that no fee is charged and the files are distributed intact. The authors maintain the copyright to the product.

Installing CU-HTML

To install CU-HTML, you must first have Word for Windows 2.0 or 6.0 installed on your computer. Then, do the following:

1. Create a **CUHTML** directory on your hard disk.

2. Uncompress the zip file into this directory.

3. Move the **CU_HTML.DLL**, **CU_HTML.INI** and **GIF.DLL** files to your **WINDOWS** directory.

4. The next and final step will differ depending on what version of Word you are using:

   - If you're using Word 2.0, copy **CU_HTML2.DOT** to your **WINWORD** directory and rename it **CU_HTML.DOT**.

   - If you are using Word 6.0, copy the **CU_HTML6.DOT** file to your **WINWORD\TEMPLATE** directory, and rename it to **CU_HTML.DOT**.

Using CU-HTML

To use CU-HTML, do the following:

1. Start up Word for Windows as you normally would.

2. Select File ➤ New to create a new document.

3. Select the **Cu_html** template.

4. If you don't see the floating toolbar, select View ➤ Toolbars and check the HTML box.

Here are some handy tips for creating a Web page with CU-HTML:

To make text bold, italic, or underlined, just select the text and mark it using the appropriate formatting button.

To mark text as a Title, Heading, or List, select the text and choose one of the styles from the Style list box.

To insert a picture, click on the GIF (Graphic) button, then select the file.

To insert a link to another .HTM file on your hard disk, select the text to be displayed for the link and click on the Link button, then select the file.

To insert a link to somewhere else on the same page, define a bookmark at that location, then click on the Local Link button, then select the bookmark.

To insert a link to a remote URL, select the text to be displayed for the link and click on the URL button, then enter the URL.

To delete a link, select the text containing the link that you want to get rid of, and click on the Delete Link button.

To convert your completed file to HTML format, save your file and click on the Write HTML button. CU-HTML will then convert your file, and save it in the same directory where your .DOC file is located, with the same name, except with the .HTM extension.

For more information about CU-HTML, check out **http://www.cuhk.hk /csc/cu_html/cu_html.htm**.

GT-HTML

GT-HTML, by Jeffrey L. Grover, John H. Davis III, and Bob Johnston of the Georgia Tech Research Institute, is another set of Word for Windows WordBasic macros for creating HTML pages (see Figure 13.7).

Figure 13.7:
GT-HTML is a set of WordBasic macros that let you create HTML pages in Word for Windows. Notice the two additional toolbars which are added when you use the GT-HTML template.

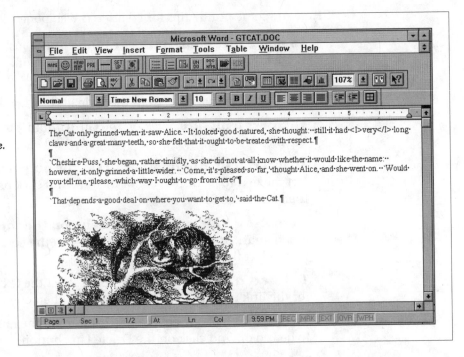

You can get GT-HTML via anonymous FTP from **ftp.gatech.edu**, in the **/pub/www directory**. The current version at the time of this writing is 6.0a, and the filename is **gt_html.zip**.

GT-HTML is currently freeware, but the copyright is maintained by the authors.

Installing GT-HTML

To install GT-HTML, you must first have Word for Windows 6.0 installed on your computer. Then, do the following:

1. Create a **GTHTML** directory on your hard disk.

2. Uncompress the zip file into this directory.

3. Move the **GT_HTML.DOT** file to your **WINWORD\TEMPLATE** directory.

4. Move the **SAMPLPIC.BMP** file to your **WINWORD** directory.

To configure GT-HTML, do the following:

1. Start up Word for Windows as you normally would.

2. Select File ➤ New to create a new document.

3. Select the **Gt_html** template.

4. If you don't see the floating toolbars, select View ➤ Toolbars and check the **Toolbar 1 (GT_HTML.DOT)** and **Toolbar 2 (GT_HTML.DOT)** boxes.

5. Click on the **SetUp** button and enter the directory where you want to store your HTML files, and the full path and filename for your preferred Web browser.

Using GT-HTML

To use GT-HTML, just create your document in Word as you would a normal document. Here are some things to remember when using GT-HTML:

To make text bold, italic, or underlined, just select the text and mark it using the appropriate formatting button.

To insert a link to somewhere else on the same page, highlight the text you want to display for the link, then click on the Name button.

To insert a picture, type the filename of the picture file, then click on the image (smiley face) button.

To mark text as a Title, Heading, or List, select the text and click on the Head button, then select the appropriate heading level.

To mark text as preformatted, which retains the tabs and spaces you have in your text, select the text and click on the Pre button.

To insert a line, click on the line button.

To open your Web browser to check a URL, select the URL and click on the WWW (globe) button.

Staking Your Claim CH. 13

353

To format text as a bulleted or numbered list, highlight the text and click on either the bullet or numbered list button.

To insert a link to another .HTM file or a URL, type the text to be displayed for the link and then the filename or URL to which it will be linked, then click on the Convert to Link button.

To delete a link, select the text containing the link that you want to get rid of, and click on the UnDo button.

To convert your completed file to HTML format, save your file and click on the DOC → HTML button. GT-HTML will then convert your file, and save it in the directory you specified in the setup.

To open the Word document version of a link file, select the filename and click on the green file open button.

To hide the HTML codes, click on the Hide button.

For more information about GT-HTML, check out **http://www.gatech.edu /word_html/release.htm**.

Word Internet Assistant

Microsoft's Word Internet Assistant is an amazingly cool idea. It transforms your everyday, ordinary copy of Word for Windows into a combination editing tool and Web browser. With just a click of a button, you're able to surf the Web right from Word.

Not only is this an easy way to make sure that your links are all correct, but it's also a great way to get ideas for Web pages. If you find one you like, you can just select File ➤ Save to save it so you can later dissect it and pick out the things that you like. Of course you can also do this from other browsers as well, but with Word Internet Assistant, you can do it all from a single application (see Figure 13.8).

The Internet connectivity portion of Word Internet Assistant comes courtesy of Booklink, the makers of InternetWorks, which I covered in Chapter 7.

Figure 13.8:
Microsoft's Word
Internet Assistant is
an innovative concept
in Web page
publishing—a
combination editor and
Web browser.

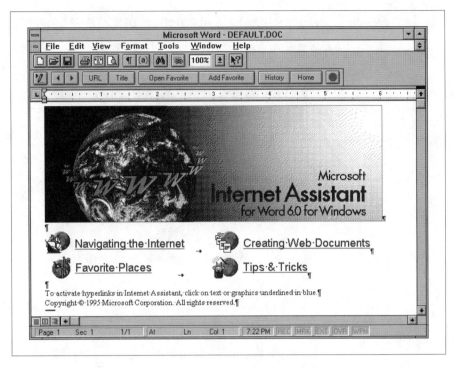

You can get Word Internet Assistant via anonymous FTP from **ftp. microsoft.com**, in the **/deskapps/word/winword-public/ia** directory. The current version is Beta 2, and the filename is **wordia.exe**, which is a self-extracting archive file.

If you're using the original release version of Word 6.0, you need to install the Word 6.0a patch before installing Word Internet Assistant. You can also get this file from **ftp.microsoft.com***, in the* **/softlib/mslfiles** *directory. The filename is* **WORD60A.EXE***. To find out which version you have, start up Word and select Help ➤ About Microsoft Word. The version number is displayed in the first line of the About screen. If it just says Microsoft Word 6.0, then you need to install the 6.0a patch.*

355

Installing Word Internet Assistant

If you're running version 6.0 of Word, you first need to install the 6.0a patch. To install the Word 6.0a patch, do the following:

1. Run the **WORD60A.EXE** self-extracting archive file in an empty directory to uncompress the setup files.

2. Run the **SETUP.BAT** file to expand the upgrade files.

3. Run the **UPGRADE.EXE** file to upgrade Word to version 6.0a.

4. Delete the upgrade files from the directory.

To install Word Internet Assistant, do the following:

1. Run the **WORDIA.EXE** self-extracting archive file into an empty directory to uncompress the setup files.

2. Close all running applications.

3. Run the **SETUP.EXE** file to install Word Internet Assistant.

Using Word Internet Assistant

To use Word Internet Assistant, do the following:

1. Start Word for Windows.

2. Select File ➤ New, and select the **Html** template.

3. Start typing.

You'll notice that the button bars change when you open an HTML document. The buttons all correspond to HTML editing functions.

Because you're in Word, you can use all of the same Word editing commands that you would use normally. In addition, you can perform some additional functions needed to create HTML documents. Here's a list of some additional commands you can use when editing HTML documents:

To switch to Web browser view, click on the eyeglasses button.

To move forward or backward through links, click on the right and left pointing arrow buttons.

To enter a ruling line, click on the horizontal line button.

To insert an image link, position the cursor where you want the link to appear and click on the Insert Picture button.

To insert a bookmark that can be used as a destination for a hyperlink, click on the bookmark button.

To insert a hypertext link, click on the Link button. The Hyperlink window appears. Select either the Local Document, URL, or Bookmark tab, depending on where you want the link to lead to.

To insert the non-printing <HEAD> and <TITLE> elements, click on the Page Information button.

For more information about Word Internet Assistant, check out **http://www. microsoft.com/pages/deskapps/word/ia/default.htm**.

With a good HTML editor at your disposal, you can create your own presence on the World Wide Web. The Web can be your canvas, and you can color it with whatever suits your fancy: art, information, sounds, and links to other places on the Web. And, once you've created it, you can share it with the world.

Staking Your Claim CH. 13

357

A

The UNIX
Shell Game

■

FOR MANY YEARS, Unix shell accounts provided the only means for the average PC user to connect to the Internet. While shell accounts do give you access to the Internet, they were only designed to support basic terminal emulation, which means the only Internet tools available were the ones you could run from the Unix server itself. If you tried to run a graphical Internet application from your PC, you'd just get error messages.

Despite the growing availability of SLIP and PPP connections, there's still a big demand for Unix shell accounts. Cost is usually the reason. In many areas, SLIP and PPP accounts still cost more than basic Unix shell accounts, although this is beginning to change, as competition for your Internet dollar increases.

Speaking in Terminals

Terminal Emulation, refers to the way your computer talks to another computer. Terminal emulation software allows you to connect a PC to a mainframe or other server that was designed to talk only to "dumb" terminals. And they don't call 'em "dumb" for nothing. Most dumb terminals consist of a monitor and a keyboard, and not much else. Because all the actual thinking went on in a big computer off in some air-conditioned room, dumb terminals didn't need to be very smart. All they had to do was display the information coming from the big computer.

And that information consisted of the basic *ASCII* character set. The ASCII character set includes your basic keyboard characters, plus a few additional characters needed to exchange information with the big computer in the air-conditioned room.

So that's why basic terminal emulation doesn't let your PC do anything more than exchange ASCII characters with a server. It doesn't matter if you're using a garage-sale XT or a 100MHz Pentium PC—the server still thinks that you're sitting at a dumb terminal.

Today, there are more options available to PC users, like *SLIP* and *PPP* connections, which allow you to access servers, and the Internet, using a more sophisticated protocol. Because these protocols are more sophisticated than basic terminal emulation, they allow you to transfer non-ASCII characters between your PC and a server, which means you can run interactive, client/server programs over your connection to servers on the Internet.

Another advantage of shell accounts is that you usually get some disk space on the provider's server. This can come in handy at times, say if you ever need to run a Unix-based program, or if you just need a little off-site, easily accessible storage space.

New options, like *SLIP Emulation*, are great for shell account users. SLIP Emulation "tricks" your PC into thinking that it's connected via a SLIP connection, when it's really just dialed in to a plain Unix shell account. What this means in practical terms is that you can run many of the same cool graphical Internet applications that SLIP and PPP users can, using your Unix shell account. See *Putting a New Face on an Old Shell: TIA* at the end of this appendix for information about setting up SLIP Emulation on your Unix shell account.

Getting Around in Unix

Even if you access the Internet from DOS or Windows, there may come a time when you'll need to use a few Unix commands in your journey through the Internet. Why? Because there just happens to be a lot of Unix systems on the Internet. For example, if you telnet to a system that speaks only Unix, you may need to know a couple of Unix commands just to be able to move around on the server.

For many years, Unix has been the de facto operating system on the Internet, mostly because *TCP/IP* is built into the Unix operating system. And TCP/IP is the language of the Internet.

Unix isn't a terribly difficult operating system, it's just different from MS-DOS. Some commands are the same; for example, "change directory" is **cd** in both DOS and Unix. But, unfortunately, the similarity pretty much ends there.

DOS and Don'ts in Unix

There are some subtle differences between Unix and DOS you should keep in mind:

- Unix uses a forward slash to separate directories (/usr/local/home/ mydir), while DOS uses the backslash, (\WINDOWS\SYSTEM).

361

- Unix systems are case sensitive, which means that File-name.txt, FILENAME.TXT, and filename.txt are all different files. DOS doesn't care whether you use UPPERCASE letters or lowercase letters.

Also, since Unix is a *multiuser* operating system, each user has their own personal space reserved on the server. This space is called your *home* directory. Typically, your directory is called something like /usr/local/home/mydir, although different systems may use different naming schemes for their user directories. Your home directory is where you always start out when you first log in. It's also where all your personal files are kept, including those that you download from other places on the Internet.

Handy Unix Commands

Overall, Unix isn't any harder to learn than DOS. It's just different. Here are a few commands you'll need to know if you want to be able to get around in Unix. To help you understand these commands, I've included the DOS equivalent for each command where applicable.

pwd	*Print Working Directory* tells you the name of the directory you're in. In DOS, you'd type **CD** by itself to get the same information.
cd	*Change Directory* switches you to the directory you specify. For example, **cd Mail** changes the current directory to the Mail subdirectory. As in DOS, if you want to change to the directory one level up, type **cd ..** (don't forget the space between **cd** and **..**).
ls	*List* is similar to the DOS DIR command, in that it displays the files in the current directory. Using ls by itself, however, only displays regular files and directories. It does not display files that begin with a dot (.), as these are usually system and configuration files.

ls -a   *List All* displays all files, including system and
                   configuration files, in the current directory.
                   Depending on your system, and what programs
                   you've run, you'll see different files listed here.
                   The (.) and (..) items are the current and parent
                   directories on the system (just like you see in DOS
                   when you run DIR).

ls -l   *List Long Name* displays the full name and
                   description of each item in the directory (see
                   Figure A.1). Unlike ls and ls -a, this command
                   allows you to distinguish between files,
                   directories, and links to other directories.

Figure A.1:
Unix file listings
dissected.

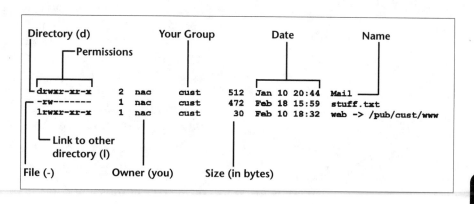

ls -la   *List Long Name, All* is simply a combination of ls
                   -l and ls -a. Of all the variations on ls, it's the
                   closest to the DOS DIR command.

cp *file filenew* *Copy* is similar to the DOS COPY command. Use
                   it to copy a file (*file*) to a new file with a
                   different name (*filenew*).

mv *file*   *Move* is similar to the DOS REN (rename)
newname*   command. Use it to change the name of a file
                   (*file*) to a new name (*newname*).

Unix Shell Game
APP. A

363

cat file	*Catalog* is similar to the DOS TYPE command. Use it to view the contents of a file (*file*). If the file is too long to display on your screen, use **cat file |more** to see the file one screen at a time.
mkdir dir-name	*Make Directory* is similar to the DOS MD command. It creates a new directory called *dirname*.
rm file	*Remove* is similar to the DOS DEL command. It deletes the file (*file*) you specify.
passwd	Use the *Change Password* command to do just that. You should change your password every month or so for security reasons. Although the odds of someone breaking into your account are pretty slim, the possibility does exist, and changing your password regularly is your best defense against dishonest hackers. Also, make sure that you choose a password that contains a combination of letters, numbers, and punctuation characters, as this kind of password is more difficult to crack.
who	*Who* lists the user IDs of all the folks who are logged into the server.

These are just a few of the commands you can use on a Unix system. There are many, many more. If you want to find out more about Unix, ask your system administrator for pointers to Unix information available on your system.

Online Help

One of the handy things about Unix is that most every command is documented online. If you want to find out more information about a particular command, use the **man** command. So, if you want to find out all about the chmod command, just type **man chmod** and you'll see everything you'd ever want to know about the **chmod** command (see Figure A.2).

Figure A.2:
You can find out all about chmod and other Unix commands by asking the man.

```
chmod(1)                    User Commands                    chmod(1)

NAME
     chmod - change the permissions mode of a file

SYNOPSIS
     chmod [ -fR ] mode filename...
     chmod [ugoa ]{ + | - | = }[ rwxlsStTugo] filename...

AVAILABILITY
     SUNWcsu

DESCRIPTION
     chmod changes or assigns the mode of a file.  The mode of  a
     file  specifies  its  permissions and other attributes.  The
     mode may be absolute or symbolic.

     An absolute mode is specified using octal numbers:

          chmod nnnn filename ...

--More--[Hit space to continue or q to stop.]
```

Permissions and How to Change Them

Permissions are a real pain. I avoided them for years, until someone explained to me that other people could read my private files in my directory if I didn't have the permissions set correctly. So I learned. If you have files on a Unix system, you ought to learn about them, too.

When you type **ls -l** at a Unix prompt, you get a whole bunch of information about the files and directories that reside in your home directory. The first character tells you whether the item is a file (-) or a directory (**d**), or a link to another directory (**l**).

The next nine characters are the *permissions* for the directory or file. The permissions determine who can read, write, and execute that file—**r** is read, **w** is write, and **x** is execute. Only programs and directories can be executed. You can't execute a program or enter a directory for which you do not have execute permission.

You can tell which permissions are granted to each type of user by looking at the three sets of three characters shown right after the first character in the file listing:

```
-rwxrwxrwx 1 owner  group  size date time filename.txt
```

Unix Shell Game
APP. A

365

The first rwx is for you, the *owner* of the file. If the file or directory is in your directory, you own it, and you have the right to set permissions for the file. The second rwx is the permissions you (or your system administrator) have set for the other people in your *group*. Your group is just a logical subset of all the people who have accounts on your system. The third rwx is for everyone else (the world), which includes anyone who isn't a part of your group.

If a permission is "on" you'll see a letter (r, w, or x) in that space. If that particular permission is "off," you'll just see a dash (−). In the following example, my file called stuff.txt can only be read and written to by me, the owner:

```
-rw------- 1 nac   cust   472 Feb 18 15:59 stuff.txt
```

All the other permissions have been removed, so all you see is dashes in those spaces.

If you want to change the permissions of a file in your home directory, you use the chmod (change mode) command. At the Unix prompt, simply follow the chmod command with one character from each of the three columns below.

u (user)   + (add)   **r** (read)

g (group)   - (remove)   **w** (write)

o (other)   **x** (execute)

a (all)

For instance, if you wanted to change the permission of the STUFF.TXT file so that anyone could read the file, you would type **chmod a+r stuff.txt**. When you check the file again with ls -l, you'll see this:

```
$ls -l stuff.txt
-rw-r--r-- 1 nac   cust   472 Nov 19 15:59 stuff.txt
```

Now, anyone can read the file. If you wanted to change the permission again, so that others could write to the file as well, you'd type **chmod a+w stuff.txt**. Now the permissions would read:

```
-rw-rw-rw- 1 nac   cust   472 Nov 19 15:59 stuff.txt
```

If you want other people to have access to your home directory, you need to add the group or world execute permission for your directory.

One last thing to remember is that as a user on a Unix system, you can only change permissions for files that you own. Normally, the files that you own are in your home directory, or in a directory that the system administrator has granted you full access to. System administrators can also change permissions for the files in your directory, but usually they will only do so for a good reason.

*If you can't remember the exact name of a command, you can use **man -k** to help you find it. So, for example, if you can't remember the change password command, you could type **man -k password**. Then, you'll see a list of all the commands that relate to passwords, including passwd.*

Putting a New Face on an Old Shell: TIA

If you take a Unix shell account at face value, it's basically pretty boring. Like DOS, it does the job, but a character-mode interface can get kind of dull after a while, especially when you've gotten used to using a graphical user interface like Microsoft Windows.

I've had an account on a Unix system for years, and used many of the Internet tools available: FTP, Gopher, and Telnet. I heard about the World Wide Web from a friend, but soon found out that although I could access it, the Unix *browser*, or client program, was strictly a character mode interface. The beauty of the Web was lost to me, because its creators designed it from the start with graphical front end client applications in mind, like the kind they use on high-end Unix workstations.

So you can imagine how I felt the first time someone showed me the NCSA Mosaic Web browser for Microsoft Windows, my jaw dropped to the floor. I thought, "Wow! This is cool!" It let you download pictures, sounds, and even programs from the World Wide Web, all by just clicking a mouse button, *and* it was a Microsoft Windows application. So I asked, "How can I get that?" Unfortunately, at the time, all I had was a Unix shell account, and was told, "Nope, sorry, can't run that from there."

367

Well, things have changed since then. There's good news for Unix shell account users—and it comes with the very un-sexy name of *SLIP Emulation*. As I mentioned earlier, SLIP Emulation "tricks" your terminal emulation Unix shell account into thinking that it's a SLIP connection, which is exactly what you need to run Mosaic, and most of the other Windows Internet tools that I've discussed in this book.

Right now, the best SLIP emulator around is The Internet Adapter (TIA) by Cyberspace Development. TIA allows you to run graphical Internet applications like Mosaic on your PC (or Macintosh) from a Unix shell account (see Figure A.3).

Figure A.3:
The Internet Adapter lets Unix shell account users run programs like NCSA Mosaic.

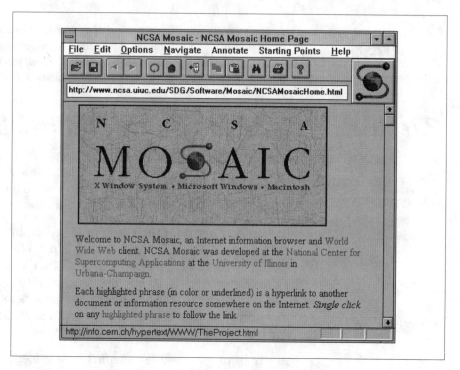

TIA doesn't run on your PC. Instead, you run it from your Unix shell account, in your home directory. But it allows you to connect to your shell account as if you were directly connected to the Internet using a SLIP connection.

A single-user license costs only $25. If you're living in an area where SLIP accounts cost considerably more than Unix shell accounts, TIA could save you that $25 in one month alone.

Cyberspace Development also offers a free 14-day trial offer, so you can check out TIA and decide if you like it before you hand over a credit card number.

Getting and Installing TIA

You can be up and running with TIA in about 30 minutes. Just follow these directions:

1. First, you'll need to use *anonymous FTP* to access the home of Cyberspace Development on the Internet, **marketplace.com**, and get the **config.guess** file, which will help you to determine the type of host system your shell account is running on. You'll need this information to help you select the right version of TIA for your shell account. Log into your Unix shell account, and type the following at a Unix prompt:

   ```
   ftp marketplace.com
   ```

2. At the login: prompt, type **anonymous**. Then, at the password: prompt, enter your e-mail address, for example, **joe@somewhere.com**.

3. Change to the TIA directory by typing **cd tia**.

4. Type **get config.guess** to retrieve the config.guess file. Once the file has been transferred, you can temporarily leave the FTP session by pressing Ctrl+Z.

5. Back at your normal Unix prompt, use the chmod command to change the mode of the file so you'll be able to execute it:

   ```
   chmod u+x config.guess
   ```

6. Now, run the file by typing **config.guess**. You should get back a response telling you what operating system your host is running, for example:

   ```
   sun.sparc.solaris2.3
   ```

Unix Shell Game APP. A

369

In this instance, config.guess told me that my Unix system is a Sun Sparc server running the Solaris operating system version 2.3. Yours may be different. Write this information down. You'll need it in a minute.

7. Now, type **fg** at the Unix prompt to go back to your ftp session, so you can get the correct binary file for your host system. When you see `ftp marketplace.com` press Enter to get back to the `ftp>` prompt.

8. Change to the TIA directory by typing **cd tia**. The next file you're going to retrieve is a binary file, so you need to type **binary** to change the transfer mode to binary. You should see the following:

```
ftp> Type set to I
```

9. Type **ls** to see a list of the files in the directory. Find the one that *most closely matches* the result you got in step 6. At the time of this writing, these are the versions of TIA that are available:

- `alpha.osf1.v2.0.tia` (DEC Alpha/OSF)
- `hp9000.hpux9.0.tia` (HP9000 HPUX)
- `irix.5.2.ta` (Silicon Graphics Inc. IRIX 5.2)
- `linux.1.1.59.tia` (Linux 1.1.59)
- `mips.dec.ultrix4.3.tia` (DEC Ultrix)
- `pc.linux.tia` (386/486 Linux)
- `pc.sco.tia` (386/486 SCO Unix)
- `rs6000.aix3.2.tia` (IBM RS/6000 AIX)
- `sgi.irix4.0.tia` (SGI Irix)
- `68k.sunos.3.tia` (Sun 3 series—68000-based—systems)
- `sparc.solaris.tia` (Sun Sparc Solaris)
- `sparc.sunos.tia` (Sun Sparc SunOS)
- `unixware.4.2.tia` (Novell Unixware 1.1.3)

10. Download the appropriate file by typing **get** and the name of the file. For example, if your server was a Sun Sparc server running SunOS, you'd type **get sparc.sunos.tia**.

11. Log out of the ftp server by typing **quit**.

12. Back at your Unix prompt, rename the file as **tia** by using the Unix **mv** (move or rename) command. For example, if you just got the sparc.sunos.tia file, you'd use the following command:

```
mv sparc.solaris.tia tia
```

13. Finally, type **chmod u+x tia** to change the mode of the file so that you can execute it.

TIA requires a special code in order to run. Cyberspace Development offers two kinds of codes: a free, 14-day evaluation code, and a permanent registration code. The 14-day evaluation code is only good for 14 days from the time you request it. After that, it will no longer work. The permanent registration code costs $25, and you can pay for it by credit card.

The Internet is not secure. Sending credit card information over the Internet can be dangerous. Although unlikely, it is possible for a dishonest person to get your credit card number by reading your mail message. Cyberspace Development understands that you may not feel comfortable sending your credit card number in a mail message, so they have an 800 number you can call to register TIA over the phone. The number is 1-800-440-6880.

To get a free 14-day evaluation code, do the following:

1. Send an e-mail message to **tia-single-user@marketplace.com**. You'll receive back a form (usually in just a few minutes), which you can fill in and send back to receive the evaluation code. Follow the instructions in the message for filling out and returning the form. After you return the form, you'll get back two messages: one containing installation and troubleshooting tips, and one containing your special evaluation code.

2. Save the evaluation code message in a file called **.tia** (the filename *must* begin with a dot). If you don't know how to save a message to a file, see the *Unix Mail Programs* section in Chapter 4.

Don't delete the e-mail message—it's the only copy of this code you're going to get.

371

3. Now you're ready to give TIA a try. From the Unix prompt, type **tia**. If you get back a message like the following, then TIA is working!

```
The Internet Adapter (tm) 1.03b for Solaris on Sun sparcs
Copyright (c) 1994 Cyberspace Development, Inc.

Ready to start your SLIP software.
```

Press Ctrl+C five times to turn it off.

If you get back an error message, read the *TIA Install & License* message that you got along with the evaluation code message from tia-single@ marketplace.com. This message contains helpful information about common problems and ways to solve them.

4. Once you have TIA working properly, type **tia -address**. This command will give you a list of *IP address* numbers for your Unix server. These IP addresses are very important. They are the actual network addresses of the servers you'll be communicating with. Write these numbers down. You'll need them when you configure your SLIP software.

Another thing you'll need to do is write down the exact characters used in your Unix prompt. Not all prompts look the same. Some use `serv-er>` and others use `{server}`. Who knows, you might even have one that says `yeah, what?:`. You'll need this information when you configure your SLIP software so that it will be able to recognize the prompt and automatically start TIA by issuing the **tia** command.

With TIA installed, you're ready to set up your SLIP software. See Appendix B for information on how to set up a SLIP connection in Windows.

B

Connecting Windows to the Internet

■

MOST WINDOWS USERS probably don't realize how lucky they are when it comes to Internet tools. Developers from all over the world are creating some of the most exciting new Internet programs for the Microsoft Windows. But even the coolest tools for Windows will be useless if you're not properly connected to the Internet.

Getting Started

Before you can turn your computer into a fully equipped Internet machine, you'll need four things:

- Windows 3.1 or Windows 95.

- A direct connection to the Internet, either via SLIP or PPP, or via a LAN.

- The Windows Sockets (Winsock) DLL (Dynamic Link Library).

- A TCP/IP protocol stack (usually included with WINSOCK.DLL).

If you have Windows 3.1, and a SLIP or PPP connection, all you need is a Winsock package that includes Winsock, TCP/IP, and connection software. Winsock is an Application Programming Interface (API) that allows Windows to communicate with TCP/IP, which is the language of the Internet. Winsock needs to be running for any Winsock application to function.

 If you accidentally start up a Winsock application when you don't have your Internet connection software running, you'll get an error message, usually something to the effect that WINSOCK.DLL could not be found.

Two of the most poplular packages for SLIP and PPP users , Chameleon Sampler and Trumpet Winsock, are both available on the Internet via anonynmous FTP. I'll tell you how to get both of these packages in the following sections.

 With Winsock running, you can run multiple Winsock applications at the same time.

If you have Windows 95, you don't need to worry about getting either of these packages, since the Winsock library and TCP/IP are both included with Windows 95. Although, if you'd like, you can use Trumpet Winsock with Windows 95.

Now, there's some information about your provider's server that you're going to need when you configure your connection software. Contact your Internet provider, and get the following information:

- The dial-up access phone number (if you're connecting with SLIP or PPP)

- The type of connection (SLIP, PPP, CSLIP)

- The IP addresses for the DNS (Domain Name Servers) used by your provider

- The host names of the mail (SMTP) and news (NNTP) servers, usually something like mail.foo.com and news.foo.com.

If your provider does not use *dynamic IP addressing*, which automatically assigns you an IP address "on the fly" when you log in, you'll also need to find out what your assigned IP address is.

Write this information down carefully. If you get one of the numbers wrong, you'll run into problems when you try to connect.

If you are on a LAN (Local Area Network) connected to the Internet, and you already have a version of TCP/IP installed on your system, such as FTP's PC/TCP software, you cannot use either the Chameleon Sampler or the Trumpet Winsock discussed in this chapter, because it's very likely that they are not compatible with your network software. However, there is probably a version of Winsock available that will run with your network software. Check with your network administrator to find out.

In the following sections, I'll describe the procedures for setting up Chameleon Sampler, Trumpet Winsock, and Windows 95 for SLIP or PPP. In each section, I'll tell you where you can get the software via anonymous FTP, how to install and configure it to access your Internet provider, and how to test your configuration using the Ping utility.

If you're just setting up a SLIP or PPP account and you don't have access to anonymous FTP, ask your provider if they can give you one of these packages (or an equivalent) on disk. Most providers would be more than happy to oblige your request.

Chameleon Sampler: Internet Access Made Easy

Chameleon Sampler is a subset of the Chameleon series of Internet tools from NetManage. The sampler includes Winsock and TCP/IP, SLIP/PPP connection software, plus a few little extras like Ping, FTP, Telnet, and a mail program. NetManage provides the sampler for free, in hopes that you'll like it enough to buy the full Internet Chameleon package for $199, which includes a Web browser, Gopher, newsreader, FTP, finger, Whois, and Archie clients, plus an FTP server.

> You can get Chameleon Sampler via anonymous FTP from, **ftp.netmanage.com**. It's in the **/pub/demos/sampler** directory, and the filename is **sampler.exe**. If your Internet provider offers dial-up access to a Unix shell, use the Unix FTP program described at the beginning of Chapter 2 to download the sampler.exe file.

The SAMPLER.EXE file is a self-extracting archive file, so you need to copy it to an empty directory and type **SAMPLER** from a DOS prompt to extract the files.

It's a good idea to keep a junk directory on your hard disk for extracting programs. Call it JUNK or STUFF or UNZIP, or whatever you like. It's especially handy for applications that come with a Setup or Install program, because you need to run these programs from a directory other than the one you're going to install the program in.

Installing Chameleon Sampler

To set up Chameleon Sampler, do the following:

1. Run the **SETUP.EXE** file. Accept the defaults, if possible.

2. Exit Windows and restart.
   The setup program will create a directory on your hard disk called **NETMANAG** (unless you change it), and will create a Chameleon Sampler group in Windows, shown in Figure B.1.

Figure B.1:
NetManage's
Chameleon Sampler
gives you a little slice
of the Internet for free.

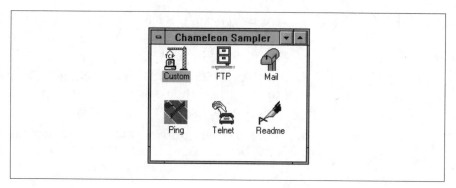

3. Double click on the Custom icon, and select File ➤ Open. Check to see if there's a configuration file for your provider included. If there is, select that file and skip to step 9.

4. If there's no configuration file for your provider, select File ➤ New. Then, save the configuration file by selecting File ➤ Save. Name the file something appropriate like **MYSLIP.CFG**.

5. Select Interface ➤ Add. Click on the Type: pull-down list in the Add Interface dialog box, and select the interface you're going to use. Use the default name (**SLIP0**, **PPP0**, OR **CSLIP0**).

Select CSLIP if you have a SLIP connection that uses VJ Header Compression. VJ Header Compression is a method of compressing, and therefore speeding up, transmissions between your PC and the server. If you aren't sure which one to choose, ask your provider.

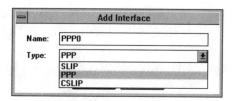

6. Select Setup ➤ IP Address. Chances are, your provider is using *dynamic IP addressing*. That means that your provider keeps a pool of addresses for people to use when they log in. When you log in, you'll be given the next available IP address. If this is the case, your provider may have given you a "dummy" address to enter

Windows
APP. B

377

here, or you can just leave it set to **0.0.0.0**. It really doesn't matter, because it's just a placeholder for the address you'll be assigned each time you log in.

7. If your provider gave you a Host Name and/or Domain name (e.g., foo.com), choose Setup ➤ Host Name and Setup ➤ Domain Name options to enter these names.

8. Now, select Services ➤ Domain Servers and enter the IP addresses of the *Domain Name Servers* (DNS) given to you by your provider in the Domain Servers dialog box.

Domain Name Servers are the "directory servers" on the Internet. It's very important that you enter the IP addresses exactly (and in the same order) as they were given to you.

9. You're now ready to set up your modem connection. Select Setup ➤ Port. The Port Settings dialog box appears. Choose the highest baud rate that your modem can support. If you're not sure, check the documentation that came with your modem. Select the COM port that your modem uses from the **Connector** list. Unless your provider has told you to change the **Data Bits**, **Stop Bits**, **Parity**, and **Flow Control**, leave these options at their default values (8, 1, None, Hardware).

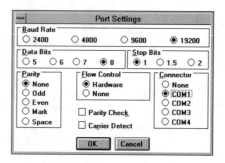

The Importance of Name Servers

Your Domain Name Server (DNS) is your best friend on the Internet. The DNS makes it possible for you to connect to someplace like **whitehouse.gov**, without having to know the exact IP address for the White House's server (198.137.241.30).

Using a DNS is much easier than having to remember all those IP addresses. And, if a server's IP address changes, you won't have to worry about it, since the DNS is responsible for keeping up with IP address changes.

If your DNS configuration isn't set up properly, you won't get very far, because there's no way for your computer to know what IP addresses to use if it can't find your DNS.

10. Select Setup ➤ Modem. If you have a Hayes-compatible modem, leave the modem settings at their defaults. Most PC modems are Hayes-compatible, so these options should work just fine. If you're not sure, check with the documentation that came with your modem.

11. Select Setup ➤ Dial. Enter your provider's dial-in number in the Dial Settings dialog box. You might also want to increase the timeout value to something higher than 30 seconds, if you think it may take longer than 30 seconds to complete the login process. You can always increase this number later if timeouts become a problem.

12. Select Setup ➤ Login and enter your user name and password. You must enter a password, or the connection will hang. If you're running TIA, don't click OK yet. Skip to the next section for special information about starting TIA.

13. Select File ➤Save to save the configuration file.

Additional Steps for TIA Users

If you're running TIA (The Internet Adapter) from a Unix shell account, you need to go through a couple of additional steps to have TIA automatically start after you log in.

1. In the Login Settings screen, enter **tia** in the Startup Command box. Click on **OK**, then save the configuration file, by selecting File ➤ Save.

2. Now, switch over to the Windows Program Manager, and start up the Windows Notepad. Select File ➤ Open, and open the **SLIP.INI** file in the **NETMANAG** directory.

3. Find the **[SLIP0]** entry. It should look something like this:

```
[SLIP0]
SCRIPT=login: $u$r word: $p$r
TYPE=SLIP
```

The **SCRIPT=** line tells Chameleon what to do when it logs in. By default, it waits for a login prompt (**login:**), then gives the script command to send your username (**$u**), and a carriage return (**$r**). Then it waits for the last half of the password prompt (**word:**) and then sends your password (**$p**), and another carriage return (**$r**).

4. To have Chameleon automatically enter the **tia** startup command that you entered in the Login Settings screen, you have to add a third prompt and script command to the SCRIPT= line. At the end of the **SCRIPT=** line, add the last character of your prompt, which is usually something like >, :, or ?. (If you aren't sure what the last character is in the prompt, log in using your normal communications software and check.) Then, after the prompt character, enter **cr** to have the script send the **tia** command (**$c**) and a carriage return (**$r**), like this:

```
SCRIPT=login: $u$r word: $p$r > $c$r
```

5. Close the SLIP.INI file.

Connecting with Chameleon

Okay, now you're ready to connect to the Internet. If Chameleon Sampler isn't open, start it by double-clicking on the Custom icon, then click on **Connect**. You'll see a message from NetManage about how to purchase the commercial version of Chameleon. Click on **OK** to close this message box.

If all goes well, you'll be connected. Minimize the Custom application. Notice the little Newt icon that just appeared on your desktop. Double-click on the little guy to see information about your connection.

If you're connected, you'll see your IP address in the Newt dialog box shown here.

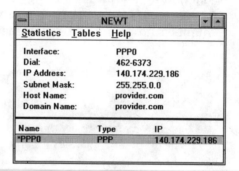

Pinging with Chameleon

Now, you need to test your connection. Why test? Because even though you are connected to the server, you won't get very far if you haven't configured Chameleon properly. The easiest way to check your connection to see if it's set up properly is with the Ping utility. (For more information about Ping, see *Ping, Your Internet Boomerang* at the end of this section.) Double-click on the Ping icon in the Chameleon Sampler group. You'll see the Ping window. The first thing you should do is to Ping your provider's name, by selecting Start, and entering the provider's name. If you get back a response like the one shown in Figure B.2, then you're connected properly.

Figure B.2:

Pinging with Chameleon.

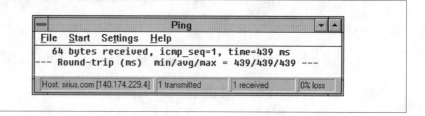

If you don't get back any response, your DNS configuration may be wrong. If this happens, double-click on the minimized Custom Icon and disconnect, then go back and double check your DNS configuration in the Domain Servers dialog box (Services ➤ Domain Servers). You may have entered one of the numbers incorrectly, or entered the numbers in the wrong order. If your numbers are correct, try exiting out of Windows and restarting. If, after doing so, you still don't get a response from Ping, contact your service provider and find out if the DNS numbers have changed, or if something is wrong on their end.

Ping, Your Internet Boomerang

Ping is a very basic utility that works sort of like a boomerang. You enter the name of something, a server or router for example, then Ping looks up its IP address on one of your provider's Domain Name Servers, which keep track of addresses on the Internet. Then Ping makes a call to that address, telling whatever computer answers to send the packet right back. Ping then figures out how long it took for the packet to make its return trip, and reports the results back to you.

Why is this useful? Well, it tells you a couple of things. First, it helps you to determine if your DNS setup is correct, because if Ping can't get an IP address for something that you know exists, like your provider's domain name (e.g., foo.com), you probably aren't talking to your DNS.

If this happens, you should try pinging the DNS itself, using the IP address that you entered in your DNS configuration. If you don't get any response back, that means that either the server is out of service, or you just aren't using the right IP address. Double-check the IP address for the DNS. If you entered it correctly, contact your provider and find out if either the IP address for the DNS has changed or if the server's just out of service at the moment.

Ping is also useful if you can't reach a host server. Say, for example, if you tried to reach an FTP server on the Internet, and your connection got refused. You can send a Ping to the FTP server, and if it answers back, you know that it's up and running, and the problem must lie somewhere else (the server may just have too many FTP connections at the moment). If it doesn't answer a Ping, then maybe you should go have lunch and try your FTP attempt later when the server's back online.

It's important to note that Ping is a very demanding protocol and can cause an excess amount of network traffic, so you shouldn't use it indiscriminately, or continually ping a host once you know that it's working. Otherwise, you could unintentionally cause problems for other users.

Trumpet Winsock

The Trumpet Winsock, by Peter Tattam, is fast becoming a standard for Winsocks. It supports modem speeds up to 115.2kbps (with a modem that supports speeds that high), offers SLIP, PPP, and CSLIP connectivity, and works with both Windows 3.1 and Windows 95.

Trumpet Winsock's biggest advantage may also be its worst disadvantage—it's very configurable. So if you're the sort who loves to roll up your sleeves and mess with configuration settings, you'll love it. But if you're the sort of person who would rather have someone else figure out all that nasty stuff, you may want to think twice before installing it.

Trumpet Winsock is shareware, and the registration fee is currently $25(US). Registering the program gives you priority support and the satisfaction of knowing that you're helping to fund further development.

You can get the latest version of the Trumpet Winsock from Trumpet Software International's anonymous FTP server, **ftp.trumpet.com.au**, in the **/ftp/pub/winsock/** directory. The current version at the time of this writing is 2.0b, and the filename is **twsk20b.zip**. When you connect to the server, download both the Trumpet Winsock file and the **winapps2.zip** file, which contains some additional useful utilities.

Setting Up Trumpet Winsock

To set up Trumpet Winsock, do the following:

1. Create a directory on your hard disk called **TRUMPWSK**.

2. Uncompress the zip file in the TRUMPWSK directory.

3. Create an icon for the **TCPMAN.EXE** file on your Windows desktop. Call it **TCPMAN**.

4. If you're using Windows 3.1, move the **WINSOCK.DLL** file to your **WINDOWS\SYSTEM** directory. If you're using Windows 95, move it to your **WINDOWS** directory. This is the file that contains the Winsock API (Applications Programming Interface), and should be kept with your other Windows .DLL files.

 ▶ *If you have already installed another Winsock package, such as Chameleon, or the Windows 95 Dial-Up Networking, you probably already have a WIN-SOCK.DLL file installed in this directory. If so, rename that file to something like WINSOCK.CHM or WINSOCK.W95 before moving the Trumpet version of WIN-SOCK.DLL to the WINDOWS\SYSTEM or WINDOWS directory. Each version of WINSOCK.DLL is different, and is written specifically for that particular Winsock package. Different versions are not interchangeable.*

5. Now, double-click on the TCPMAN icon you created in step 3. You'll see a blank Network Configuration window, as shown in Figure B.3.

6. Select **Internal SLIP** if you have a SLIP connection, or **Internal PPP** if you have a PPP connection. Notice that several of the fields are now grayed out. As long as you're connecting over a modem, and you aren't going to be using Trumpet Winsock over a dedicated network, you don't have to worry about these fields.

7. Enter the IP address of your provider's Domain Name Server (DNS) in the **Name server** field. If your provider has more than one DNS, separate them by using a space.

8. If your provider has a time server, enter this number in the **Time server** field.

9. Enter your provider's domain name (e.g., foo.com) in the **Domain suffix** field.

Figure B.3:

Setting up Trumpet
Winsock from the
Network Configuration
dialog box.

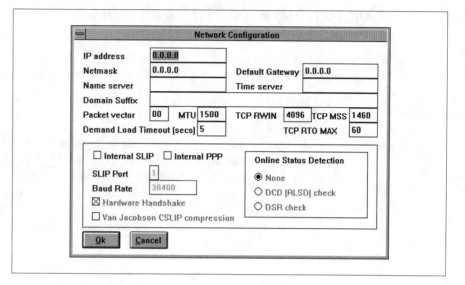

10. If your provider uses CSLIP, or VJ header compression, check the
    Van Jacobson CSLIP compression box.

11. The **MTU** (Maximum Transmission Unit), **TCP RWIN** (TCP
    Receive Window), and **TCP MSS** (TCP Maximum Segment Size)
    values are currently the subject of much debate among users and
    developers alike. Keeping them at their default values, which are
    quite high, tends to help speed up file transfers, but slows down in-
    teractive applications, and can even cause some applications to
    freeze up completely. I recommend starting with lower values—
    MTU=256, TCP RWIN=848, TCP MSS=212. If your provider
    has any suggestions, you should probably heed their advice. If
    you're interested in experimenting with these settings, see Chap-
    ter 12 for more information about configuring Trumpet Winsock.

12. When you're done with the Network Configurations window,
    click on OK.

13. If you are using PPP, you'll probably need to configure the PPP op-
    tions. Select File ➤ PPP Options. The PPP Authentication Options
    window appears. Check the **PAP Authentication Protocol**
    box, enter your username and password, and click on **OK**. This
    option may be required for you to be able to log into your mail
    server. If you aren't sure, check with your provider.

Windows
APP. B

385

Connecting with Trumpet Winsock

Now you're ready to connect to the Internet. If you're using TIA on a Unix shell account, skip this step and go on to the next section. To connect with Trumpet Winsock, do the following:

1. Choose Dialler ➤ Login and enter the phone number for your provider.

2. Enter your user name at the **Login username** prompt, and enter your password at the **Login password** prompt. This is the only time you'll be prompted to enter this information—Trumpet saves it in the **TRUMPWSK.INI** file. Then the Trumpet Winsock starts dialing. Once you're connected, you'll see a **PPP ENABLED** or **SLIP ENABLED** message and your IP address in the Trumpet Winsock window.

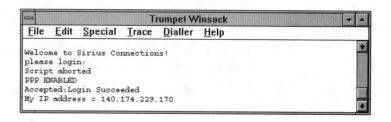

3. Finally, minimize the Trumpet Winsock application.

 If you want to configure Trumpet Winsock so that it will automatically dial when you start TCPMan or automatically log out when you quit TCPMan, click on Dialler ➤ Options. Select one of the three login options: **No automatic login, Automatic login on startup only,** *or* **Automatic login and logout on demand**.

Additional Steps for TIA Users

If you're using TIA on a Unix shell account, you need to dial the number manually. Select Dialler ➤ Manual login. Then type **ATDT** and the phone number of your provider. Log in to your shell account. When you get a prompt, type **tia** and press Enter. After you see the message stating that TIA is running, press Esc. Now, you're connected and you can minimize the Trumpet Winsock application.

Pinging with Trumpet

Now you can use Trumpet's Ping Utility to check your connection. (For more information about Ping, see *Ping, Your Internet Boomerang* earlier in this chapter.) You'll find the **PINGW.EXE** application in your **TRUMPWSK** directory. Start it up and enter your provider's host name after the **host:** prompt, and you should start seeing responses appear, like those shown in Figure B.4. Once you're sure that you're connected, press Esc to stop pinging, and close the Ping window.

Figure B.4:
Pinging with Trumpet.

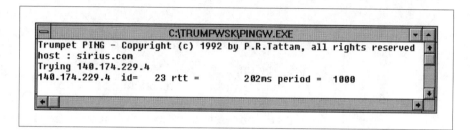

If you don't get a response from the host , check your DNS configuration. Double-click on the minimized TCPMAN icon and select File ➤ Setup. Check the IP address numbers you entered in the **Name server** field.

Windows 95

One of the nicest things about Windows 95 is that it comes with both Winsock and SLIP/PPP connectivity built-in. Although you'll probably still need to install the additional software from your original disks, it is nice knowing that you really don't need to get anything else.

 If you want, you can also use Trumpet Winsock under Windows 95. Just follow the directions for installing Trumpet Winsock in the previous section.

Setting Up SLIP or PPP in Windows 95

Setting up a SLIP or PPP connection in Windows 95 is a little complicated, but once you've got it set up, it's real easy to use. It's a three part process:

- Modem setup
- Dial-Up Networking setup
- TCP/IP setup, which enables Winsock support

I'll take you through each setup procedure, one at a time.

Setting up Your Modem

Unlike previous versions of Windows, Windows 95 wants to know everything about your hardware. So, before you can use a modem with any Windows 95 program, you need to configure Windows 95 for your modem. If you haven't yet installed a modem in Windows 95, follow these directions to set up yours. If you already have a modem set up in Windows 95, you can skip this step and go on to the "Dial-up Networking" section.

1. From the Start menu, select Settings ➤ Control Panel. Then double click on the Modems icon (see Figure B.5). You'll be asked if you want Windows to find your modem. Windows is pretty good at figuring out what kind of modem you have, so it's probably best to let it determine what kind of modem you've got.

2. Windows then scans your COM ports, looking for a modem. When it finds one, it queries the modem to find out what kind it is. Once it determines the modem type, check it to make sure that it's correct. If it's not, click on the Change button to select the correct modem from the list.

3. Next, enter your location (for example, North America) and area code. If you need to dial a number before being able to dial outside (like a 9), you can enter that too.

Figure B.5:
The Windows 95
Control Panel.

Dial-Up Networking

Now you're ready to set up Dial-Up Networking support. If you installed and configured the Dial-Up Networking support when you first installed Windows 95, go ahead and skip to the *Installing TCP/IP Support* section. If you installed it, but haven't yet configured it, skip to Step 2.

1. First, you'll need to locate your installation CD ROM or disks. From Control Panel, select the Add/Remove Programs icon, then select the **Windows Setup** tab. Choose **Dial-up Networking** from the list of components. When prompted, insert the appropriate disk or CD ROM. Complete the software installation procedure.

2. Now you need to configure Dial-up Networking. From the Start menu, select Programs ➤ Accessories ➤ Dial-up Networking. If

Windows
APP. B

389

this is the first time you've selected this option, you're prompted to configure a Dial-up Networking connection (see Figure B.6).

3. You're prompted next to enter the name of the computer you're dialing. It's probably best to name it something descriptive, like "PPP Connection," or "Internet Connection," or "Joe's House of Unix." If you have more than one modem installed, select the modem you want to use, then click on **Next>**. Enter the area code and phone number in the spaces provided, and click on **Next>**. When you're done, just click on **Finish**.

Figure B.6:
Windows 95's Dial-Up Networking option lets you set up a SLIP or PPP connection without any additional software.

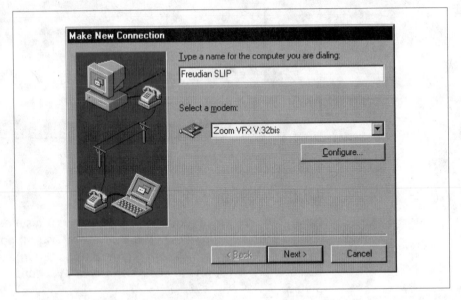

4. Now, the Dial-Up Networking window will appear, containing an icon for your connection. Click on the icon with your right mouse button, then select **Properties** from the pop-up menu. The properties window appears.

5. Click on the **Server Type** button at the bottom of the properties window. The Server Types window appears.

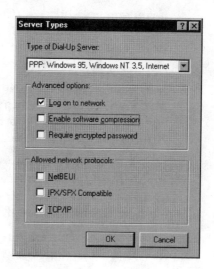

6. Select the correct type of connection for your provider (SLIP, PPP, or CSLIP) from the **Type of Dial-Up Server** pull-down list. If you're using TIA, uncheck the **Log on to network** option. The **Enable Software Compression** option enables *VJ Header Compression* or CSLIP. Only enable this option if your provider supports it. Under **Allowed network protocols**, uncheck **NetBEUI** and **IPX/SPX compatible**. Click on **OK** to return to the properties window.

If you're using TIA, click on the **Configure** *button at the bottom of the configuration properties window. A modem properties window appears. Click on the Options tab at the top of the window and select* **Bring up terminal window after dialing**. *This will enable you to issue the* **tia** *command to start up TIA after you log in to your account. Click on* **OK** *to return to the properties window.*

7. Close the properties window by clicking on **OK**.

Installing TCP/IP and Winsock Support

To install TCP/IP and Winsock support, do the following:

1. From the Start menu, select Settings ➤ Control Panel, and double-click on the **Network** icon. The Network window appears.

391

2. If you don't already see TCP/IP Protocol listed, click on **Add**. Then click on **Protocol**, select **Microsoft** and **TCP/IP**, and click on **OK**. You'll be prompted to enter the appropriate installation diskette or CD-ROM. Follow the prompts to install the TCP/IP drivers.

3. Now, you'll see a list of Network adapters. Double-click on the **Microsoft Dial-up Adapter** in the network components list. The Dial-Up Adapter Properties window appears. Click on the **Bindings** tab, and make sure that **TCP/IP** is checked.

4. Next click on the **Advanced** tab, and check the setting for **Use IP header compression** (see Figure B.7). If your provider uses CSLIP or VJ header compression, select **Yes**. Otherwise, select **No**. Click on **OK** to return to the Network window.

5. Now, you need to configure TCP/IP. Double-click on **TCP/IP**. The TCP/IP window appears, with the **IP Address** tab displayed.

Figure B.7:
Configuring the Dial Up Adapter Settings for your SLIP or PPP connection.

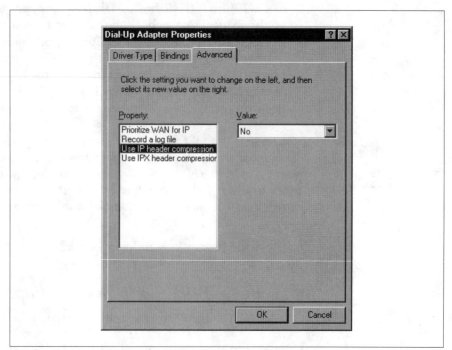

6. The IP Address tab lets you specify the IP address for your computer. Chances are, your provider is using dynamic IP addressing. That means that you are given the next available IP address when you log in. If you have a pre-assigned IP address, enter it here.

7. Click on the **Gateway** tab. Enter the IP address of the gateway given to you by your provider in the **New Gateway** field, and click on **Add** (*don't* press Enter).

8. Click on the **DNS Configuration** tab. Select **Enable DNS**, and enter your provider's host and domain names in the spaces provided. Enter the IP address of the first Domain Name Server given to you by your provider (see Figure B.8). Click on the **Add** button (*don't* press Enter). If your provider gave you more than one address, add the remaining ones in the order given to you by your provider.

Figure B.8:

Setting up Domain Name Servers in Windows 95.

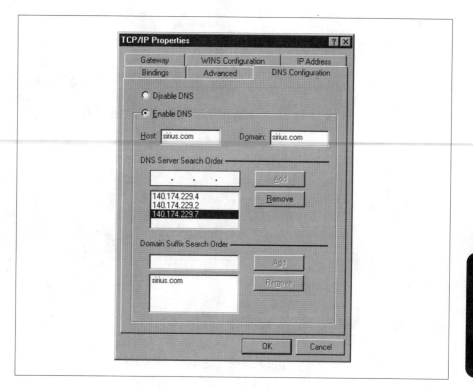

Windows
APP. B

9. Under **Domain suffix search order**, enter your provider's domain name (e.g., foo.com). Just like with the DNS entries, click on **Add** after you add the suffix name.

10. Click on **OK** to close the Properties window, and go back to the Network window, as shown in Figure B.9.

11. Click on **OK**—this is *very* important. Don't just close the window, or you'll lose the configuration settings you just entered. Now Windows 95 will prompt you to shut down and restart. After Windows reboots, you'll be ready to try out your connection.

Figure B.9:

When you're done configuring TCP/IP and the Dial Up Adapter, save your settings by clicking on OK.

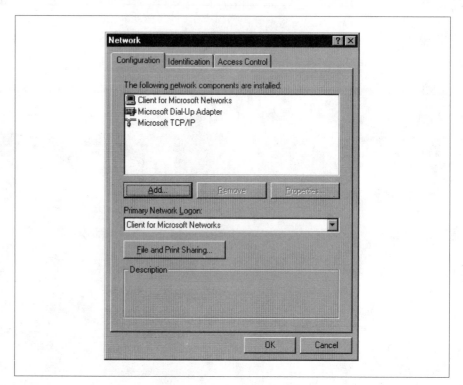

Connecting with Windows 95

Start up Dial-Up Networking by clicking on the Start menu and selecting Programs ➤ Accessories ➤ Dial-Up Networking. The Dial Up Networking window appears. Double-click on the connection you just created.

Check to make sure that your login name and password are correct. (If you're using TIA, these fields should be blank.) If you like, you can click on the **Save password** box to have Windows 95 save your login name and password so that you won't need to type it in again.

Now, click on **Connect**. Windows 95 will dial up your provider and log you in. If your password or user name is not correct, you'll be prompted to change it.

> *If you're using TIA, you will need to log in manually, and issue the* **tia** *command from the Terminal window. If you haven't yet configured your connection to bring up the Terminal window, you can do so from the Dial-Up Networking Properties dialog box. See Dial-Up Networking earlier in this appendix for more information.*

Pinging with Windows 95

To Ping in Windows 95, open up a DOS prompt by clicking on the Start menu, then selecting Programs ➤ MS-DOS prompt.

At the prompt, type **ping** followed by the name of your provider. If you get a series of replies back, like those shown in Figure B.10, you're connected.

Figure B.10:
Pinging with
Windows 95.

```
COMMAND                                                    _ □ ✕
Auto     ▼  ▢ ▤ ▤ ▨  ▣▤▤  A

Microsoft(R) Windows 95
    (C)Copyright Microsoft Corp 1981-1994.

C:\WIN95>ping sirius.com

Pinging sirius.com [140.174.229.201] with 32 bytes of data:

Reply from 140.174.229.201: bytes=32 time=1ms TTL=32
Reply from 140.174.229.201: bytes=32 time<10ms TTL=32
Reply from 140.174.229.201: bytes=32 time=2ms TTL=32
Reply from 140.174.229.201: bytes=32 time<10ms TTL=32

C:\WIN95>_
```

If you don't get anything back, go back to the Start menu, and select Settings ➤ Control Panel, and double-click on **Network**. Double-click on **TCP/IP**. Then click on the **DNS Configuration** tab and check your DNS configuration.

Index

Note to the Reader: Throughout this index **boldfaced** page numbers indicate primary discussions of a topic. *Italicized* page numbers indicate illustrations.

GET A FREE CATALOG JUST FOR EXPRESSING YOUR OPINION.

Help us improve our books and get a *FREE* full-color catalog in the bargain. Please complete this form, pull out this page and send it in today. The address is on the reverse side.

Name _____ Company _____

Address _____ City _____ State ____ Zip _____

Phone ( ) _____

1. **How would you rate the overall quality of this book?**

   ❏ Excellent
   ❏ Very Good
   ❏ Good
   ❏ Fair
   ❏ Below Average
   ❏ Poor

2. **What were the things you liked most about the book? (Check all that apply)**

   ❏ Pace
   ❏ Format
   ❏ Writing Style
   ❏ Examples
   ❏ Table of Contents
   ❏ Index
   ❏ Price
   ❏ Illustrations
   ❏ Type Style
   ❏ Cover
   ❏ Depth of Coverage
   ❏ Fast Track Notes

3. **What were the things you liked *least* about the book? (Check all that apply)**

   ❏ Pace
   ❏ Format
   ❏ Writing Style
   ❏ Examples
   ❏ Table of Contents
   ❏ Index
   ❏ Price
   ❏ Illustrations
   ❏ Type Style
   ❏ Cover
   ❏ Depth of Coverage
   ❏ Fast Track Notes

4. **Where did you buy this book?**

   ❏ Bookstore chain
   ❏ Small independent bookstore
   ❏ Computer store
   ❏ Wholesale club
   ❏ College bookstore
   ❏ Technical bookstore
   ❏ Other _____

5. **How did you decide to buy this particular book?**

   ❏ Recommended by friend
   ❏ Recommended by store personnel
   ❏ Author's reputation
   ❏ Sybex's reputation
   ❏ Read book review in _____
   ❏ Other _____

6. **How did you pay for this book?**

   ❏ Used own funds
   ❏ Reimbursed by company
   ❏ Received book as a gift

7. **What is your level of experience with the subject covered in this book?**

   ❏ Beginner
   ❏ Intermediate
   ❏ Advanced

8. **How long have you been using a computer?**

   years _____
   months _____

9. **Where do you most often use your computer?**

   ❏ Home
   ❏ Work

   ❏ Both
   ❏ Other _____

10. **What kind of computer equipment do you have? (Check all that apply)**

    ❏ PC Compatible Desktop Computer
    ❏ PC Compatible Laptop Computer
    ❏ Apple/Mac Computer
    ❏ Apple/Mac Laptop Computer
    ❏ CD ROM
    ❏ Fax Modem
    ❏ Data Modem
    ❏ Scanner
    ❏ Sound Card
    ❏ Other _____

11. **What other kinds of software packages do you ordinarily use?**

    ❏ Accounting
    ❏ Databases
    ❏ Networks
    ❏ Apple/Mac
    ❏ Desktop Publishing
    ❏ Spreadsheets
    ❏ CAD
    ❏ Games
    ❏ Word Processing
    ❏ Communications
    ❏ Money Management
    ❏ Other _____

12. **What operating systems do you ordinarily use?**

    ❏ DOS
    ❏ OS/2
    ❏ Windows
    ❏ Apple/Mac
    ❏ Windows NT
    ❏ Other _____

13. On what computer-related subject(s) would you like to see more books?

_____

_____

_____

14. Do you have any other comments about this book? (Please feel free to use a separate piece of paper if you need more room)

_____

_____

_____

_____

- - - - - - - - - - - PLEASE FOLD, SEAL, AND MAIL TO SYBEX - - - - - - - - - - -

SYBEX INC.
Department M
2021 Challenger Drive
Alameda, CA
94501

Let us hear from you.

 **T**alk to SYBEX authors, editors and fellow forum members.

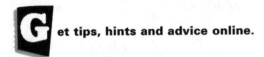 **G**et tips, hints and advice online.

Download magazine articles, book art, and shareware.

What Kind of File Is That?

Filename Extension	What Is It?
.AU	Unix sound file.
.AVI	Microsoft Video for Windows.
.FLI or .FLC	AutoDesk Flic video.
.GIF	CompuServe compressed image.
.JPG	JPEG image.
.LZH	LHarc archive.
.MOV	Apple Quicktime video.
.MPG	MPEG video.
.PDF	Adobe Acrobat hypertext document.
.PS	Adobe Postscript document.
.SIT	Macintosh compressed archive.
.TAR	Unix Tape Archive.
.tar.Z	Unix Tape Archive, compressed.
.VOC	SoundBlaster sound.
.WAV	Wave sound file.
.Z or .GZ	Unix compressed file
.ZIP	Zip archive.